MW01170238

PICTURE DICTIONARY

ITALIAN-ENGLISH

ITALIAN-ENGLISH PICTURE DICTIONARY

Illustrated by Kathryn Adams, Pat Gangnon, Colin Gillies, David Shaw and Yvonne Zan.
Designed by David Shaw and Associates.

Typesetting by Osgoode Technical Translations and Ray's Typographics.

Color separations by New Concept Limited.

Printed in Canada by Metropole Litho Inc.

English language editors: P. O'Brien-Hitching, R. LeBel, P. Rényi, K. C. Sheppard.

Italian editors: A Sarzotti, C. Pella.

Originally published by Éditions Rényi Inc., Toronto, Canada

Distributed exclusively in trade and education in the United States of America by Langenscheidt Publishers, Inc., Maspeth, New York 11378

Hardcover	ISBN 0-88729-853-2
Softcover	ISBN 0-88729-859-1

Distributed outside the USA by Éditions Rényi Inc., Toronto, Canada

Hardcover	ISBN 0-921606-24-9
Softcover	ISBN 0-921606-99-0

INTRODUCTION

Some of Canada's best illustrators have contributed to this Picture Dictionary, which has been carefully designed to combine words and pictures into a pleasurable learning experience.

Its unusually large number of terms (3336) makes this Picture Dictionary a flexible teaching tool. It is excellent for helping young children acquire language and dictionary skills. Because the vocabulary it encompasses is so broad, this dictionary can also be used to teach new words to older children and adults as well. Further, it is also an effective tool for teaching English as a second language.

THE VOCABULARY

The decision on which words to include and which to leave out was made in relation to three standards. First, a word-frequency analysis was carried out to include the most common words. Then a thematic clustering analysis was done to make sure that words in common themes (animals, plants, activities etc.) were included. Finally, the vocabulary was expanded to include words which children would likely hear, ask about and use. This makes this dictionary's vocabulary more honest than most. 'To choke', 'greedy', 'to smoke' are included, but approval is withheld.

This process was further complicated by the decision to *systematically* illustrate the meanings. Although the degree of abstraction was kept reasonably low, it was considered necessary to include terms such as 'to expect' and 'to forgive', which are virtually impossible to illustrate. Instead of dropping these terms, we decided to provide explanatory sentences that create a context.

Where variations occur between British and North American English, both terms are given, with an asterisk marking the British version (favor/favour*, gas/petrol*).

USING THIS DICTIONARY

Used at home, this dictionary is an enjoyable book for children to explore alone or with their parents. The pictures excite the imagination of younger children and entice them to ask questions. Older children in televisual cultures often look to visual imagery as an aid to meaning. The pictures help them make the transition from the graphic to the written. Even young adults will find the book useful, because the illustrations, while amusing, are not childish.

The dictionary as a whole provides an occasion to introduce students to basic dictionary skills. This work is compatible with school reading materials in current use, and can serve as a 'user-friendly' reference tool.

Great care has been taken to ensure that any contextual statements made are factual, have some educational value and are compatible with statements made elsewhere in the book. Lastly, from a strictly pedagogical viewpoint, the little girl featured in the book has not been made into a paragon of virtue; young users will readily identify with her imperfections.

A te e a tutti i miei amici

Forse questo è il tuo primo dizionario italiano. . . Sono sicura che lo troverai divertente.

Io mi chiamo Sabrina. Vado a scuola volentieri e ho tanti amici. Al giovedì prendo lezioni di nuoto. Sono molto ghiotta. Ho un fratellino e ho le mie idee su tante cose. Se vuoi incontrare mio papà, che è un ammiraglio, guarda al fondo della pagina, verso destra. Mamma è alla pagina seguente, in alto. Se vuoi fare la mia conoscenza, devi cercare nel dizionario la parola ''calm''.

Vieni con me e scoprirai tante parole nuove e interessanti. Ti farai anche delle belle risate.

Le illustrazioni sono state disegnate da cinque persone adulte, che si sono divertite un mondo. Io le ho aiutate, disegnando una figura (quella della zebra). Ho anche scelto io l'ultima parola del dizionario: indovina quale è!

Questo dizionario è stato composto apposta per te, per i tuoi amici e le tue amichette. Spero che ti piacerà proprio tanto.

Sabrina

l'abbaco, il pallottoliere

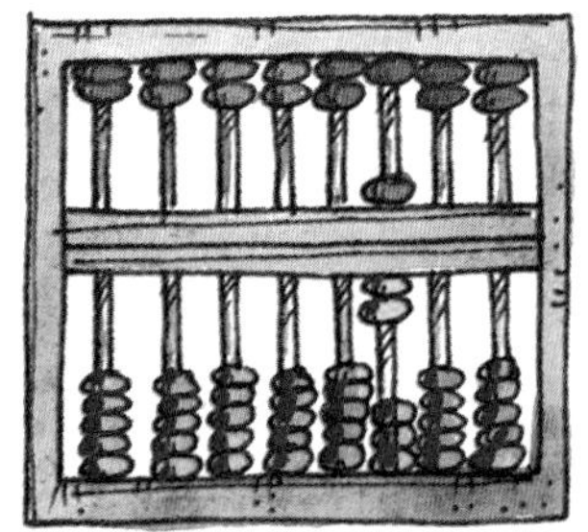

1 abacus

di, circa, attorno

Parlami **di** tua madre.
Ci vuole **circa** un'ora.
Mario si guarda **attorno**.

Tell me about your mother.
It takes about an hour.
Mario looks about him.

2 about

La mela è **sopra** la sua testa.

3 above

Paolo è **assente** oggi.

4 absent

Questo è il pedale dell'**acceleratore**.

5 accelerator

un accento

John parla con **un accento** inglese.
Città ha **l'accento** sull'ultima vocale.

John speaks with a British accent.
Città has an accent on the last vowel.

6 accent

un incidente

7 accident

la fisarmonica

8 accordion

Tutti **accusano** Mirella.

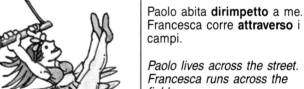

9 to accuse

un asso di picche

10 ace

Mi **duole** la testa.

11 My head **aches.**

Un acido può bruciare la pelle.

12 acid

La ghianda è prodotta dalla quercia.

13 acorn

un'acrobata

14 acrobat

dirimpetto, attraverso

Paolo abita **dirimpetto** a me.
Francesca corre **attraverso** i campi.

Paolo lives across the street.
Francesca runs across the fields.

15 across

addizionare, fare l'addizione

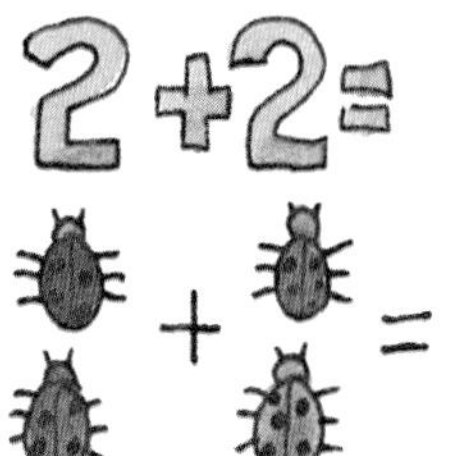

16 to add

Questo è **l'indirizzo** di Sabrina.

17 address

Il papà di Sabrina è **un ammiraglio**.

18 admiral

Ernesto **adora** Sonia.

19 to **adore**

Gli adulti sono bambini cresciuti.
20 adult
Avanza il re!
21 to advance
Essere alti talvolta è **un vantaggio**.
22 advantage
La mamma di Sabrina ama **l'avventura**.
23 adventure
Filippo è **impaurito.**
24 He is afraid.
L'Africa è un continente.
25 Africa
dopo, **dietro**
Puoi giocare **dopo** cena.
Sta correndo **dietro** alla palla.
You can play after dinner.
He is running after the ball.
26 after
Il pomeriggio comincia a mezzogiorno.
27 afternoon
di nuovo, **nuovamente**
L'hai fatto **di nuovo**!
E' **nuovamente** il tuo turno!
You did it again!
It is your turn again.
28 again
Micio **si strofina** contro le gambe del signor Francesco.
29 to rub against
C'è una certa differenza d'**età**.
30 age
una persona **agile**
31 agile person
La caravella **si è arenata**.
32 aground
davanti, **in anticipo**
Elena è seduta **davanti a** Pierino.
Combina **in anticipo** per le tue vacanze!
Elena sits ahead of Pierino.
Plan ahead for your next holiday.
33 ahead
soccorrere, **venire in aiuto**
34 to provide aid
Cerca di **mirare** al bersaglio!
35 to aim
L'aquilone vola nell' **aria**.
36 air
Fido dorme sul **materassino pneumatico**.
37 air mattress
L'insetto è sotto una cupola **ermetica.**
38 airtight
Questo **aeroplano** sembra in difficoltà.
39 airplane/aeroplane*

Gli aerei atterrano all'**aeroporto**.
40 airport
Il passaggio separa le file di poltrone.
41 aisle
la sveglia
42 alarm clock
un albo fotografico
43 album
La casa è **in fiamme**.
44 alight
Certamente, uno dei pesci è **vivo**.
45 alive
Voglio **tutti** i dolci!
46 I want them **all**.
Un gatto in **un vicolo** cieco.
47 alley
un alligatore
48 alligator
la mandorla
49 almond
Baffo arriva **quasi** ad addentare l'osso.
50 almost
Perché è tutto **solo**?
51 alone
Camminano **lungo** il fiume.
52 along
forte, ad alta voce
53 aloud
l'alfabeto
a b c d e f g h i l m n o p q r s t u v z
54 alphabet
Devo **già** andare via?
55 Do I have to go **already**?
Sto bene, non ho niente.
56 I am **alright**.
Anch' io ne voglio.
57 I **also** want some.
la scala **d'alluminio**
58 **aluminum/aluminium*** ladder
Cado **sempre**.
59 I **always** fall down.

un'ambulanza
60 ambulance
un lupo tra gli agnelli
61 wolf among sheep
un'ancora
62 anchor
un monumento antico
63 ancient
un angolo retto
64 angle
Tito è adirato.
65 He is angry.
gli animali
66 animals
la caviglia
67 ankle
annunciare
68 to announce
un altro panino
69 another sandwich
La risposta giusta è...
2
+2
=
70 The answer is...
la formica
71 ant
l'Antartico
72 Antarctic
un'antilope
73 antelope
le corna
74 antlers
Non ho denaro.
75 I do not have any money.
Mangia qualunque cosa.
76 It eats anything.
Tito non può andare
in nessun posto.
77 He cannot go anywhere.
Un acino è separato
dal grappolo.
78 apart
la scimmia
79 ape

un alveare 80 apiary	**chiedere scusa, scusarsi** **Chiedere scusa** significa dire: mi dispiace! **Scusate** il mio ritardo! *To apologize is to say you are sorry.* *I apologize for being late!* 81 to apologize/apologise*	**comparire, apparire** Il prestigiatore ha fatto **comparire** un coniglietto. La regina è **apparsa** in televisione. *The magician made a rabbit appear.* *The Queen appeared on television.* 82 to appear	**applaudire** 83 to applaud
la mela 84 apple	**il torsolo della mela** 85 apple core	**avvicinarsi** 86 to approach	**un'albicocca** 87 apricot
In **aprile**, ogni goccia un barile! 88 April	**il grembiule** 89 apron	**un acquario** 90 aquarium	**un arco** 91 arch
un architetto 92 architect	Nell'**Artico** fa molto freddo. 93 Arctic	**discutere** 94 to argue	**il braccio** 95 arm
la poltrona 96 armchair	Lancillotto porta **l'armatura.** 97 armor/armour*	**un'ascella** 98 armpit	**attorno, circa, verso** **Attorno** al mondo in ottanta giorni. Un autocarro pesa **circa** 6 tonnellate. Arriveremo **verso** mezzogiorno. *Around the world in eighty days* *A truck weighs around 6 tons.* *We will be there around noon.* 99 around

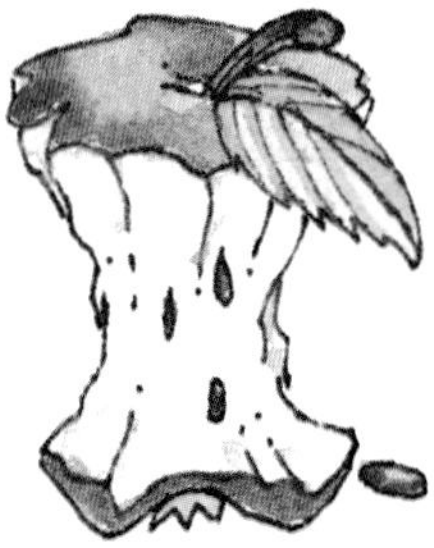

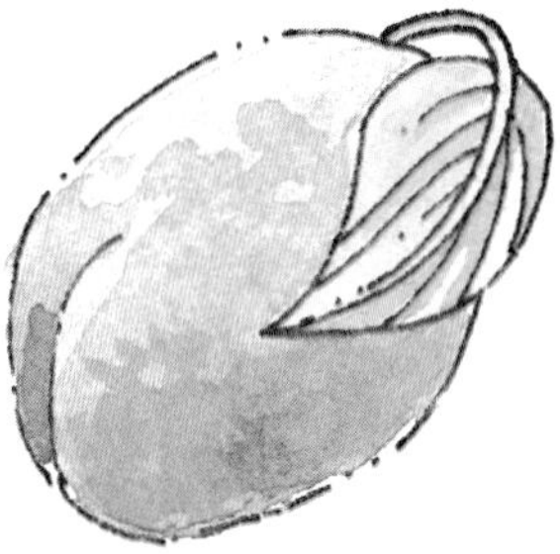

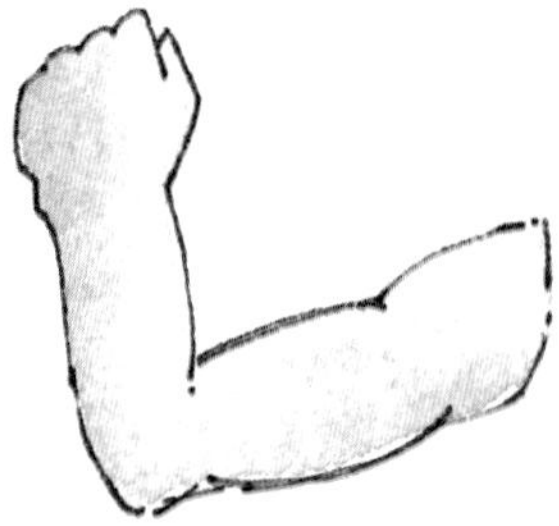

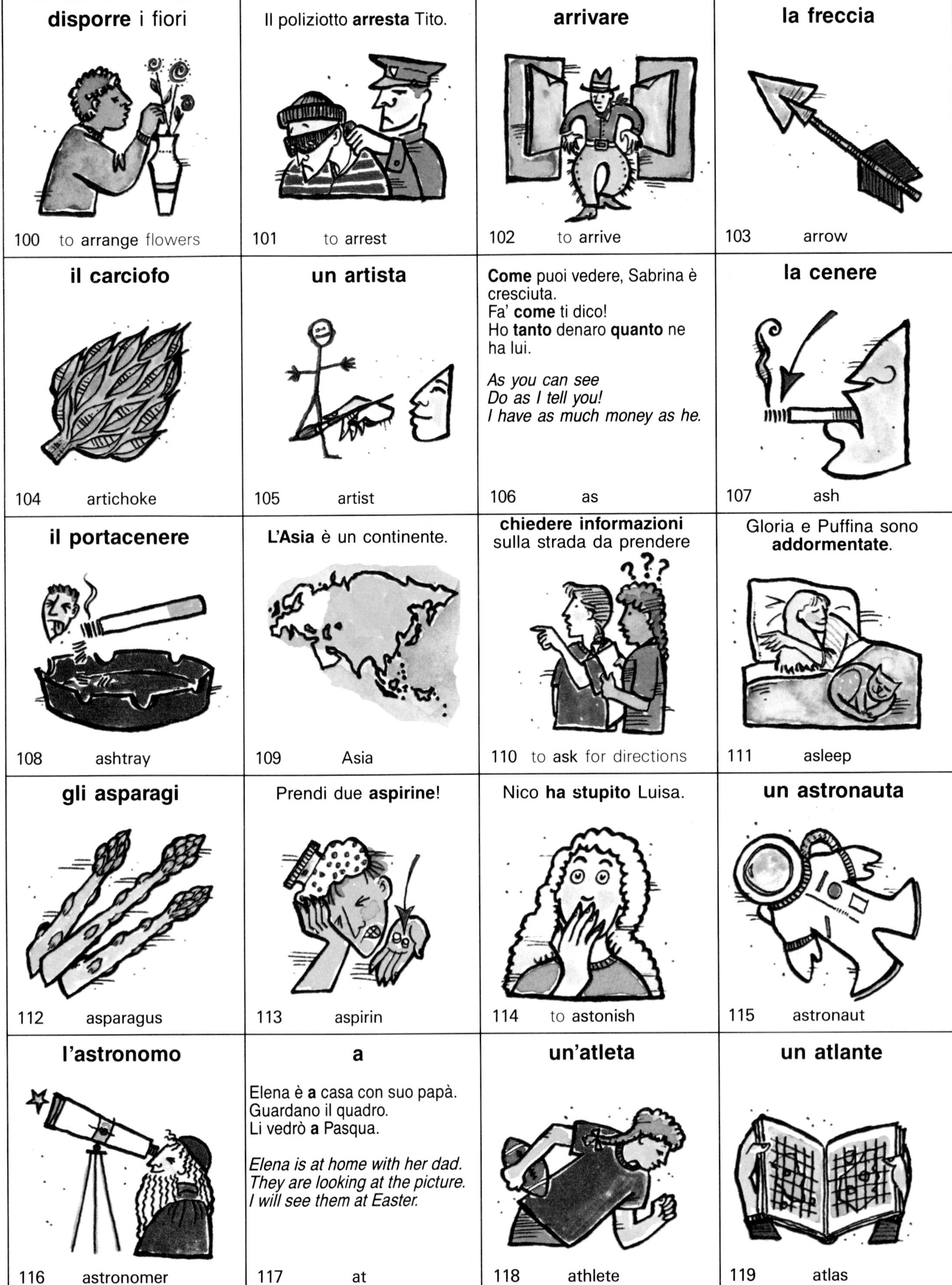
disporre i fiori
100 to arrange flowers
Il poliziotto arresta Tito.
101 to arrest
arrivare
102 to arrive
la freccia
103 arrow
il carciofo
104 artichoke
un artista
105 artist
Come puoi vedere, Sabrina è cresciuta.
Fa' come ti dico!
Ho tanto denaro quanto ne ha lui.
As you can see
Do as I tell you!
I have as much money as he.
106 as
la cenere
107 ash
il portacenere
108 ashtray
L'Asia è un continente.
109 Asia
chiedere informazioni sulla strada da prendere
???
110 to ask for directions
Gloria e Puffina sono addormentate.
111 asleep
gli asparagi
112 asparagus
Prendi due aspirine!
113 aspirin
Nico ha stupito Luisa.
114 to astonish
un astronauta
115 astronaut
l'astronomo
116 astronomer
a
Elena è a casa con suo papà.
Guardano il quadro.
Li vedrò a Pasqua.
Elena is at home with her dad.
They are looking at the picture.
I will see them at Easter.
117 at
un'atleta
118 athlete
un atlante
119 atlas

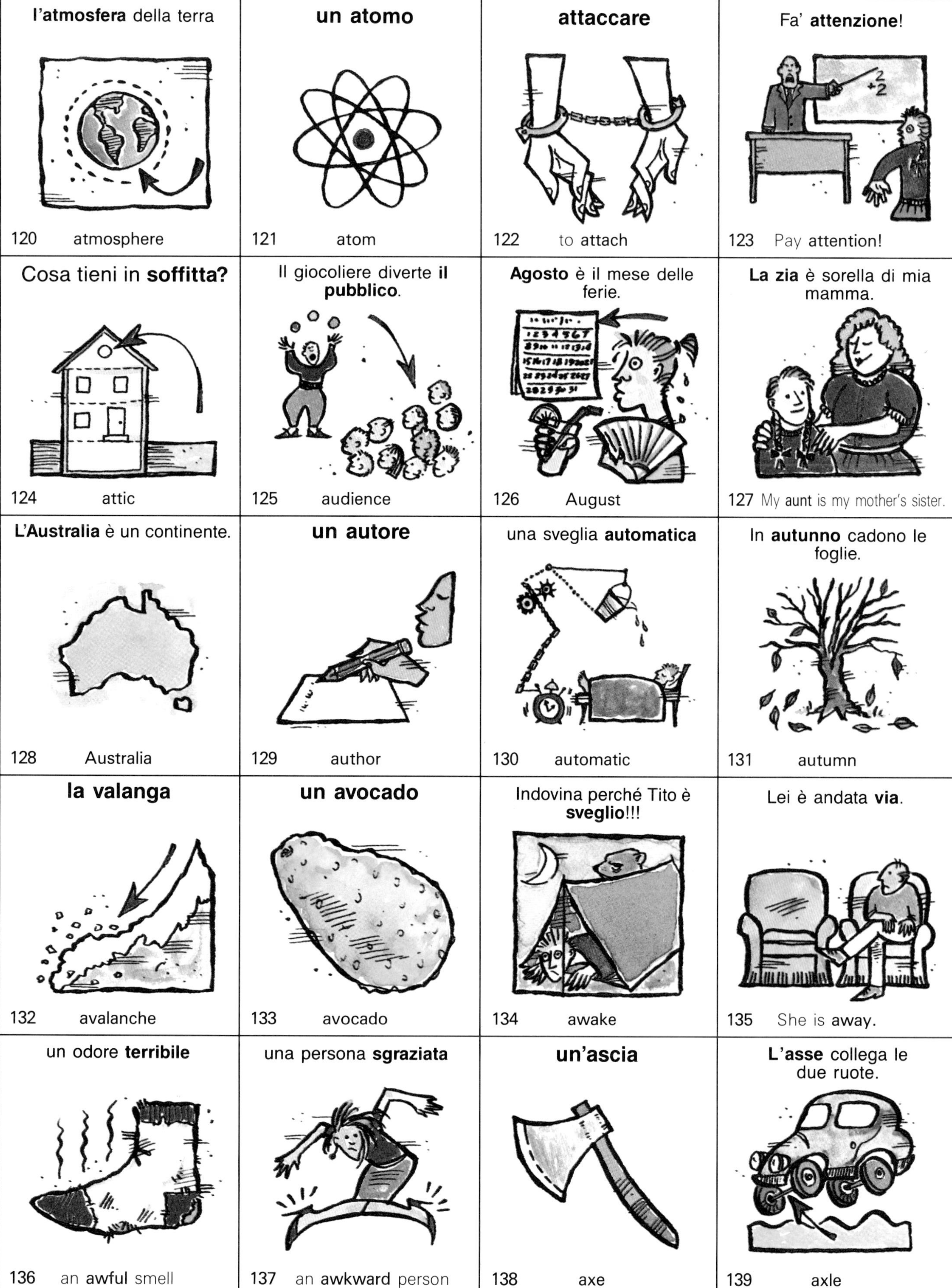
l'atmosfera della terra
120 atmosphere
un atomo
121 atom
attaccare
122 to attach
Fa' attenzione!
123 Pay attention!
Cosa tieni in soffitta?
124 attic
Il giocoliere diverte il pubblico.
125 audience
Agosto è il mese delle ferie.
126 August
La zia è sorella di mia mamma.
127 My aunt is my mother's sister.
L'Australia è un continente.
128 Australia
un autore
129 author
una sveglia automatica
130 automatic
In autunno cadono le foglie.
131 autumn
la valanga
132 avalanche
un avocado
133 avocado
Indovina perché Tito è sveglio!!!
134 awake
Lei è andata via.
135 She is away.
un odore terribile
136 an awful smell
una persona sgraziata
137 an awkward person
un'ascia
138 axe
L'asse collega le due ruote.
139 axle

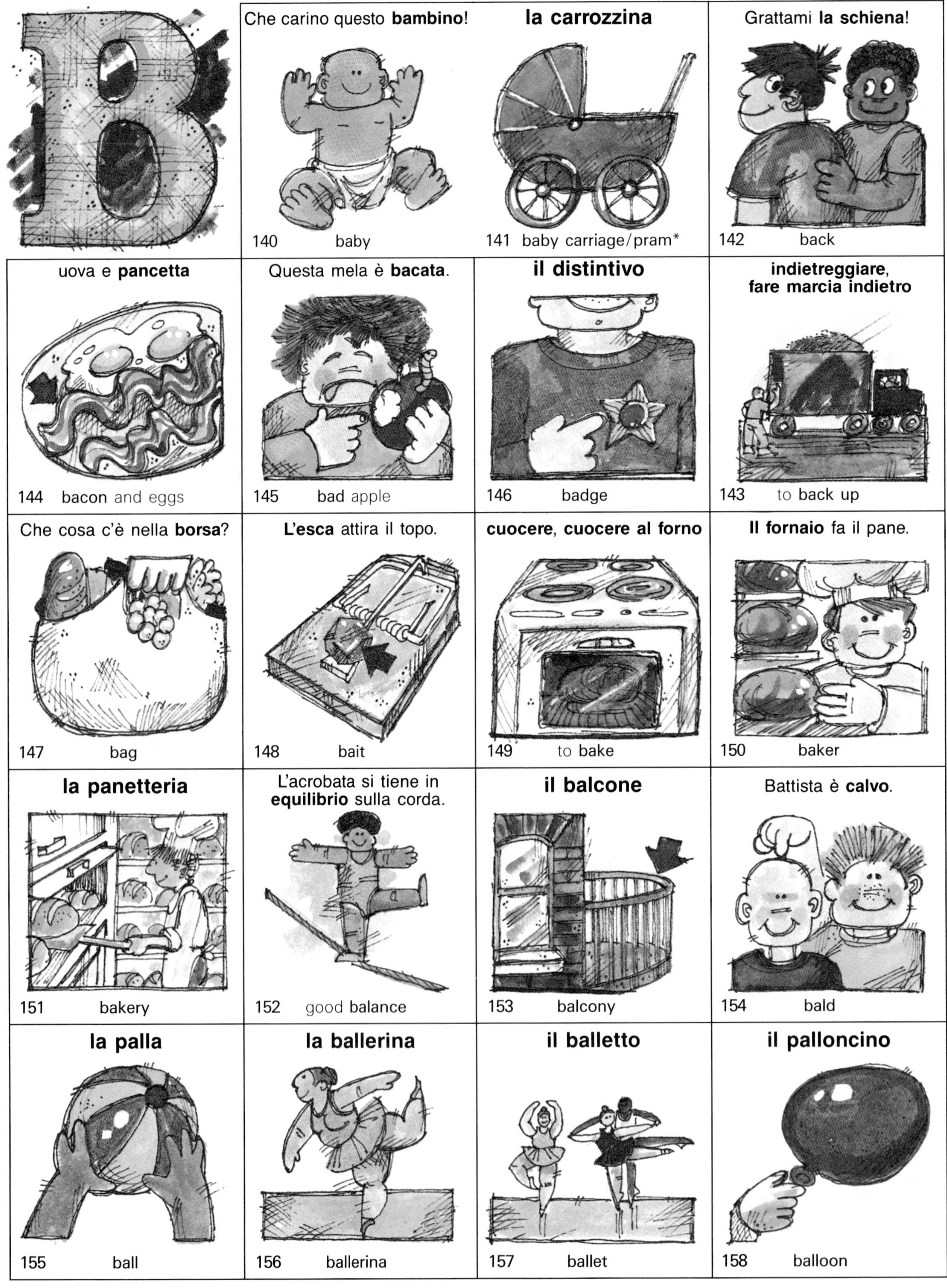
B
Che carino questo **bambino**!
140 baby
la carrozzina
141 baby carriage/pram*
Grattami **la schiena**!
142 back
uova e **pancetta**
144 bacon and eggs
Questa mela è **bacata**.
145 bad apple
il distintivo
146 badge
indietreggiare, fare marcia indietro
143 to back up
Che cosa c'è nella **borsa**?
147 bag
L'esca attira il topo.
148 bait
cuocere, **cuocere al forno**
149 to bake
Il fornaio fa il pane.
150 baker
la panetteria
151 bakery
L'acrobata si tiene in **equilibrio** sulla corda.
152 good balance
il balcone
153 balcony
Battista è **calvo**.
154 bald
la palla
155 ball
la ballerina
156 ballerina
il balletto
157 ballet
il palloncino
158 balloon

un pallone aerostatico, una mongolfiera
159 hot air balloon
la banana
160 banana
il nastro
161 band
un'orchestra
162 musical band
La benda ha fatto passare il male.
163 bandage
battere
164 to bang
Rino scende scivolando sul corrimano.
165 banister
Rosvaldo porta i suoi soldi in banca.
166 bank
una sbarra di ferro
167 bar
I bar sono riservati agli adulti.
168 bar/pub*
il filo spinato
169 barbed wire
Il barbiere taglia i capelli a Michele.
170 barber
un piede nudo
171 one bare foot
il fienile, la stalla
172 bargain
$100.00
la chiatta
173 barge
abbaiare
174 to bark
L'orzo cresce nei campi.
176 barley
il capannone agricolo, il fienile
177 barn
I soldati abitano in una caserma.
178 barracks
la corteccia di un albero
175 bark

un barile d'olio d'oliva
179 barrel
la canna della pistola
180 barrel
la molletta
181 barrette/hair slide*
la sbarra di un passaggio a livello
182 barrier
la base della colonna
183 base
una base del gioco del baseball
184 base
il baseball
185 baseball
17
il seminterrato
186 basement/cellar*
il basilico
187 basil
il canestro
188 basket
la pallacanestro
189 basketball
due mazze da gioco
190 bats
Sto facendo il bagno.
192 I am having a bath.
il bagno
193 bathroom
la vasca da bagno
194 bathtub
Il pipistrello vola di notte.
191 bat
una pila per la tua radiolina
195 battery
La barca veleggia nella baia.
196 bay
La mamma usa le foglie d'alloro per l'arrosto.
197 bay leaves
il bazar
198 bazaar

essere Prometti di **essere** buona? **Sono** buona! Pierino e Luca **sono** bravi, ma Sabrina **è** brava? *Do you promise to be good?* *I am good.* *Pierino and Luca are good, but is Sabrina good?* 199 to be	**la spiaggia** 200 beach	**una perla** della collana 201 bead	**il becco** 202 beak
un raggio di luce 203 beam of light	**i fagioli** 204 beans	Quest'**orso** sa andare in bicicletta. 205 bear	**una barba** molto lunga 206 beard
una bestia orribile, **una bestiaccia** 207 beast	Marina **batte** il tamburo. 208 to beat	Fufi è **bella**! 209 beautiful	**il castoro** 210 beaver
Piango **perché**. . . 211 I am crying because...	**diventare** Il bruco **diventa** una farfalla 212 to become	**il letto** 213 bed	**la lampada da notte** 214 bed lamp/reading light*
la camera da letto 215 bedroom	**L'ape** è un insetto molto utile. 216 bee	**il faggio** 217 beech	Le api vivono in **un alveare**. 218 beehive

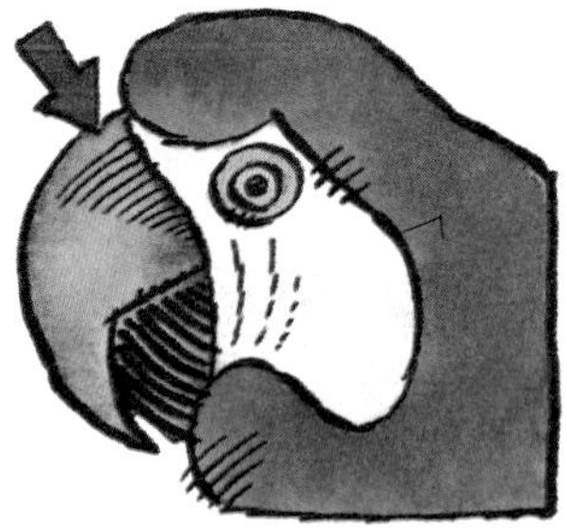

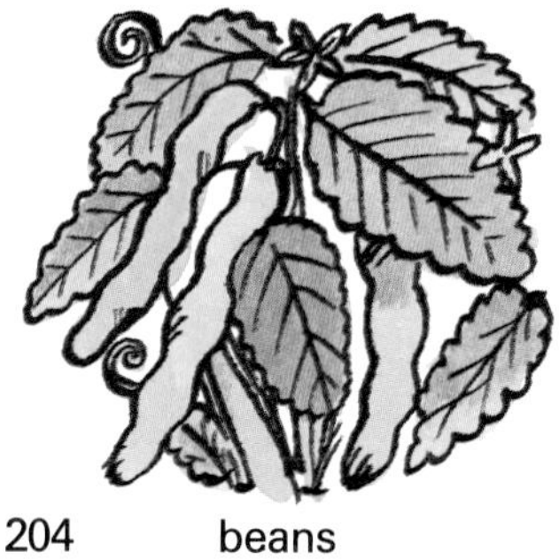

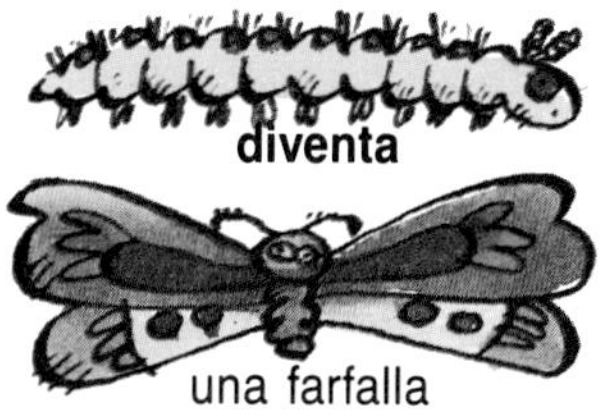

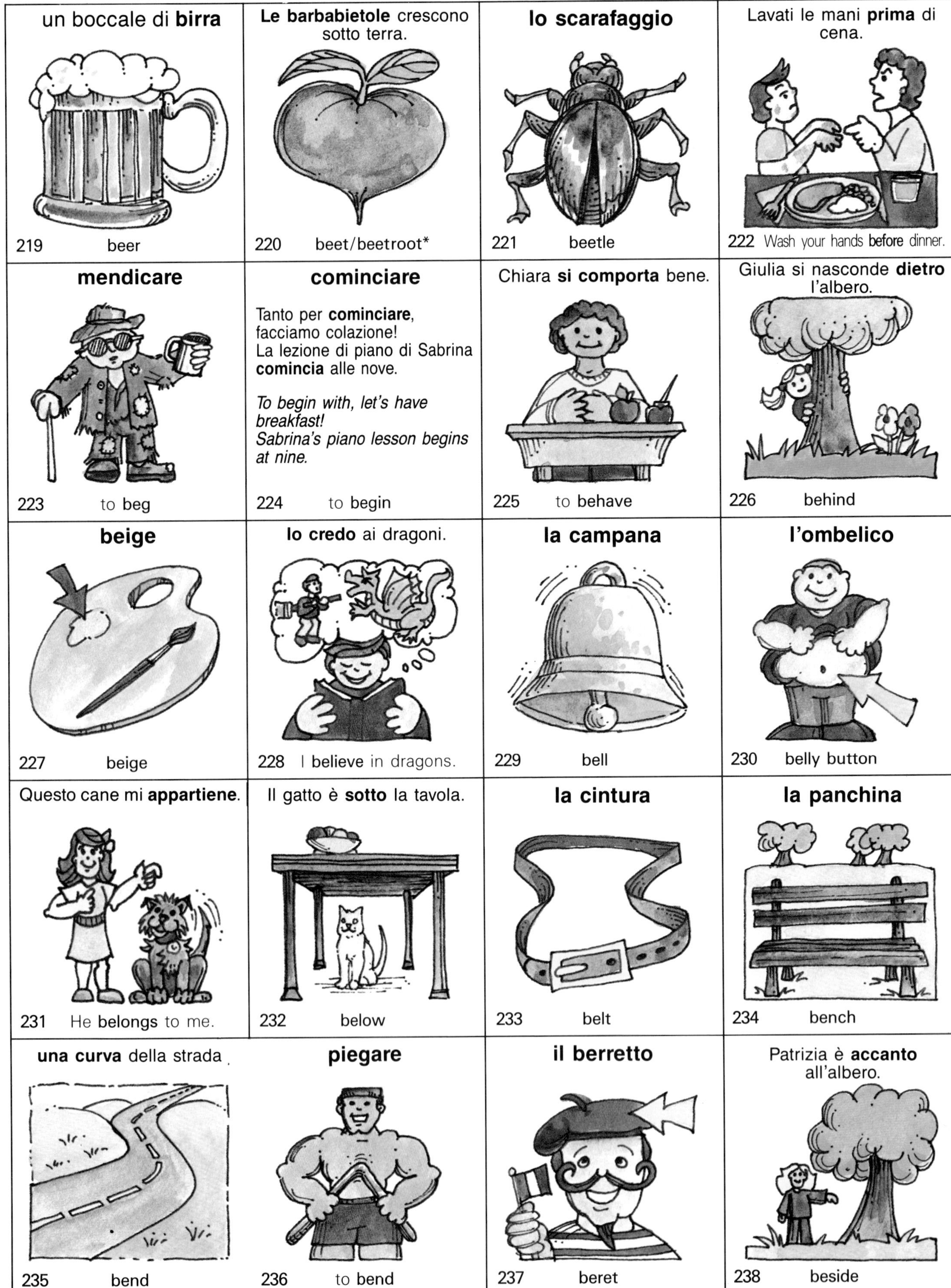

un boccale di **birra**
219 beer

Le barbabietole crescono sotto terra.
220 beet/beetroot*

lo scarafaggio
221 beetle

Lavati le mani **prima** di cena.
222 Wash your hands **before** dinner.

mendicare
223 to beg

cominciare

Tanto per **cominciare**, facciamo colazione!
La lezione di piano di Sabrina **comincia** alle nove.

To begin with, let's have breakfast!
Sabrina's piano lesson begins at nine.

224 to begin

Chiara **si comporta** bene.
225 to behave

Giulia si nasconde **dietro** l'albero.
226 behind

beige
227 beige

Io credo ai dragoni.
228 I **believe** in dragons.

la campana
229 bell

l'ombelico
230 belly button

Questo cane mi **appartiene**.
231 He **belongs** to me.

Il gatto è **sotto** la tavola.
232 below

la cintura
233 belt

la panchina
234 bench

una curva della strada
235 bend

piegare
236 to bend

il berretto
237 beret

Patrizia è **accanto** all'albero.
238 beside

inoltre, oltre a

Inoltre, non dovresti mangiare tanto zucchero!
C'erano molti altri studenti, **oltre a** lui.

Besides, you should not eat so much sugar!
There were many other pupils besides him.

239 besides

la migliore

240 best

meglio, migliore

Giulia scrive **meglio** di Davide.
Questo libro è **migliore** del primo.

Giulia writes better than Davide.
This book is better than the first one.

241 better

Filippo cammina **tra** due massi.

242 between

il bavaglino

243 bib

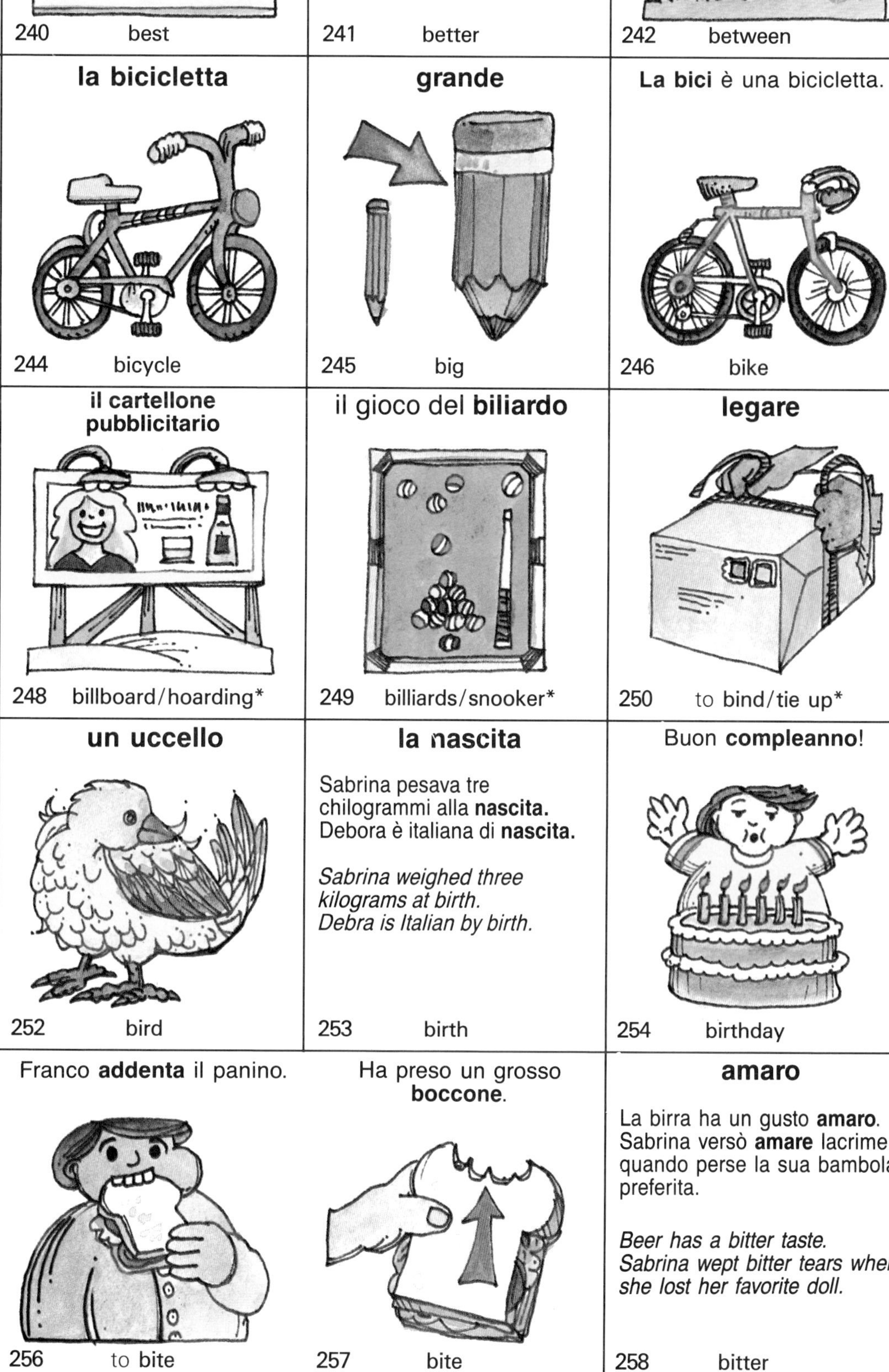

la bicicletta

244 bicycle

grande

245 big

La bici è una bicicletta.

246 bike

il biglietto di banca

247 bill/banknote*

il cartellone pubblicitario

248 billboard/hoarding*

il gioco del **biliardo**

249 billiards/snooker*

legare

250 to bind/tie up*

il binocolo

251 binoculars

un uccello

252 bird

la nascita

Sabrina pesava tre chilogrammi alla **nascita.**
Debora è italiana di **nascita.**

Sabrina weighed three kilograms at birth.
Debra is Italian by birth.

253 birth

Buon **compleanno**!

254 birthday

il biscotto

255 biscuit

Franco **addenta** il panino.

256 to bite

Ha preso un grosso **boccone**.

257 bite

amaro

La birra ha un gusto **amaro**.
Sabrina versò **amare** lacrime quando perse la sua bambola preferita.

Beer has a bitter taste.
Sabrina wept bitter tears when she lost her favorite doll.

258 bitter

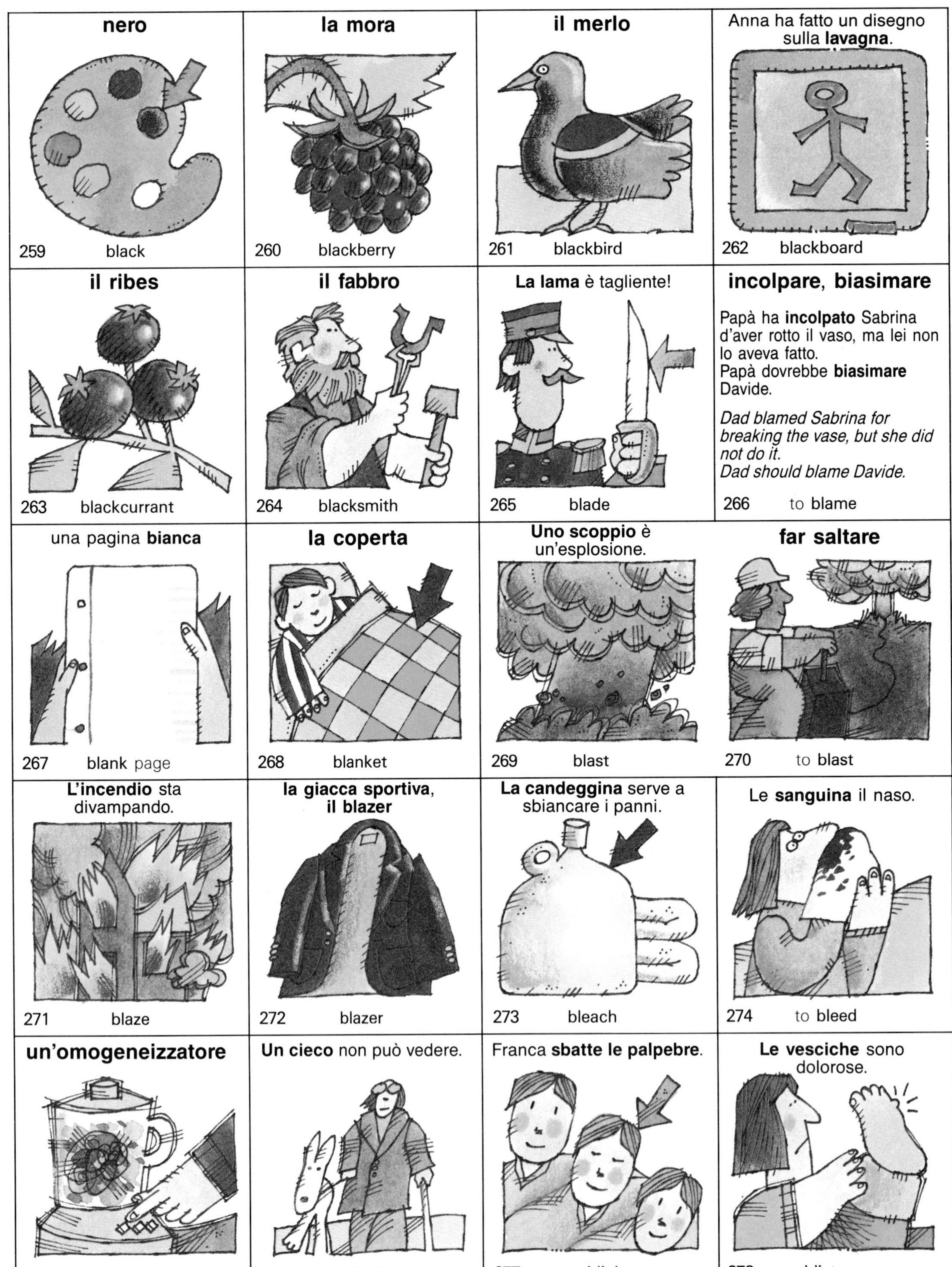

nero
259 black

la mora
260 blackberry

il merlo
261 blackbird

Anna ha fatto un disegno sulla **lavagna**.
262 blackboard

il ribes
263 blackcurrant

il fabbro
264 blacksmith

La lama è tagliente!
265 blade

incolpare, biasimare

Papà ha **incolpato** Sabrina d'aver rotto il vaso, ma lei non lo aveva fatto.
Papà dovrebbe **biasimare** Davide.

Dad blamed Sabrina for breaking the vase, but she did not do it.
Dad should blame Davide.

266 to blame

una pagina **bianca**
267 blank page

la coperta
268 blanket

Uno scoppio è un'esplosione.
269 blast

far saltare
270 to blast

L'incendio sta divampando.
271 blaze

la giacca sportiva, il blazer
272 blazer

La candeggina serve a sbiancare i panni.
273 bleach

Le **sanguina** il naso.
274 to bleed

un'omogeneizzatore
275 blender

Un cieco non può vedere.
276 blind

Franca **sbatte le palpebre**.
277 to blink

Le vesciche sono dolorose.
278 blister

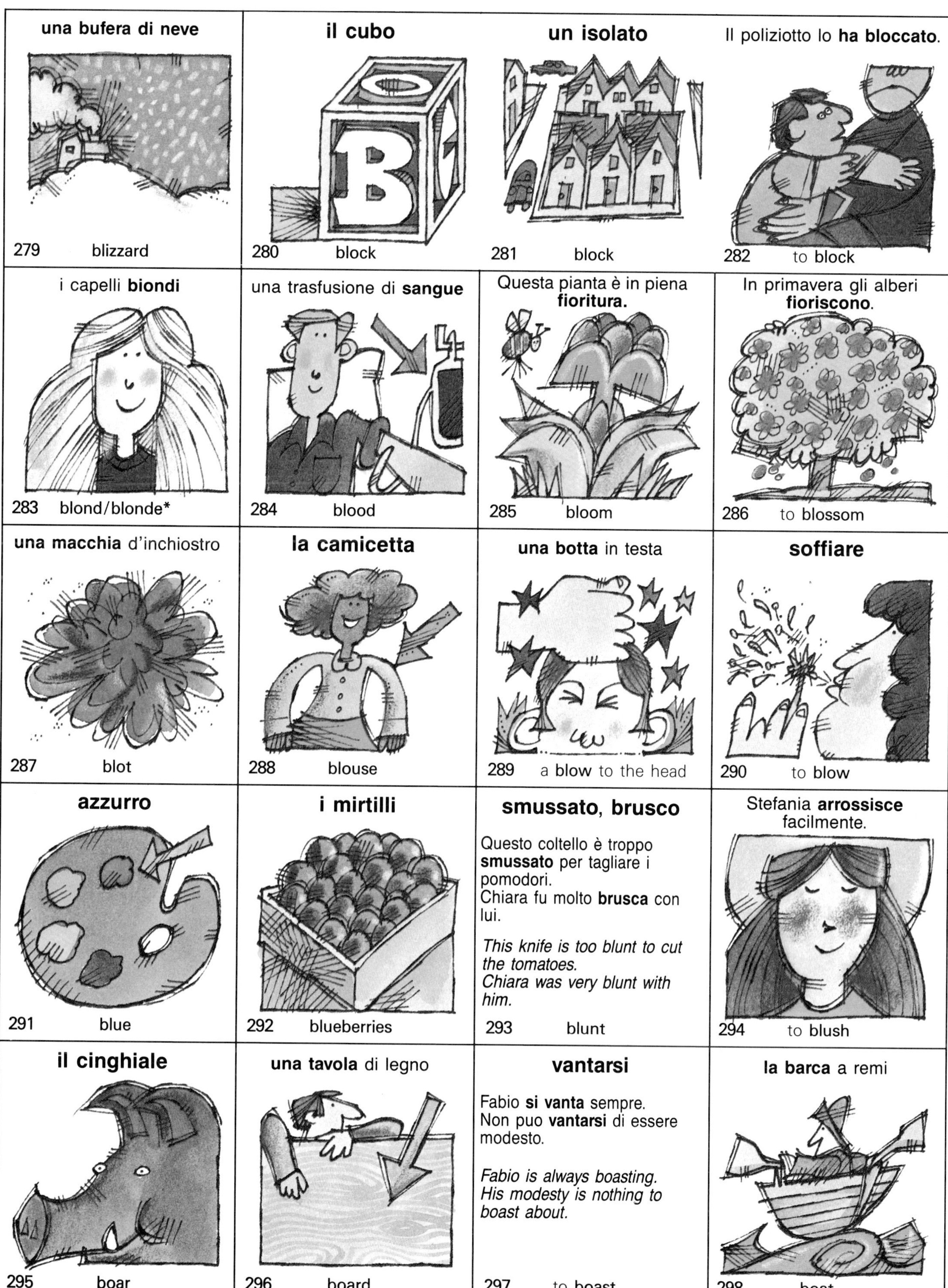
una bufera di neve
279 blizzard
il cubo
280 block
un isolato
281 block
Il poliziotto lo ha bloccato.
282 to block
i capelli biondi
283 blond/blonde*
una trasfusione di sangue
284 blood
Questa pianta è in piena fioritura.
285 bloom
In primavera gli alberi fioriscono.
286 to blossom
una macchia d'inchiostro
287 blot
la camicetta
288 blouse
una botta in testa
289 a blow to the head
soffiare
290 to blow
azzurro
291 blue
i mirtilli
292 blueberries
smussato, brusco
Questo coltello è troppo smussato per tagliare i pomodori.
Chiara fu molto brusca con lui.
This knife is too blunt to cut the tomatoes.
Chiara was very blunt with him.
293 blunt
Stefania arrossisce facilmente.
294 to blush
il cinghiale
295 boar
una tavola di legno
296 board
vantarsi
Fabio si vanta sempre.
Non puo vantarsi di essere modesto.
Fabio is always boasting.
His modesty is nothing to boast about.
297 to boast
la barca a remi
298 boat

una forcina da capelli

299 bobby pin/hairgrip*

il corpo umano

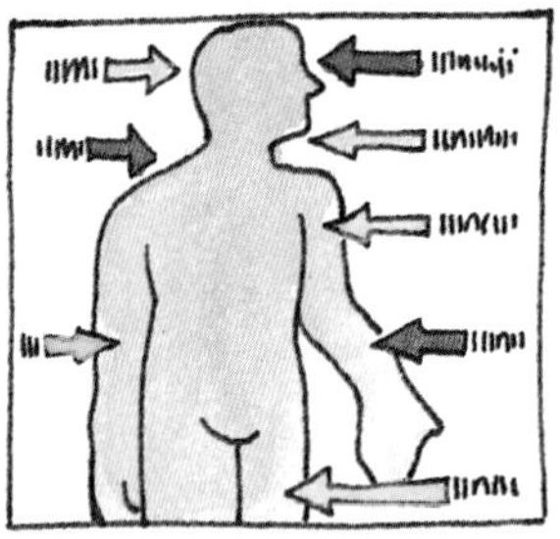

300 body

bollire

301 to boil

il bullone

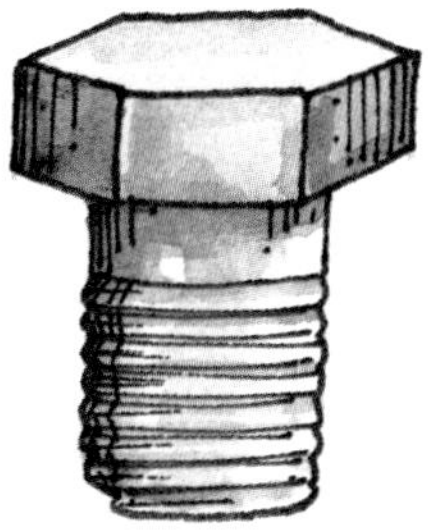

302 bolt

un osso per il cane

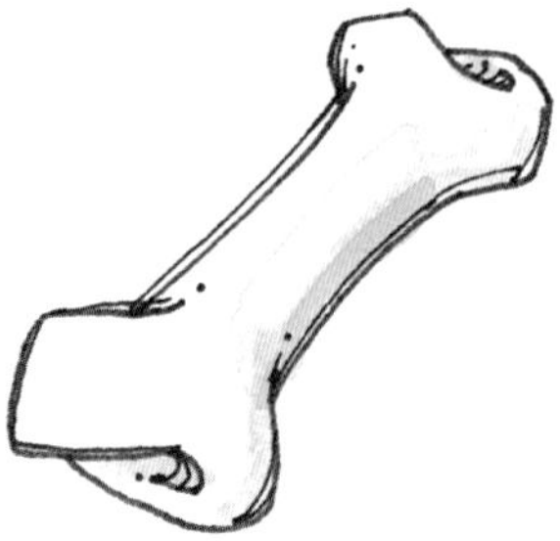

303 bone

il falò

304 bonfire

il libro

305 book

uno scaffale per i libri

306 bookshelf

il boomerang

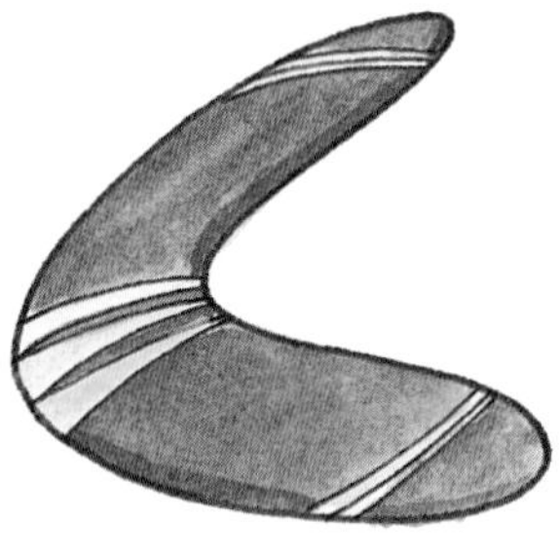

307 boomerang

lo stivale

308 boot

il confine, la frontiera

309 border

Il cemento è difficile da **perforare**.

310 to bore

nato

In che anno sei **nata**?
E' un poeta **nato**.

What year were you born?
He is a born poet.

312 born

prendere in prestito

Sabrina sovente **prende in prestito** la bicicletta di suo fratello.
Posso **prendere in prestito** il tuo libro?

Sabrina often borrows her brother's bike.
Can I borrow your book?

313 to borrow

il padrone

314 boss

annoiare

Sabrina qualche volta **annoia** da morire.
Luca mi **annoia**, perché parla troppo.

Sabrina can bore people to death.
Luca bores me because he talks too much.

311 to bore

ambedue, sia . . . che

Enzo e Renato sono **ambedue** graziosi.
Sia l'uno **che** l'altro hanno un bel sorriso.

Enzo and Renato are both cute.
Both have a nice smile.

315 both

la bottiglietta

316 bottle

un apribottiglie

317 bottle opener

il fondo dell'acquario

318 bottom

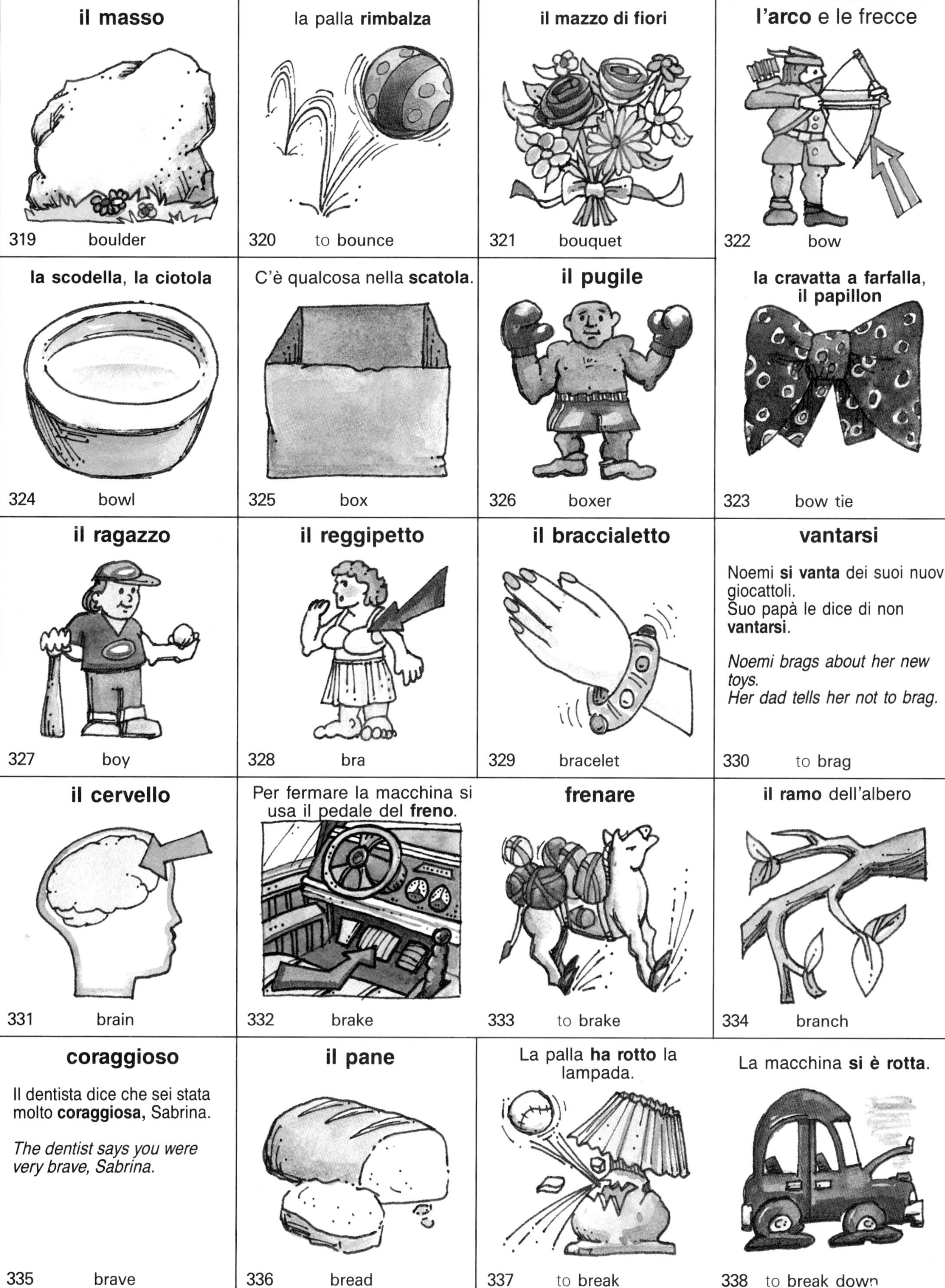
il masso
319 boulder
la palla rimbalza
320 to bounce
il mazzo di fiori
321 bouquet
l'arco e le frecce
322 bow
la scodella, la ciotola
324 bowl
C'è qualcosa nella scatola.
325 box
il pugile
326 boxer
la cravatta a farfalla, il papillon
323 bow tie
il ragazzo
327 boy
il reggipetto
328 bra
il braccialetto
329 bracelet
vantarsi
Noemi si vanta dei suoi nuovi giocattoli.
Suo papà le dice di non vantarsi.
Noemi brags about her new toys.
Her dad tells her not to brag.
330 to brag
il cervello
331 brain
Per fermare la macchina si usa il pedale del freno.
332 brake
frenare
333 to brake
il ramo dell'albero
334 branch
coraggioso
Il dentista dice che sei stata molto coraggiosa, Sabrina.
The dentist says you were very brave, Sabrina.
335 brave
il pane
336 bread
La palla ha rotto la lampada.
337 to break
La macchina si è rotta.
338 to break down

Il ladro **ha scassinato** la gioielleria.
339 to break in
la colazione
340 breakfast
Che **alito** cattivo!
341 breath
respirare
342 to breathe
La tua casa è fatta di **mattoni**?
343 brick
Questo **muratore** si chiama Pamela.
344 bricklayer
La sposa è un po' timida.
345 bride
Anche **lo sposo** è timido.
346 bridegroom
il ponte
347 bridge
la briglia del cavallo
348 bridle
la borsa di cuoio
349 briefcase
Il sole è **splendente**.
350 bright sun
Baffo mi **porta** le ciabatte.
351 to bring
Sabrina **riporta** i libri alla biblioteca.
352 to bring back
un vetro **fragile**
353 brittle glass
i broccoli
354 broccoli
la spilla
355 brooch
Un ruscello è un fiume piccolino.
356 brook
la scopa
357 broom
Voglio bene a mio **fratello**.
358 I love my brother.

il sopracciglio
359 brow
marrone
360 brown
Angelo ha bisogno di **spazzolarsi** i capelli.
362 to brush
la spazzola
363 brush
Che brutto **livido**!
361 bruise
i cavolini di Bruxelles
366 brussels sprouts
il pennello
364 paintbrush
lo spazzolino da denti
365 toothbrush
A Susanna il bagno piace con tante **bolle** di sapone.
367 bubble
il secchio
368 bucket
la fibbia della cintura
369 belt buckle
il bocciolo
370 bud
il bisonte
371 buffalo
un insetto
372 bug
la tromba dei soldati
373 bugle
costruire
374 to build
il toro
375 bull
il bulldozer
376 bulldozer
Le pallottole sono molto pericolose.
377 bullet
il megafono
378 bullhorn/megaphone*

Leone è un **attaccabrighe**.
379 bully

Osvaldo ha **un bernoccolo** sulla testa.
380 bump

i paraurti
381 bumpers

un mazzo di asparagi
382 bunch

una fascina di legna da ardere
383 bundle

la boa
384 buoy

lo scassinatore
385 burglar

bruciare, ardere
386 to burn

Il palloncino **è scoppiato**.
387 to burst

sotterrare
388 to bury

un autobus
389 bus

la fermata dell'autobus
390 bus stop

Un cespuglio è più piccolo di un albero.
391 bush

In questo momento sono **occupato**.
392 I am busy now.

ma

Vorrei andare, **ma** sono impegnato.
Paolo è alto, **ma** sua sorella è più alta di lui.

I would like to go, but I am busy.
Paolo is tall, but his sister is taller.
393 but

il macellaio
394 butcher

Spalmo **il burro** sul pane.
395 butter

la farfalla
396 butterfly

i bottoni
397 buttons

Filippo si **compra** un gelato.
398 to buy

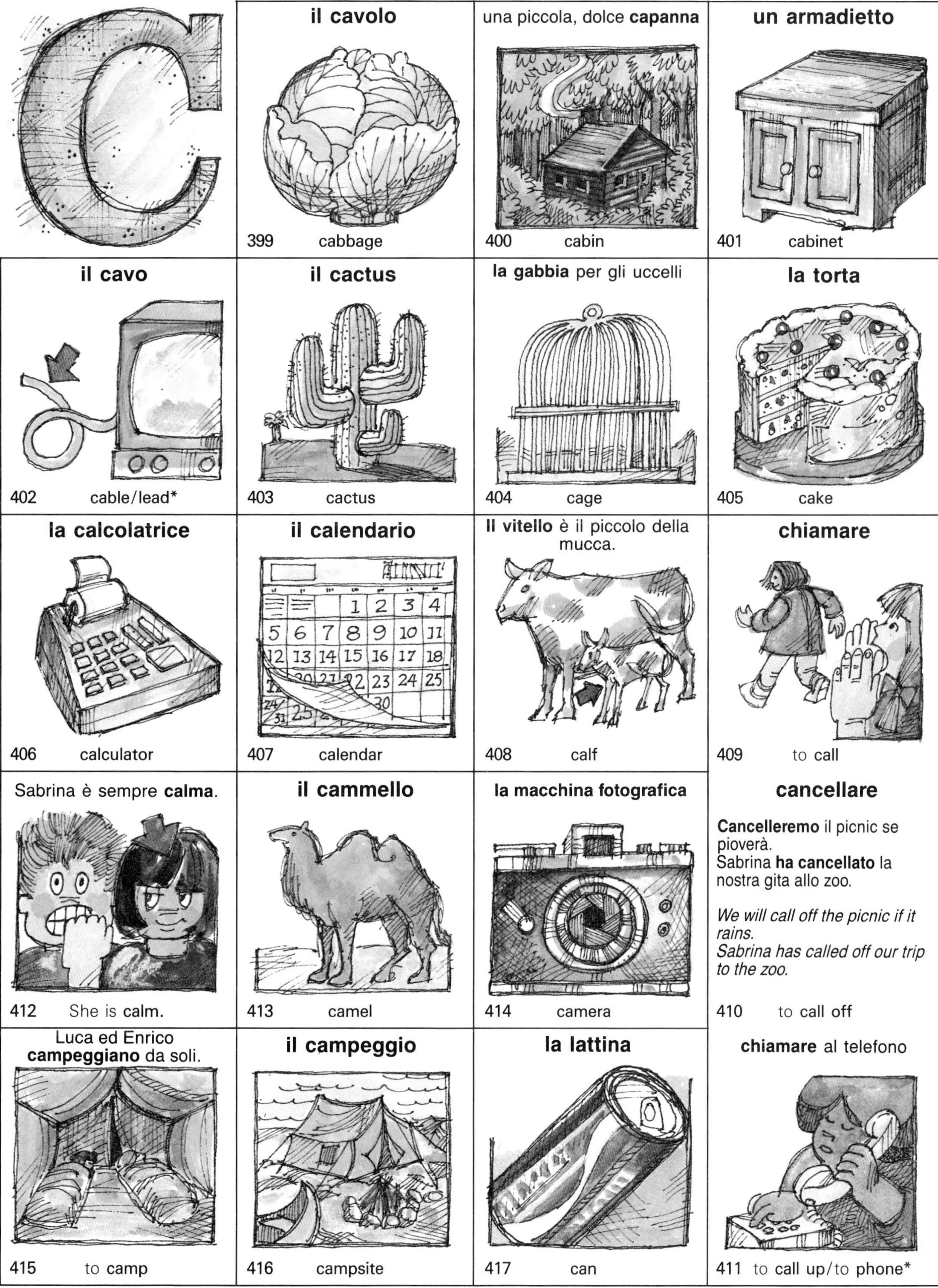
il cavolo
399 cabbage
una piccola, dolce capanna
400 cabin
un armadietto
401 cabinet
il cavo
402 cable/lead*
il cactus
403 cactus
la gabbia per gli uccelli
404 cage
la torta
405 cake
la calcolatrice
406 calculator
il calendario
407 calendar
Il vitello è il piccolo della mucca.
408 calf
chiamare
409 to call
Sabrina è sempre calma.
412 She is calm.
il cammello
413 camel
la macchina fotografica
414 camera
cancellare
Cancelleremo il picnic se pioverà.
Sabrina ha cancellato la nostra gita allo zoo.
We will call off the picnic if it rains.
Sabrina has called off our trip to the zoo.
410 to call off
Luca ed Enrico campeggiano da soli.
415 to camp
il campeggio
416 campsite
la lattina
417 can
chiamare al telefono
411 to call up/to phone*

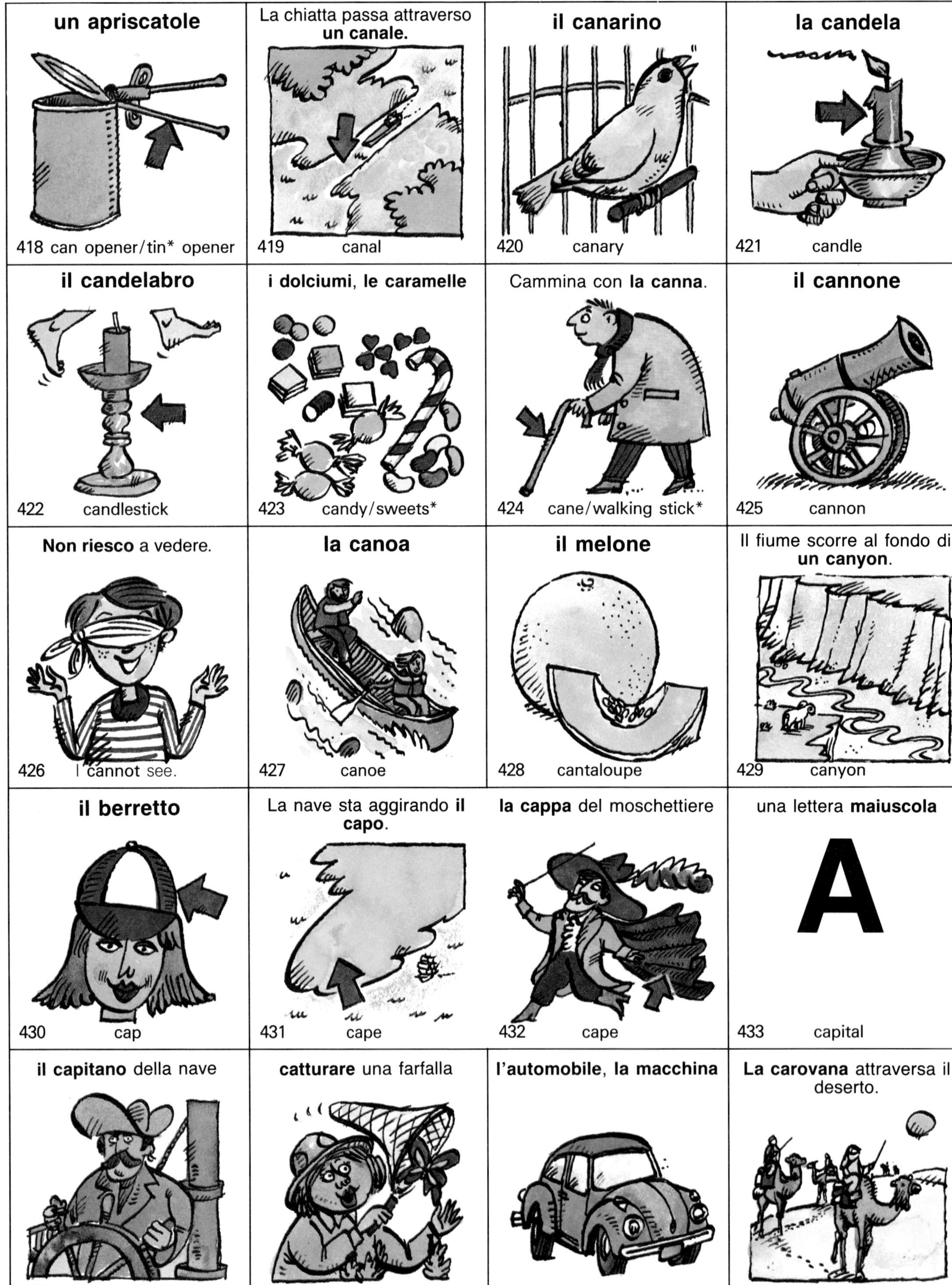
un apriscatole
418 can opener/tin* opener
La chiatta passa attraverso un canale.
419 canal
il canarino
420 canary
la candela
421 candle
il candelabro
422 candlestick
i dolciumi, le caramelle
423 candy/sweets*
Cammina con la canna.
424 cane/walking stick*
il cannone
425 cannon
Non riesco a vedere.
426 I cannot see.
la canoa
427 canoe
il melone
428 cantaloupe
Il fiume scorre al fondo di un canyon.
429 canyon
il berretto
430 cap
La nave sta aggirando il capo.
431 cape
la cappa del moschettiere
432 cape
una lettera maiuscola
A
433 capital
il capitano della nave
434 captain
catturare una farfalla
435 to capture
l'automobile, la macchina
436 car
La carovana attraversa il deserto.
437 caravan

le carte
438 cards
la scatola di cartone
439 cardboard
L'infermiera si prende cura dei malati.
440 to care
Sebastiano è sconsiderato
441 He is careless.
il carico dell'aereo
442 cargo
i garofani
443 carnation
Carnevale, che allegria!
444 carnival
il falegname
445 carpenter
il tappeto
446 carpet
la carrozzina
447 carriage/pram*
la carota
448 carrot
Il Signor Fortini porta una grossa cassa.
449 to carry
il carretto
450 cart
Le viti sono confezionate in scatole da 100.
100
451 carton
trinciare un pollo
452 to carve
il baule
453 case
denaro contante
454 cash
noci di acagiù
455 cashew nuts
il castello
456 castle
il gatto
457 cat

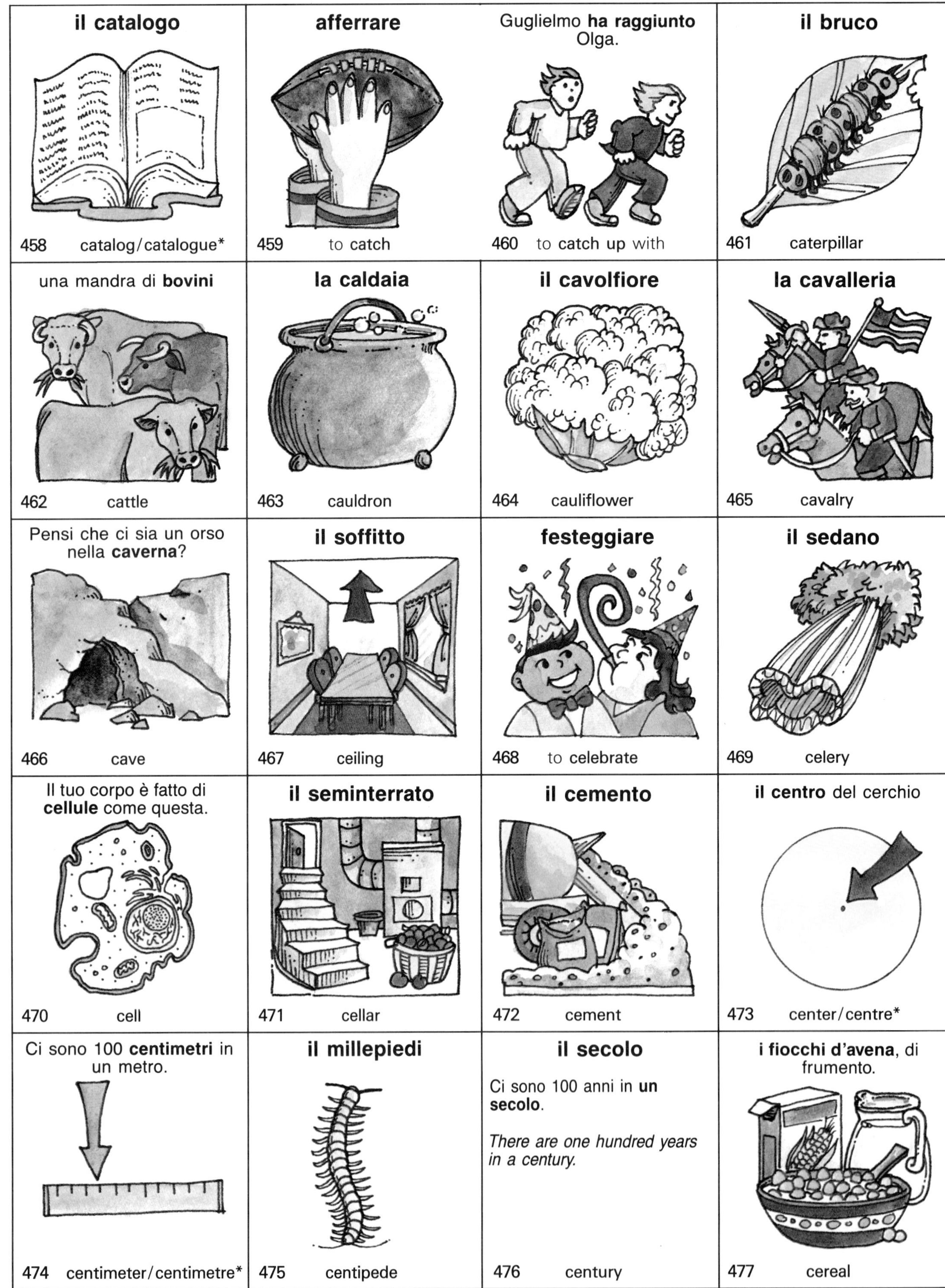
il catalogo
458 catalog/catalogue*
afferrare
459 to catch
Guglielmo ha raggiunto Olga.
460 to catch up with
il bruco
461 caterpillar
una mandra di bovini
462 cattle
la caldaia
463 cauldron
il cavolfiore
464 cauliflower
la cavalleria
465 cavalry
Pensi che ci sia un orso nella caverna?
466 cave
il soffitto
467 ceiling
festeggiare
468 to celebrate
il sedano
469 celery
Il tuo corpo è fatto di cellule come questa.
470 cell
il seminterrato
471 cellar
il cemento
472 cement
il centro del cerchio
473 center/centre*
Ci sono 100 centimetri in un metro.
474 centimeter/centimetre*
il millepiedi
475 centipede
il secolo
Ci sono 100 anni in un secolo.
There are one hundred years in a century.
476 century
i fiocchi d'avena, di frumento.
477 cereal

certo

Sabrina è **certa** d'aver ragione.
Sabrina prova un **certo** sentimento per Filippo.

Sabrina is certain that she is right.
Sabrina has a certain feeling for Filippo.

478 certain

il certificato

479 certificate

la catena

480 chain

la sega a motore

481 chainsaw

la sedia

482 chair

Il gesso serve a scrivere sulla lavagna.

483 chalk

la campionessa

484 champion

gli spiccioli

485 change

un canale navigabile

487 channel

Questo è **il** dodicesimo **capitolo** del libro.

488 chapter

il carattere

Sabrina ha **un caratterino**.
Che cosa significa questo **carattere** cinese?

Sabrina has a strong character.
What does this Chinese character mean?

489 character

Carlo **si è cambiato** i vestiti.

486 to change

il carbone di legna

490 charcoal

il cardo

491 chard

accusare, **ricaricare**

La polizia **ha accusato** Tito di furto.
Il tuo giocattolo si è fermato perchè mi sono scordato di **ricaricare** la batteria.

The police charged Tito with robbery.
Your toy has stopped because I forgot to charge the battery.

492 to charge

il cocchio

493 chariot

il grafico

494 chart

rincorrere

495 to chase

chiacchierare

496 to chat

una matita **a buon mercato**, una corona molto cara

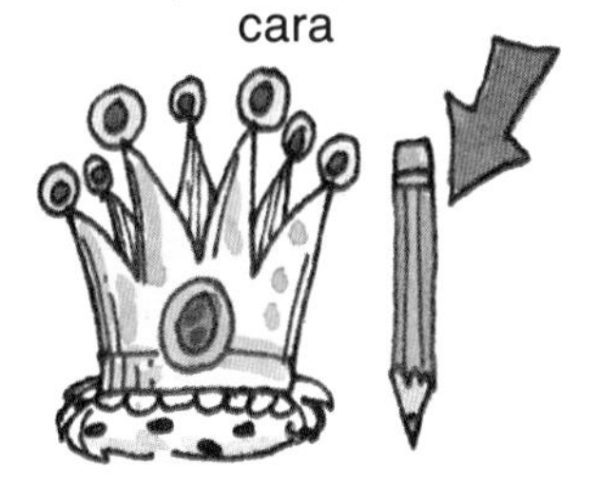

497 **cheap** pencil, expensive crown

Nico **imbroglia**, perché sta copiando.
498 to cheat
controllare, **depositare**
Hai controllato le tue addizioni?
Favorite **depositare** il cappotto all'entrata.
Did you check your addition?
Check your coat at the entrance, please.
499 to check
la guancia
500 cheek
Il formaggio si ricava dal latte.
501 cheese
un assegno
502 cheque*/check
le ciliegie
503 cherries
a **petto** nudo
504 chest
una castagna
505 chestnut
Mastica bene prima di inghiottire.
506 to chew
i ceci
507 chick peas
il pollo
508 chicken
la varicella
509 chicken-pox
Il capo saluta i suoi soldati.
510 chief
la bambina
511 child
una giornata **rigida**
512 a chilly day
il camino
513 chimney
lo scimpanzè
514 chimpanzee
il mento
515 chin
tazze e piattini di **porcellana**
516 china/crockery*
una scheggia di legno
517 chip

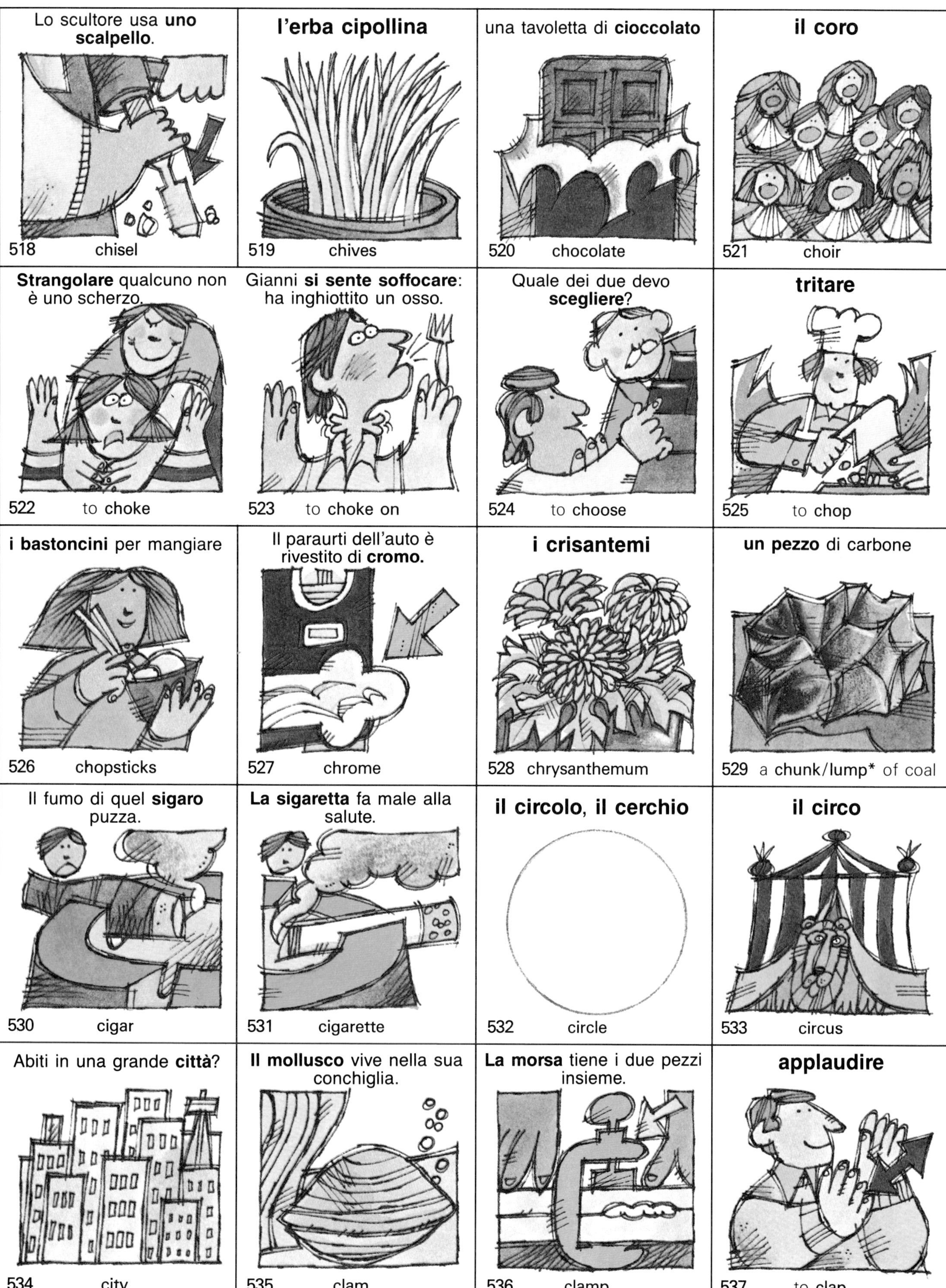
Lo scultore usa **uno scalpello**.
518 chisel
l'erba cipollina
519 chives
una tavoletta di **cioccolato**
520 chocolate
il coro
521 choir
Strangolare qualcuno non è uno scherzo.
522 to choke
Gianni **si sente soffocare**: ha inghiottito un osso.
523 to choke on
Quale dei due devo **scegliere**?
524 to choose
tritare
525 to chop
i bastoncini per mangiare
526 chopsticks
Il paraurti dell'auto è rivestito di **cromo.**
527 chrome
i crisantemi
528 chrysanthemum
un pezzo di carbone
529 a chunk/lump* of coal
Il fumo di quel **sigaro** puzza.
530 cigar
La sigaretta fa male alla salute.
531 cigarette
il circolo, **il cerchio**
532 circle
il circo
533 circus
Abiti in una grande **città**?
534 city
Il mollusco vive nella sua conchiglia.
535 clam
La morsa tiene i due pezzi insieme.
536 clamp
applaudire
537 to clap

l'aula scolastica 538 classroom	Il granchio ha **chele** molto robuste. 539 claw	**l'argilla** **L'argilla** si usa per fare i mattoni. Si possono anche fare vasi e piatti con **l'argilla**. *Clay is used to make bricks. You can also make pots and dishes out of clay.* 540 clay	La bambina è **pulita**. 541 She is all **clean**.
Zia Anna **sparecchia** la tavola. 542 to clear	**la rupe** 543 cliff	**arrampicarsi**, **scalare** 544 to climb	**la clinica** 545 clinic
tagliare 546 to clip	**un orologio** da tavolo 547 clock	Nina **chiude** il libro. 548 to close	**Il** tuo **guardaroba** è in ordine? 549 closet/cupboard*
la stoffa, **lo strofinaccio** I vestiti sono fatti di **stoffa**. La mamma usa uno **strofinaccio** da cucina per lavare i piatti. *Clothes are made out of cloth. Mother uses a dishcloth to wipe the dishes.* 550 cloth	**i vestiti** 551 clothes	**il filo per stendere** i panni 552 clothes line	**la nuvola** 553 cloud
Un trifoglio con quattro foglie porta fortuna. 554 clover	**il pagliaccio** 555 clown	Thal usa **la clava** per cacciare. 556 club	**l'indizio**, **il suggerimento** La polizia ha trovato **un indizio** per il delitto. Ti darò un **suggerimento**. *The police found a clue to the crime.* *I will give you a clue.* 557 clue

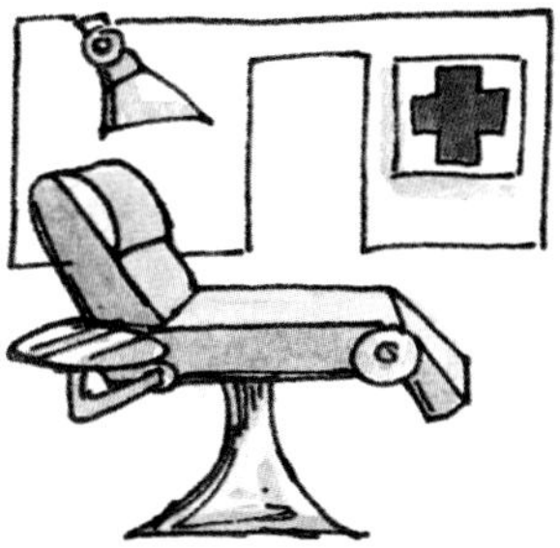

Per inserire la marcia, si schiaccia **la frizione.**

558 clutch

Afferra la corda!

559 to clutch

E' **il** nostro **allenatore**.

560 coach

Abbiamo viaggiato in **corriera.**

561 coach

Il carbone viene estratto nelle miniere.

563 coal

ruvido, **grossolano**

Questa stoffa è molto **ruvida**.
Non usare parole **grossolane**!

This cloth is very coarse.
Do not use coarse language!

564 coarse

la costa

565 coast

allenare

Teresa **allena** la squadra due volte alla settimana.

Teresa coaches the team twice a week.

562 to coach

D'inverno occorre **un cappotto** pesante.

566 coat

Il ragno tesse **la ragnatela**.

567 cobweb

una tazza di **cacao** caldo

568 cocoa

la noce di cocco

569 coconut

il merluzzo

570 cod

Con questi chicchi si fa del buon **caffè.**

571 coffee

la cassa da morto

572 coffin

la serpentina

573 coil

la moneta

574 coin

Ho **freddo**.

575 I am cold.

il colletto

576 collar

La sorella di Sabrina **colleziona** francobolli.

577 to collect

Il collegio è una scuola per studenti grandi.

578 college

Le automobili **si scontrano** se i guidatori s'addormentano.

579 to collide

uno scontro frontale

580 collision

Qual'è **il colore** che preferisci?

581 color/colours*

una cavalla col suo **puledro**

582 colt

due **colonne** di marmo

583 column

il pettine

584 comb

Sandra **si pettina** i capelli.

585 to comb

mescolare gli ingredienti

586 combine

venire

Sabrina **è venuta** alla festa in autobus.
Dile di **venire** a casa!

Sabrina came to the party by bus.
Tell her to come home.

587 to come

La maniglia **si è staccata**.

588 to come off

E' svenuto, ma **si sta riprendendo**.

589 to come to

comodo

590 comfortable

Una virgola in realtà non è così grossa.

591 comma

comandare, dare un comando

592 to command

la comunità

La scuola è stata costruita con l'impegno dell'intera **comunità**.

The school was built thanks to the effort of the entire community.

593 community

due **compagni** inseparabili

594 companion

Sono in buona **compagnia**.

595 I am in good company.

paragonare

596 to compare

La mia **bussola** indica il nord.

597 My compass points north.

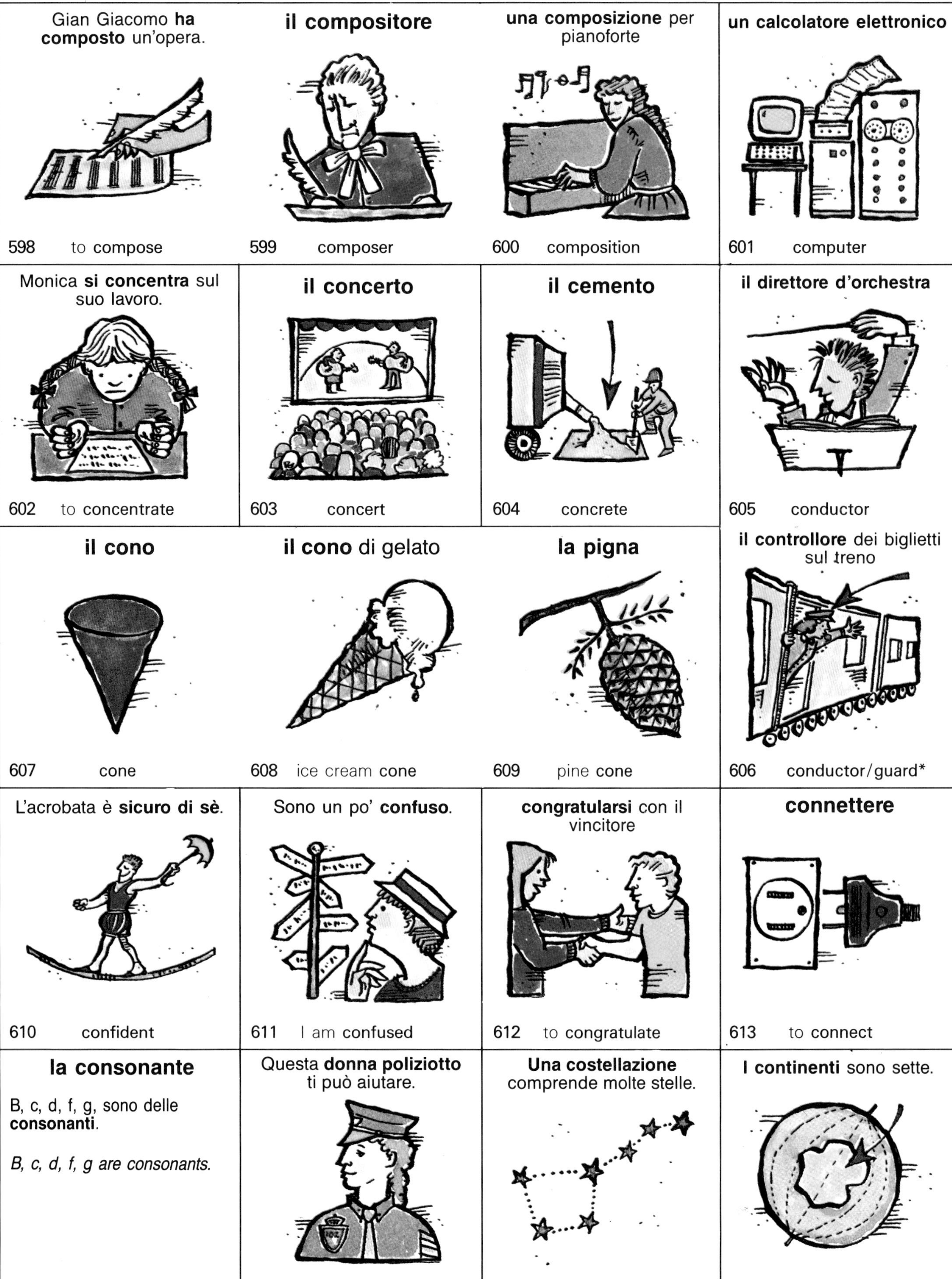
Gian Giacomo **ha composto** un'opera.
598 to compose
il compositore
599 composer
una composizione per pianoforte
600 composition
un calcolatore elettronico
601 computer
Monica **si concentra** sul suo lavoro.
602 to concentrate
il concerto
603 concert
il cemento
604 concrete
il direttore d'orchestra
605 conductor
il cono
607 cone
il cono di gelato
608 ice cream cone
la pigna
609 pine cone
il controllore dei biglietti sul treno
606 conductor/guard*
L'acrobata è **sicuro di sè**.
610 confident
Sono un po' **confuso**.
611 I am confused
congratularsi con il vincitore
612 to congratulate
connettere
613 to connect
la consonante
B, c, d, f, g, sono delle **consonanti**.
B, c, d, f, g are consonants.
614 consonant
Questa **donna poliziotto** ti può aiutare.
615 constable
Una costellazione comprende molte stelle.
616 constellation
I continenti sono sette.
617 continent

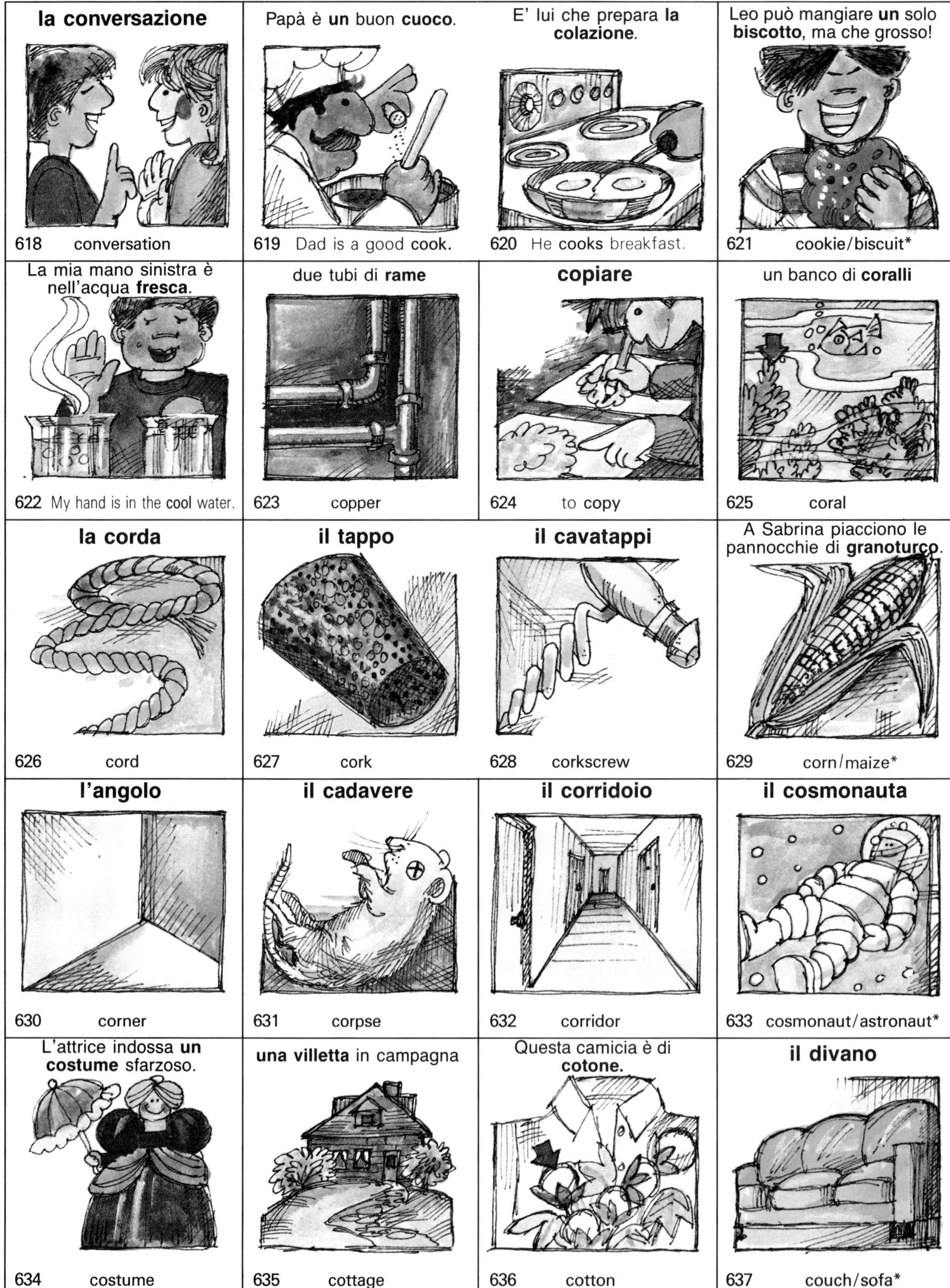
la conversazione
618 conversation
Papà è **un** buon **cuoco**.
619 Dad is a good **cook**.
E' lui che prepara **la colazione**.
620 He **cooks** breakfast.
Leo può mangiare **un** solo **biscotto**, ma che grosso!
621 cookie/biscuit*
La mia mano sinistra è nell'acqua **fresca**.
622 My hand is in the **cool** water.
due tubi di **rame**
623 copper
copiare
624 to copy
un banco di **coralli**
625 coral
la corda
626 cord
il tappo
627 cork
il cavatappi
628 corkscrew
A Sabrina piacciono le pannocchie di **granoturco**.
629 corn/maize*
l'angolo
630 corner
il cadavere
631 corpse
il corridoio
632 corridor
il cosmonauta
633 cosmonaut/astronaut*
L'attrice indossa **un costume** sfarzoso.
634 costume
una villetta in campagna
635 cottage
Questa camicia è di **cotone.**
636 cotton
il divano
637 couch/sofa*

Livia **tossisce** educatamente.
638 to cough
contare
639 to count
il contatore
1234
640 counter
Mettilo sul **banco**!
641 counter
Vai spesso in **campagna**?
642 country
Questo **paese** è il Canada.
643 country
Mamma e papà fanno **una** bella **coppia.**
644 couple
Ci vuole **un** bel **coraggio** per combattere un drago.
645 courage
il campo da tennis
646 court
La mia **cugina** è figlia dello zio Carlo.
647 My **cousin** is my uncle's daughter.
coprire
648 to cover
il coperchio
649 cover
la mucca, la vacca
650 cow
Questo ragazzo è **un codardo**.
651 This boy is a **coward**.
il cow-boy
652 cowboy
un grosso **granchio**
653 crab
Il vaso ha **un'incrinatura**.
654 crack
il cracker
655 cracker
la culla
656 cradle
La gru è un uccello migratore.
657 crane

una gru in un cantiere edile
658 crane

schiantarsi, scontrarsi
659 to crash

Che cosa c'è nella **gabbia**?
660 crate

camminare carponi, strisciare
661 to crawl

il gambero
662 crayfish

i pastelli, le matite colorate
663 crayons

la panna, **la crema**
A papà piace **la panna** nel caffè.
La **crema** solare previene le scottature.
Dad likes cream in his coffee.
Sun cream prevents sunburn.
664 cream

la piega
665 crease

Che strana **creatura**!
666 creature

Un torrente è un piccolo fiume.
667 creek

l'equipaggio della nave
668 the crew

un lettino per bimbi
669 crib/cot*

il grillo
670 cricket

un criminale dietro le sbarre
671 criminal

il coccodrillo
672 crocodile

Quando spunta **il croco**, la primavera è alle porte.
673 crocus

Quell'imbrogliona ha rubato una mela.
674 crook

un palo **storto**
675 crooked post

La torre è diritta, ma il quadro è **inclinato**.
676 crooked painting, upright tower

un buon **raccolto**
677 crop

la croce
678 cross
Guarda prima di attraversare.
679 to cross
Il 6 è cancellato.
680 to cross out
il corvo
681 crow
Che folla in cosi poco spazio!
682 A big crowd in a small space.
la corona
683 crown
Messer Baldo incorona la nuova regina.
684 to crown
le briciole
685 crumb
Per fare il vino, Ermenegildo pigia l'uva.
686 to crush
Sabrina preferisce la crosta.
687 crust
la gruccia
688 crutch
piangere
689 to cry
una sfera di cristallo
690 crystal
il cucciolo di un'orsa
691 cub
il cubo
692 cube
il cuculo
693 cuckoo
il cetriolo
694 cucumber
il polsino della camicia
695 cuff
una tazza di tè
696 cup
La brocca è sulla credenza.
697 cupboard

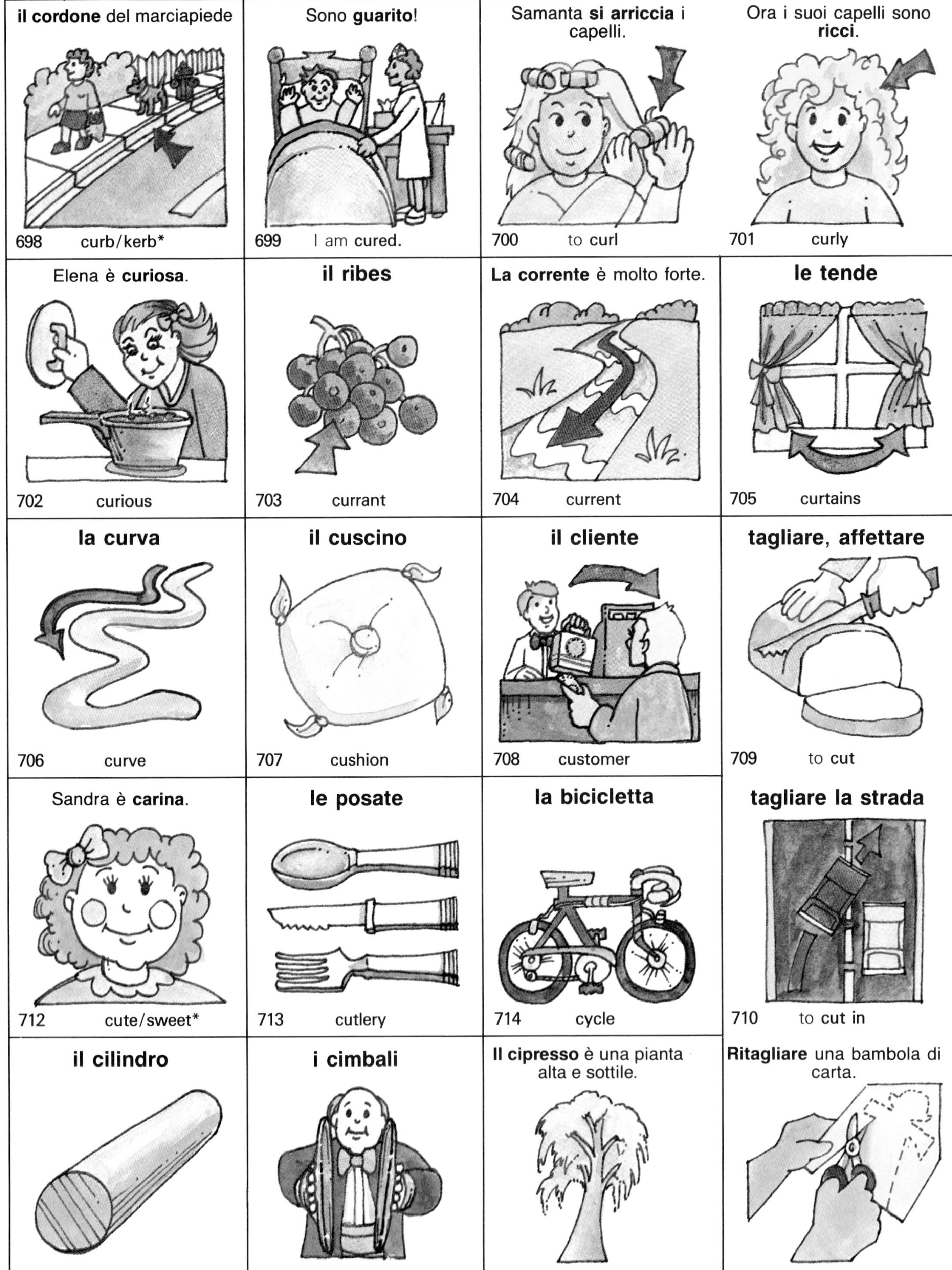

il cordone del marciapiede 698 curb/kerb*	Sono **guarito**! 699 I am **cured**.	Samanta **si arriccia** i capelli. 700 to **curl**	Ora i suoi capelli sono **ricci**. 701 **curly**
Elena è **curiosa**. 702 curious	**il ribes** 703 currant	**La corrente** è molto forte. 704 current	**le tende** 705 curtains
la curva 706 curve	**il cuscino** 707 cushion	**il cliente** 708 customer	**tagliare, affettare** 709 to cut
Sandra è **carina**. 712 cute/sweet*	**le posate** 713 cutlery	**la bicicletta** 714 cycle	**tagliare la strada** 710 to **cut in**
il cilindro 715 cylinder	**i cimbali** 716 cymbals	**Il cipresso** è una pianta alta e sottile. 717 cypress	**Ritagliare** una bambola di carta. 711 to **cut out**

La giunchiglia fiorisce in primavera.
718 daffodil
il pugnale
719 dagger
un giornale quotidiano
720 daily
un'azienda che produce latte
721 dairy
Sfogliamo insieme una margherita.
722 daisy
Una diga sbarra il fiume.
723 dam
un pacco danneggiato
724 damaged
umido
725 damp
danzare, ballare
726 to dance
la ballerina
727 dancer
Il dente di leone è un'erbaccia dannosa.
728 dandelion
Attenzione, pericolo!
729 danger
Leone non ha paura del buio.
730 dark
il gioco dei dardi
731 dart
il cruscotto
732 dashboard
Qual'è la data di oggi?
1 2 3 4 5
6 7 8 9 10 11 12
13 14 15 16 17 18 19
20 21 22 23 24 25 26
27 28 29 30 31
733 date
E' mia figlia Grazia.
734 daughter
l'inizio di una bella giornata
735 the start of a nice day
un topo morto
736 dead mouse

I sordi non ci sentono.

737 deaf

caro

Carlo è un **caro** amico.
Cara mamma, al campeggio mi diverto tanto.

Carlo is a dear friend.
Dear Mom, camp is fun!

738 dear

Dicembre è l'ultimo mese dell'anno.

739 December

decidere

Sabrina non riesce a **decidere** che cosa indossare. Forse la mamma dovrà **decidere** per lei.

Sabrina cannot decide what to wear.
Mom may have to decide for her.

740 to decide

il ponte della nave

741 deck

Il pirata **decora** l'albero di Natale.

742 to decorate

la decorazione

743 decoration

Alberto evita il lato **profondo** della piscina.

744 deep end

C'è **un cervo** nella foresta!

745 deer

consegnare

746 to deliver

Battista mi **ha ammaccato** la macchina.

747 to dent

la dentista

748 dentist

un grande magazzino

749 department store

il deserto

750 desert

Chi mi ha messo **la scrivania** nel deserto?

751 desk

il dessert

752 dessert

Godzilla **distrugge** la città.

753 to destroy

Il cacciatorpediniere è una nave militare.

754 destroyer

l'investigatore

755 detective

Al mattino le foglie sono coperte di **rugiada**.

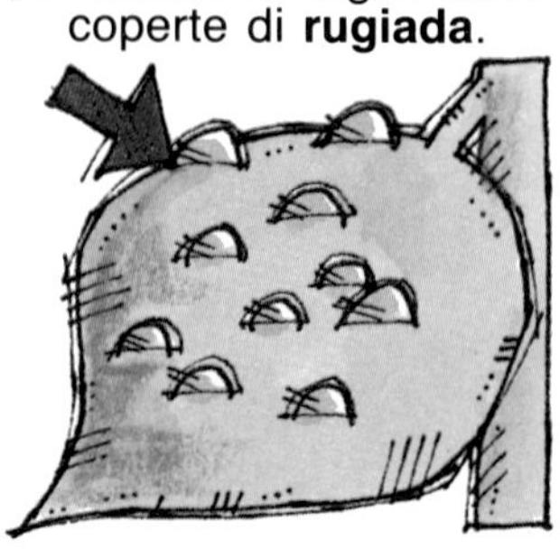

756 dew

la diagonale 757 diagonal	**il diagramma** 758 diagram	**il diamante** 759 diamond	I bebè hanno bisogno di **pannolini.** 760 diaper/nappy*
Tieni **un diario**? 761 diary	Sta cercando una parola nel **dizionario**. 762 dictionary	**morire** 763 to die	**differenza** Tutti nascono uguali, non c'è nessuna **differenza.** C'è molta **differenza** tra la notte e il giorno. *All people are born equal, there is no difference. There is quite a difference between night and day.* 764 difference
gente **diversa** 765 different people	**vangare** 766 to dig	Il serpente **digerisce** un elefante. 767 The snake **digests** an elephant.	La luce nella stanza è **fioca**. 768 dim
Sabrina ha due **fossette** nelle guance. 769 dimple	**il canotto** 770 dinghy	**la sala da pranzo** 771 dining room	**una cena** a luce di candela 772 dinner
il dinosauro 773 dinosaur	**La direzione** è questa! 774 direction	Papà ha camminato tra **l'immondizia**. 775 dirt	I suoi pantaloni sono **sporchi**. 776 dirty

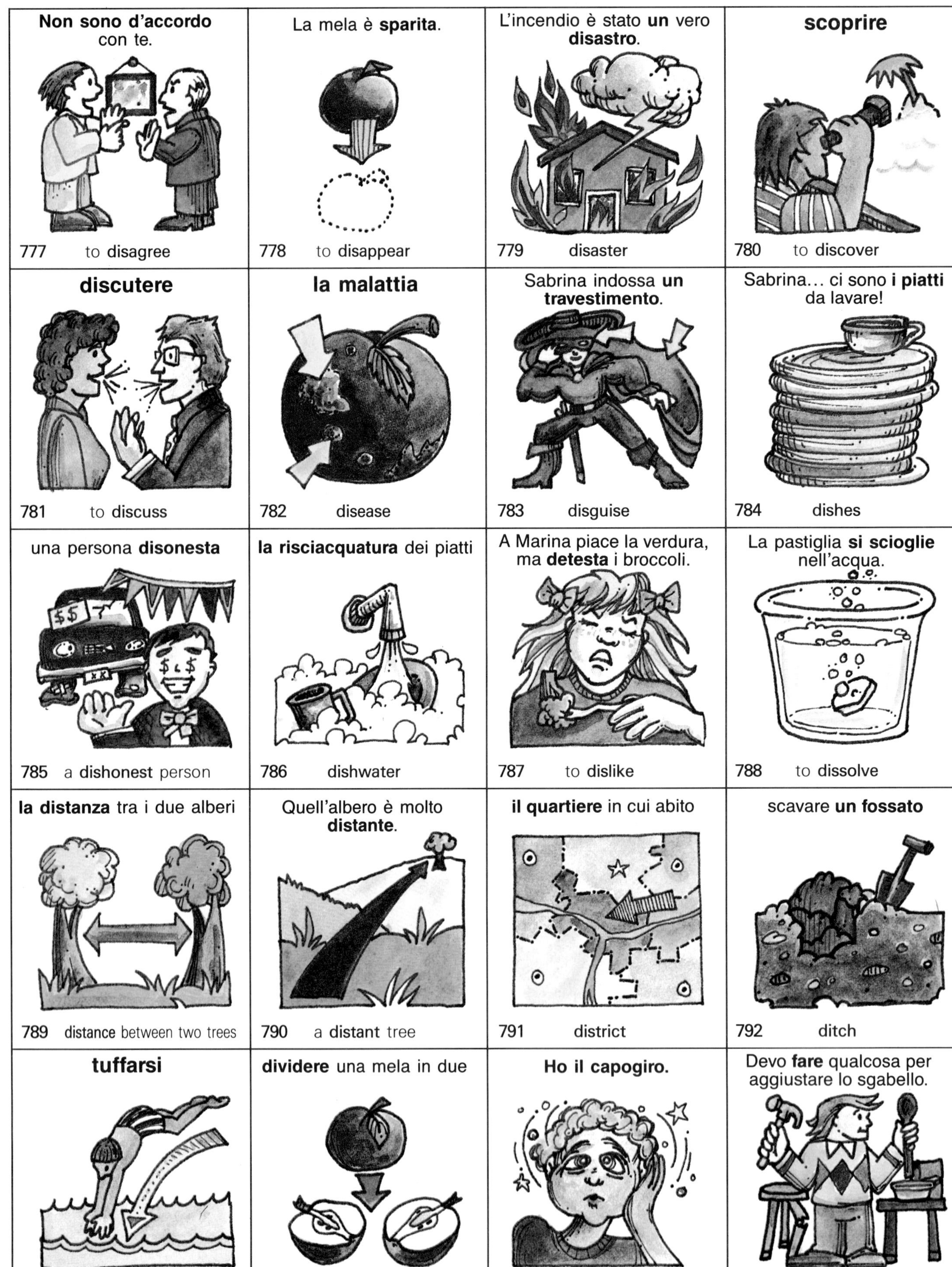
Non sono d'accordo con te.
777 to disagree
La mela è **sparita**.
778 to disappear
L'incendio è stato **un** vero **disastro**.
779 disaster
scoprire
780 to discover
discutere
781 to discuss
la malattia
782 disease
Sabrina indossa **un travestimento**.
783 disguise
Sabrina... ci sono **i piatti** da lavare!
784 dishes
una persona **disonesta**
785 a dishonest person
la risciacquatura dei piatti
786 dishwater
A Marina piace la verdura, ma **detesta** i broccoli.
787 to dislike
La pastiglia **si scioglie** nell'acqua.
788 to dissolve
la distanza tra i due alberi
789 distance between two trees
Quell'albero è molto **distante**.
790 a distant tree
il quartiere in cui abito
791 district
scavare **un fossato**
792 ditch
tuffarsi
793 to dive
dividere una mela in due
794 to divide
Ho il capogiro.
795 I feel dizzy.
Devo **fare** qualcosa per aggiustare lo sgabello.
796 What shall I do?

797	**il pontile**	dock
798	**il dottore**	doctor
799	**il cane**	dog
800	**la bambola**	doll
801	**il delfino**	dolphin
802	**la cupola**	dome
803	Farfarello è **un asino** fortissimo.	donkey
804	**la porta**	door
805	**la maniglia**	doorknob
806	**doppio**	double
807	**la pasta**	dough
808	**La colomba** è il simbolo della pace.	dove
809	Sabrina ha un cuscino di **piume.**	down
810	Come mai Samanta **sonnecchia** a scuola?	to doze
811	**una dozzina** di uova	dozen
812	Non **trascinare** la borsa per terra!	to drag
813	**il drago**	dragon
814	**la libellula**	dragonfly
815	**lo scarico**	drain/plug hole*
816	Roberto **disegna** bene.	to draw

Alzate il **ponte levatoio**!
817 drawbridge

Le calze di Sabrina non sono in questo **cassetto**.
818 drawer

un bel **sogno**
819 a nice **dream**

Sta sognando delle pecore.
820 I **dream** of sheep.

il vestito
821 dress

vestirsi
822 to dress

Forse le calze di Sabrina sono in questo **cassettone**.
823 dresser/chest of drawers*

sbavare
824 to dribble

Andare alla deriva non è molto divertente.
825 to drift

Patrizia **sta forando** una tavola.
826 to drill

il trapano electtrico
827 drill

una bevanda alcoolica
828 drink

gocciolare
830 to drip

Io **guido** con prudenza.
831 I **drive** carefully.

un guidatore imprudente
832 crazy **driver**

bere
829 to drink

pioggerella

La pioggerella è una pioggia leggera.

Drizzle is a light rain.
833 drizzle

Il Griso **sbava** alla vista del pollo.
834 to drool

una goccia di medicina
835 drop

L'ospite **ha lasciato cadere** il bicchiere.
836 to drop

Vieni a **farmi visita** in qualunque momento.
837 to drop in
Papà **lascia** il gatto dal veterinario.
838 Dad **drops off** the cat at the vet.
abbandonare la gara
839 to **drop out**
Sono assonnato.
840 I feel **drowsy**.
il tamburo
841 drum
una maglietta **asciutta**
842 dry
asciugare, far asciugare
843 to dry
una lavanderia a secco
844 dry cleaner
un essicatoio
845 dryer
la duchessa
846 duchess
un'anitra
847 duck
Un duello non è un bel modo di discutere.
848 duel
il duca
849 duke
il deposito dei rifiuti
850 dump
scaricare
851 to dump
un autocarro ribaltabile
852 dumptruck/lorry*
Il prigioniero è rinchiuso in **una cella sotterranea**.
853 dungeon
il crepuscolo
854 dusk
la polvere
855 dust
il nano
856 dwarf

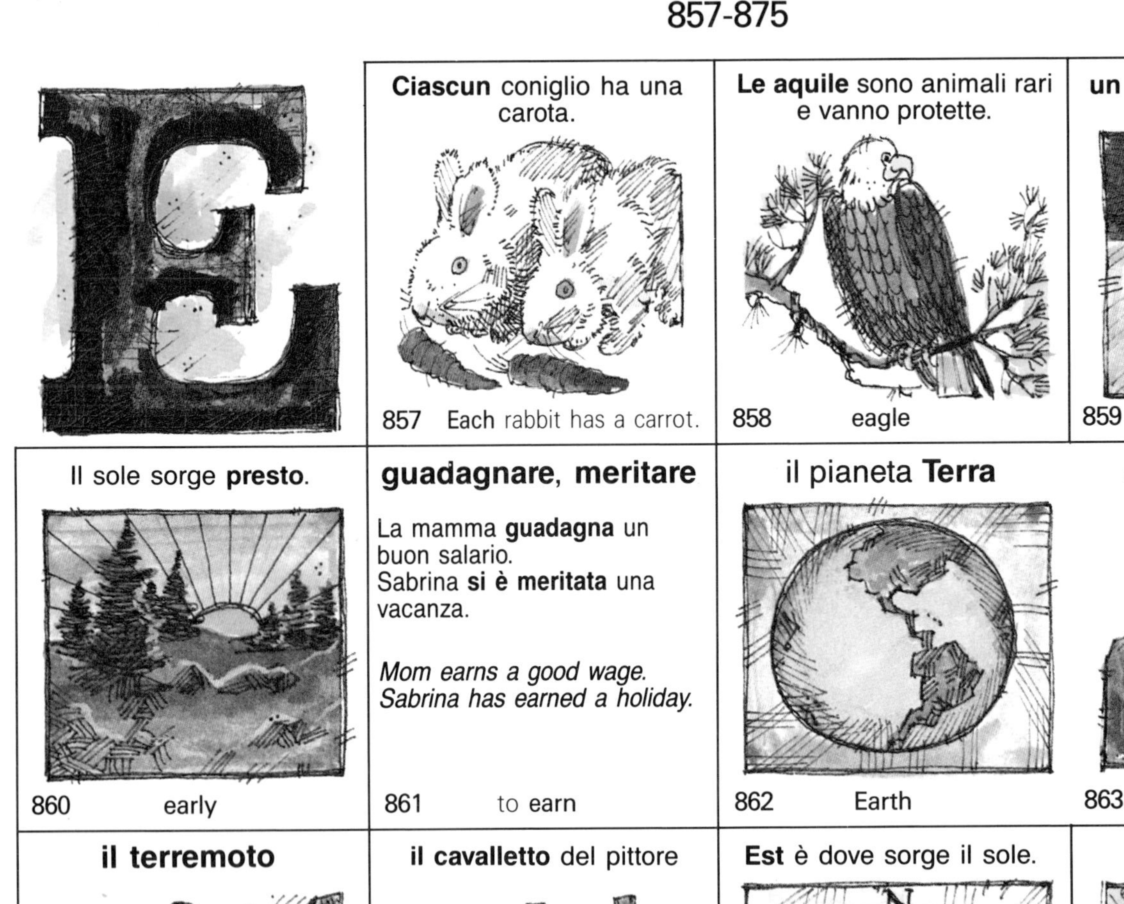

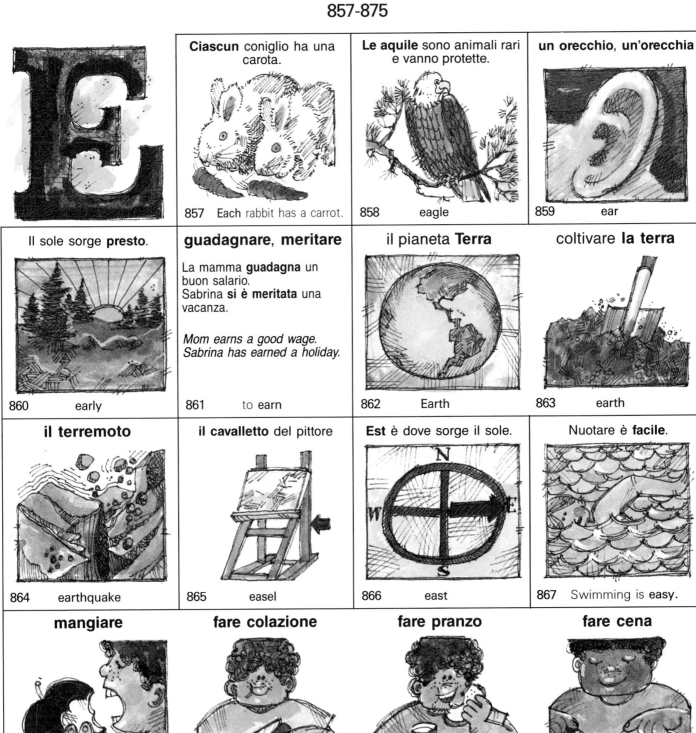

Ciascun coniglio ha una carota.

857 Each rabbit has a carrot.

Le aquile sono animali rari e vanno protette.

858 eagle

un orecchio, **un'orecchia**

859 ear

Il sole sorge **presto**.

860 early

guadagnare, meritare

La mamma **guadagna** un buon salario.
Sabrina **si è meritata** una vacanza.

Mom earns a good wage.
Sabrina has earned a holiday.

861 to earn

il pianeta **Terra**

862 Earth

coltivare **la terra**

863 earth

il terremoto

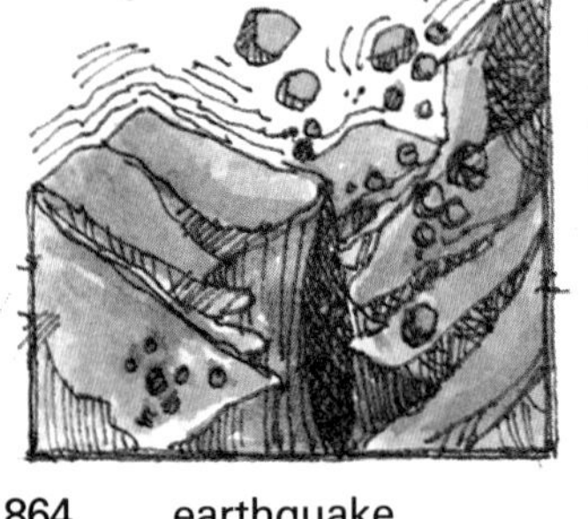

864 earthquake

il cavalletto del pittore

865 easel

Est è dove sorge il sole.

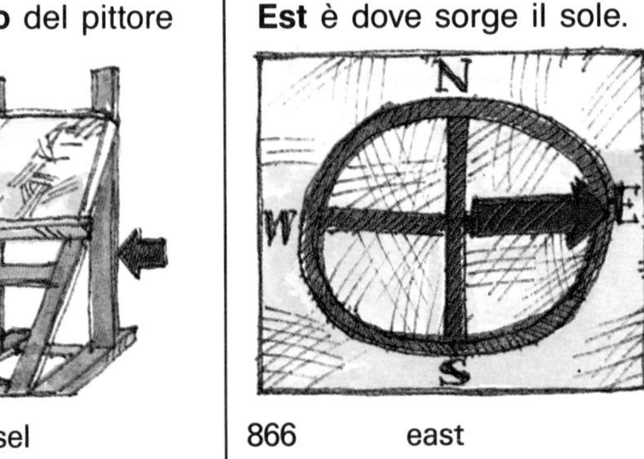

866 east

Nuotare è **facile**.

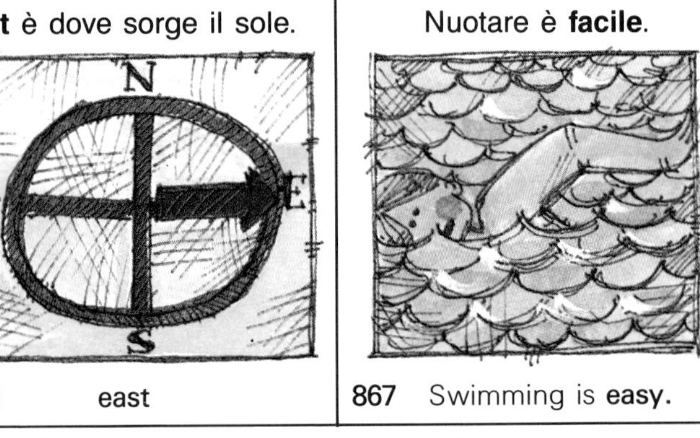

867 Swimming is **easy**.

mangiare

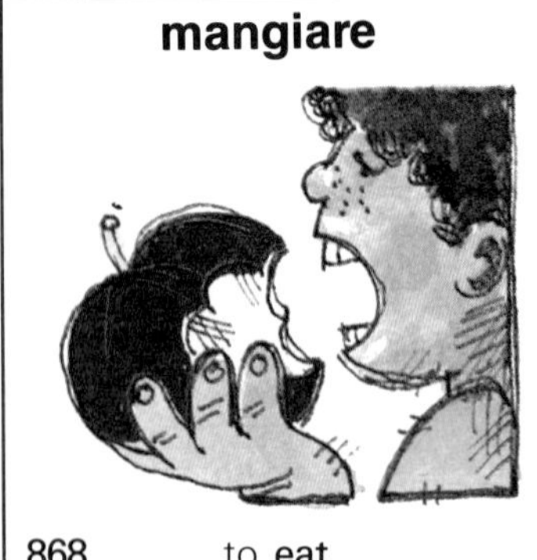

868 to eat

fare colazione

869 to eat breakfast

fare pranzo

870 to eat lunch

fare cena

871 to eat dinner/supper*

L'eco rimanda la voce.

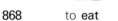

872 echo

un'eclisse di sole

873 eclipse

L'albero è sul **ciglio** del burrone.

874 The tree is at the **edge**.

un'anguilla

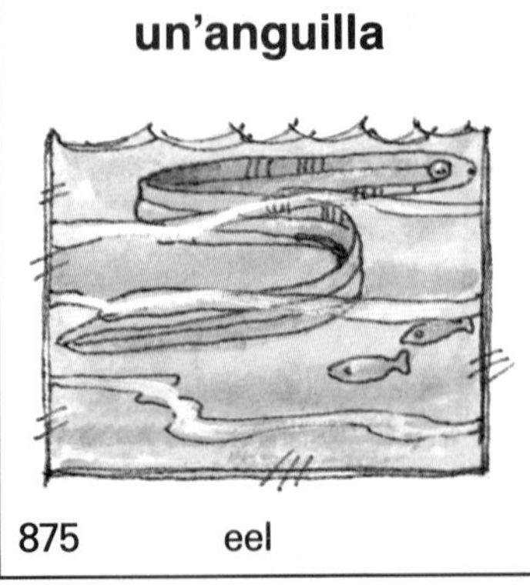

875 eel

La gallina ha fatto **un uovo**.
876 egg

una melanzana di color violetto
877 eggplant/aubergine*

otto insetti
878 eight

L'ottavo pesce è rosso.
879 eighth

Pippo gioca con **l'elastico**.
880 elastic

il gomito
881 elbow

le elezioni
Si tengono **le elezioni** per scegliere il governo.
Chi ha vinto **le elezioni**?
Elections are held to choose the government.
Who won the election?
882 election

un elettricista
883 electrician

l'elettricità
884 electricity

un elefante
885 elephant

un ascensore
886 elevator/lift*

l'alce
887 elk

un olmo
888 elm

Giorgio l'ha **imbarazzato.**
889 to embarrass

abbracciare
890 to embrace

il ricamo
891 embroidery

un'emergenza
892 emergency

La scatola è **vuota**.
893 The jar is **empty**.

E' **la fine** della strada.
894 This is the **end**.

Un giorno non saranno più **nemici.**
895 enemies

il motore di un'automobile
896 engine

il macchinista del treno
897 engineer/engine driver*

godere, godersi
898 to enjoy

I dinosauri erano animali **enormi.**
899 enormous dinosaur

abbastanza, basta
900 That is enough.

Fido **entra** dalla porta.
901 to enter

l'entrata
902 entrance

la busta
903 envelope

La loro forza è **uguale**.
904 equal

l'equatore
905 equator

la commissione

Sabrina sta facendo **una commissione** per suo papà.
Ha molte **commissioni** da fare questa mattina.

Sabrina is running an errand for Dad.
She has many errands this morning.

906 errand

la scala mobile
907 escalator

Ce l'ha fatta a **scappare**.
908 to escape

L'Europa è un continente.
909 Europe

Il sole causa **l'evaporazione** dell'acqua.
910 evaporation

Quattro è un numero **pari**.
911 Four is an **even** number.

una superficie **piana**
912 an **even** surface

Il pino è una pianta **sempreverde**.
913 evergreen

ogni

Sabrina si fa il letto **ogni** mattina.
Devo dirtelo **ogni** volta?

Sabrina makes her bed every day.
Must I tell you every time?

914 every

un esame difficile
915 exam

esaminare con la lente

916 to examine

un esempio

Qualche volta Sabrina non dà buon **esempio**.
E' più facile capire quando si fa **un esempio**.

Sometimes Sabrina does not set a good example.
Things are easier to understand when you give an example.

917 example

il punto esclamativo

918 exclamation mark

Mi scusi!

919 Excuse me!

Giunone **fa ginnastica**.

920 to exercise

esistere

Esistere vuol dire essere.
I dinosauri non **esistono** più.

To exist is to be.
Dinosaurs no longer exist.

921 to exist

uscire

922 to exit/leave*

Il pallone **si dilata** finché scoppia.

923 to expand

aspettare, aspettarsi

Vi aspettiamo alle due.
Papà **si aspetta** che tu sia brava, Sabrina.

We expect you at two o'clock.
Dad expects you to be good, Sabrina.

924 to expect

caro, costoso

925 expensive

un esperimento

926 experiment

un'esperta

927 expert

Adesso te lo **spiego.**

928 to explain

L'avventuriero **esplora** la giungla.

929 to explore

un'esplosione

930 explosion

un estintore

931 extinguisher

un occhio

932 eye

il sopracciglio

933 eyebrow

gli occhiali

934 eyeglasses/spectacles*

le ciglia

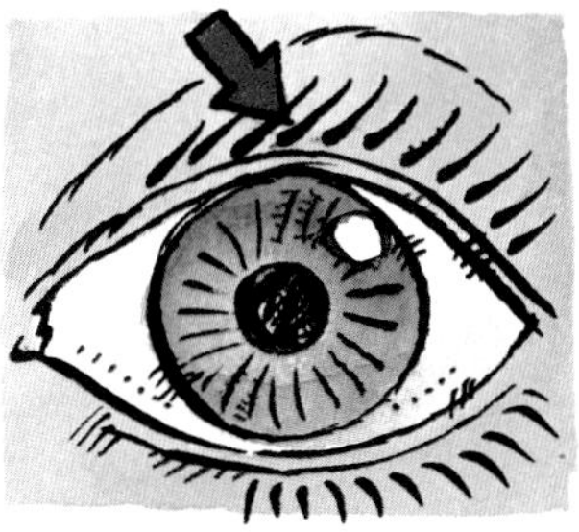

935 eyelash

F
la favola della cicala e della formica
936 fable
la faccia, il viso
937 face
la fabbrica
938 factory
Pierino **è stato bocciato**.
939 to fail
La macchina **si è rotta**.
940 to fail
la fiera
941 fair
La fata accoglierà un tuo desiderio.
942 fairy
fede, fiducia
Abbiamo **fiducia** in te.
Sabrina l'ha accettato **in buona fede**.
We have faith in you.
Sabrina accepted it in good faith.
943 faith
Questo quadro è **falso**.
944 fake painting
In **autunno** le foglie cadono.
945 fall/autumn*
cadere
946 to fall
Per fortuna, era un **falso** allarme.
949 false alarm
la famiglia
950 family
cadere, cascare
947 to fall down
cascare, fare una caduta
948 to fall off
Marilyn è un'attrice **famosa.**
951 famous actress
il ventilatore
952 fan
i costumi **eleganti**
953 fancy clothes
le zanne del leone
954 fang

La città è **lontana**.
955 The city is **far** away.
Addio!
956 Farewell !
Molti alimenti provengono dalle **fattorie.**
957 farm
il contadino, **l'agricoltore**
958 farmer
veloce
959 fast
allacciare la cintura di sicurezza
960 I **fasten** my seatbelt.
Brentano è **grasso** perché mangia troppi dolci.
961 fat
Il veleno è **mortale**.
962 fatal
il padre
963 father
Il rubinetto perde.
964 faucet/tap*
Di chi è **la colpa**?
965 Whose **fault** is it?
il favore
Posso chiederti **un favore**? Sabrina è gentile: fa volentieri **favori** alla gente.
Can I ask you a favor? Sabrina is nice; she likes doing people favors.
966 favor/favour*
Il mio gusto **preferito**!
967 favorite/favourite*
temere il peggio
968 to **fear** the worst
il banchetto
969 feast
E' **la piuma** di un canguro?
970 feather
Febbraio è il secondo mese dell'anno.
971 February
dar da mangiare
972 to **feed**
Mi sento bene.
973 I **feel** well.
La femmina dell'uccello fa le uova.
974 female

la staccionata
975 fence
il parafango
976 fender/wing*
la felce
977 fern
Meglio prendere il traghetto che nuotare!
978 ferry
la festa, la celebrazione
979 festival
Paolo ha la febbre alta.
980 fever
Pochi erano presenti.
981 Few people came.
il campo
982 field
Chiara è la quinta.
1 2 3 4
983 fifth
Questi sciocchi bisticciano sempre.
984 to fight
Fiorella si lima le unghie.
985 to file
riempire, colmare
986 to fill
una pellicola per la macchina fotografica
988 film
un maiale molto sporco
989 filthy
la pinna di uno squalo
990 fin
fare il pieno
987 to fill up
Il poliziotto le dà una multa per eccesso di velocità.
991 fine
Io sto bene.
992 I am fine.
il dito
993 finger
l'impronta digitale
994 fingerprint

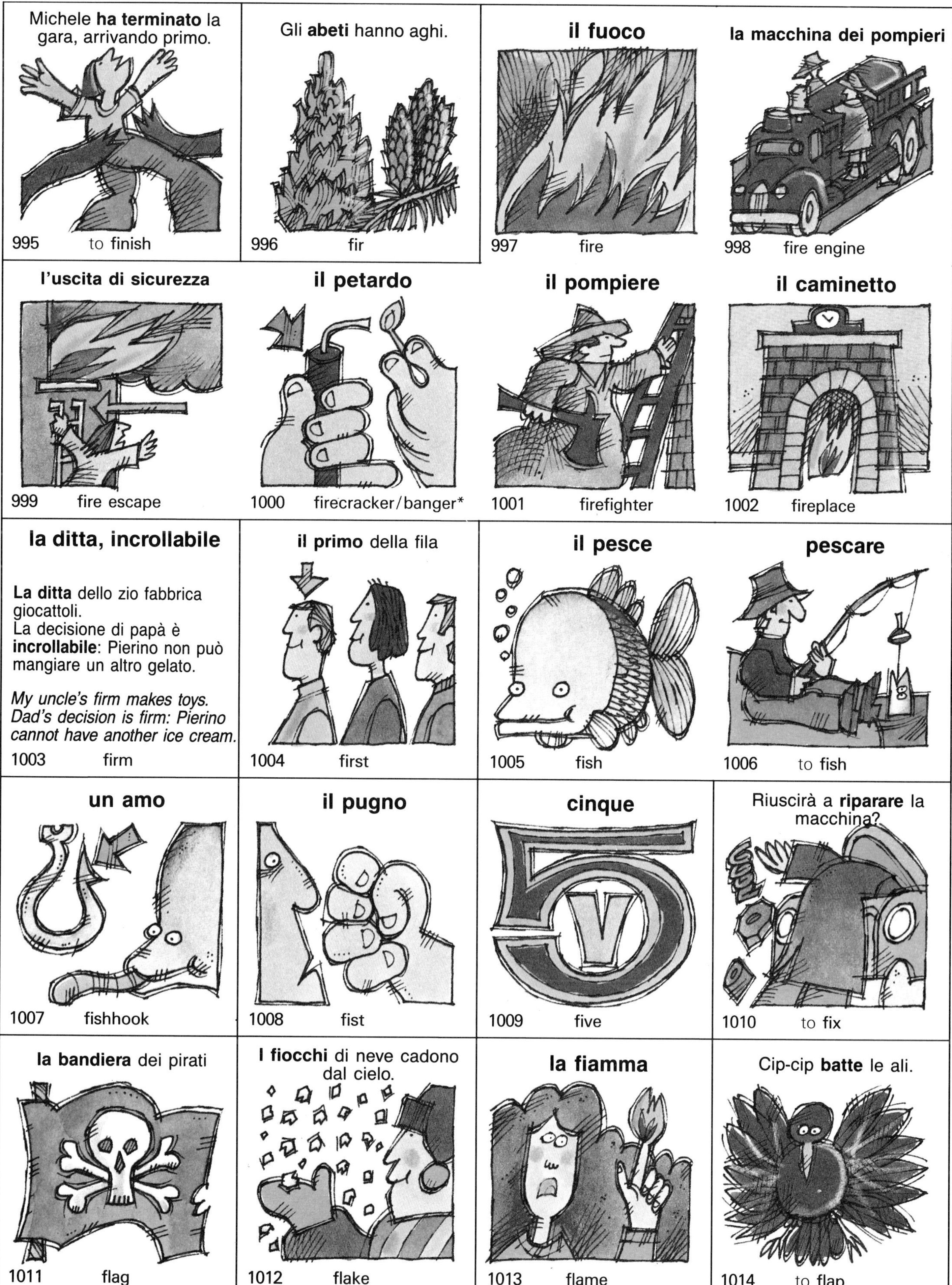
Michele **ha terminato** la gara, arrivando primo.
995 to finish
Gli **abeti** hanno aghi.
996 fir
il fuoco
997 fire
la macchina dei pompieri
998 fire engine
l'uscita di sicurezza
999 fire escape
il petardo
1000 firecracker/banger*
il pompiere
1001 firefighter
il caminetto
1002 fireplace
la ditta, incrollabile
La ditta dello zio fabbrica giocattoli.
La decisione di papà è **incrollabile**: Pierino non può mangiare un altro gelato.
My uncle's firm makes toys.
Dad's decision is firm: Pierino cannot have another ice cream.
1003 firm
il primo della fila
1004 first
il pesce
1005 fish
pescare
1006 to fish
un amo
1007 fishhook
il pugno
1008 fist
cinque
1009 five
Riuscirà a **riparare** la macchina?
1010 to fix
la bandiera dei pirati
1011 flag
I fiocchi di neve cadono dal cielo.
1012 flake
la fiamma
1013 flame
Cip-cip **batte** le ali.
1014 to flap

Un razzo può rischiarare la notte.
1015 flare
il lampo della macchina fotografica
1016 flash
una lampada elettrica portatile
1017 flashlight/torch*
il matraccio
1018 flask
piatto, liscio
1019 flat
spianare
1020 to flatten
Quale **gusto** preferisci?
1021 flavor/flavour*
Baffo ha **una pulce** sulla schiena.
1022 flea
fuggire
1023 to flee
il vello
1024 fleece
E' bene in **carne**.
1025 flesh
galleggiare
1026 to float
uno stormo d'uccelli
1027 flock
un'inondazione
1028 flood
il pavimento
1029 floor
Il fornaio fa il pane con **la farina**.
1030 flour
Il sangue **scorre.**
1031 to flow
il fiore
1032 flower
Ugo ha preso **l'influenza**.
1033 flu
il batuffolo, **la lanugine**
1034 fluff

L'acqua è **un liquido**.
1035 fluid

la mosca
1036 fly

la pattina dei pantaloni
1037 fly

Gli uccelli e gli aeroplani **volano.**
1038 to fly

la schiuma
1039 foam

La nebbia oscura la veduta.
1040 fog

Piegare seguendo le indicazioni.
1041 to fold

L'oca **segue** Battista ovunque.
1042 to follow

il cibo
1043 food

il piede
1044 foot

la palla da **football**
1045 American football

un'impronta nella neve
1046 footprint

Queste sono **le impronte** di Alberto.
1047 footsteps

per

Tutti **per** uno e uno **per** tutti.
Se non era **per** te, avremmo perso la partita.

One for all and all for one.
But for you, we would have lost the game.

1048 for

forzare la porta
1049 to force

la fronte
1050 forehead

La foresta ospita molti animali.
1051 forest

dimenticare, scordarsi

Papà **si è dimenticato** di comprare il latte.
Il cane **ha dimenticato** il suo nome.
Scordatelo!

Dad forgot to buy milk.
Our dog has forgotten his name.
Forget it!

1052 to forget

perdonare

Ti **perdono** se prometti di star buono.
Sabrina **ha perdonato** il cane che aveva mangiato la sua bambolina preferita.

I forgive you if you promise to be good.
Sabrina forgave her dog for eating her favorite doll.

1053 to forgive

la forchetta
1054 fork

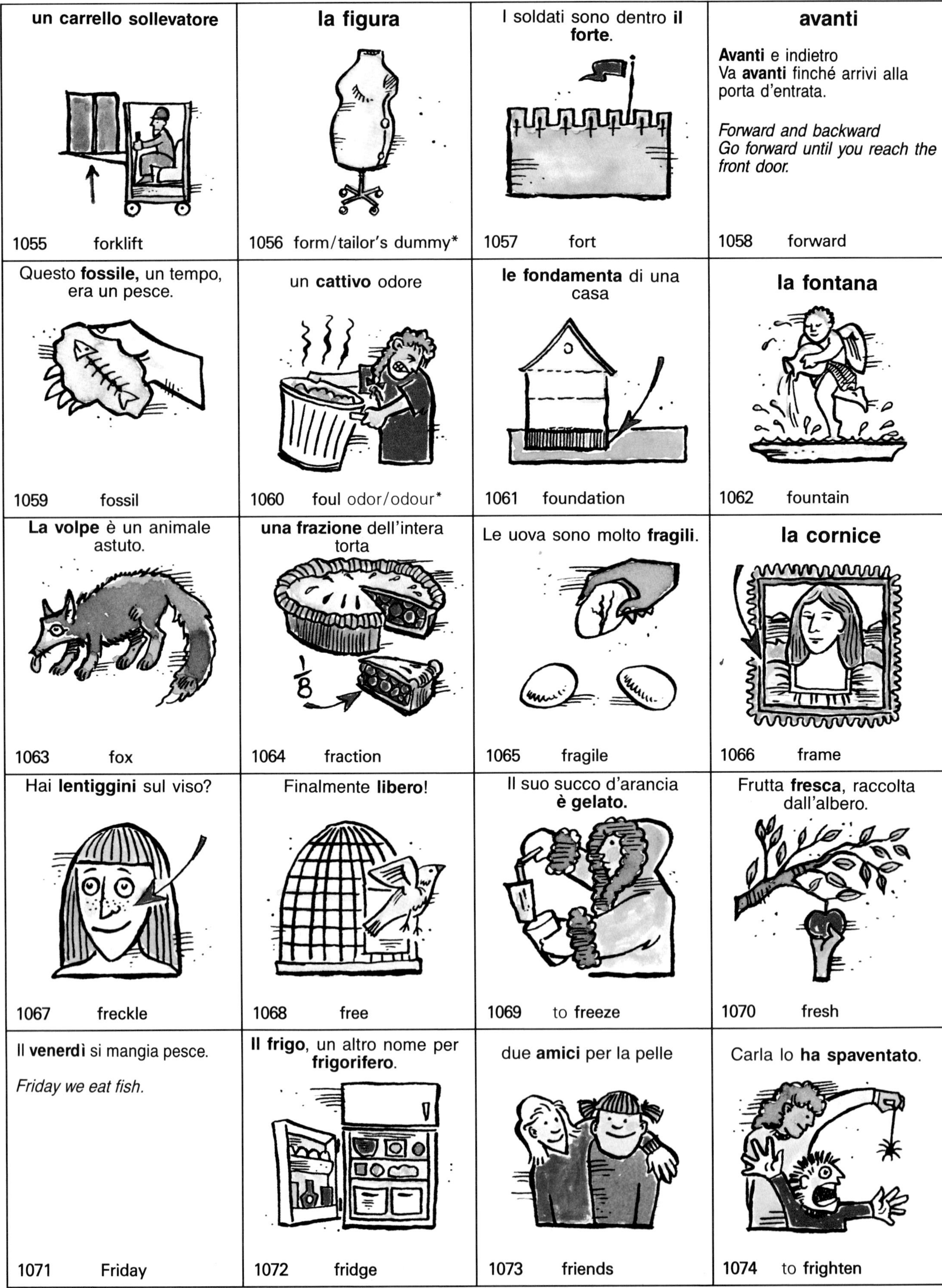

un carrello sollevatore
1055 forklift

la figura
1056 form/tailor's dummy*

I soldati sono dentro **il forte**.
1057 fort

avanti
Avanti e indietro
Va **avanti** finché arrivi alla porta d'entrata.
Forward and backward
Go forward until you reach the front door.
1058 forward

Questo **fossile,** un tempo, era un pesce.
1059 fossil

un **cattivo** odore
1060 foul odor/odour*

le fondamenta di una casa
1061 foundation

la fontana
1062 fountain

La volpe è un animale astuto.
1063 fox

una frazione dell'intera torta
1064 fraction

Le uova sono molto **fragili**.
1065 fragile

la cornice
1066 frame

Hai **lentiggini** sul viso?
1067 freckle

Finalmente **libero**!
1068 free

Il suo succo d'arancia **è gelato.**
1069 to freeze

Frutta **fresca**, raccolta dall'albero.
1070 fresh

Il **venerdì** si mangia pesce.
Friday we eat fish.
1071 Friday

Il frigo, un altro nome per **frigorifero**.
1072 fridge

due **amici** per la pelle
1073 friends

Carla lo **ha spaventato**.
1074 to frighten

la rana
1075 frog
Io vengo **da** Marte.
1076 I am **from** Mars.
il davanti, la parte anteriore
1077 front
Il gelo copre parte della finestra.
1078 frost
accigliarsi, corrugare la fronte
1079 to frown
La frutta è meglio dei dolciumi.
1080 fruit
friggere
1081 to fry
la padella
1082 frying pan
Le auto hanno bisogno di **carburante**.
1083 Cars need **fuel**.
pieno
1084 full
divertirsi
1085 having **fun**
la cassetta delle offerte
1086 charity **fund**
Un funerale è sempre triste.
1087 funeral
un imbuto
1088 funnel
divertente
Mamma non lo trova **divertente**.
Ci è capitata una cosa **divertente** mentre andavamo a scuola.
Mother does not think that is funny.
A funny thing happened on the way to school.
1089 funny
Una pelliccia d'estate?
1090 **fur** coat
la caldaia del riscaldamento
1092 furnace/boiler*
i mobili
1093 furniture
La luce è mancata: sono saltati **i fusibili**.
1094 fuse
un gatto **dal pelo lungo**
1091 furry
0 0 0 1 2

un forte vento

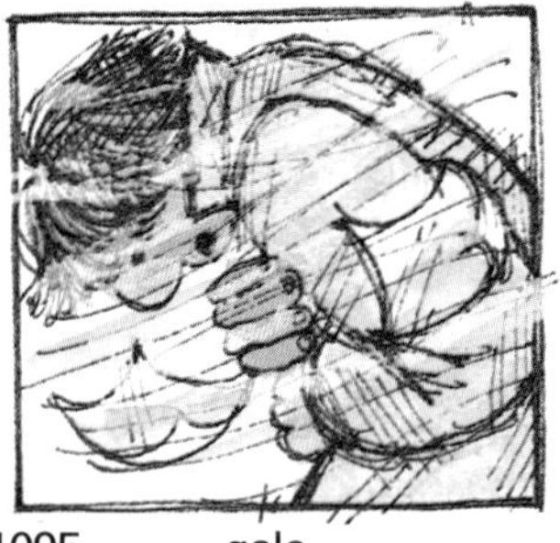

1095 gale

una galleria d'arte

1096 gallery

Un cavallo può trottare o **galoppare.**

1097 to gallop

il gioco delle palline

1098 game

Il papero è il maschio dell'oca.

1099 gander

una banda di delinquenti

1100 gang

Sabrina ha **uno spazio** tra gli incisivi.

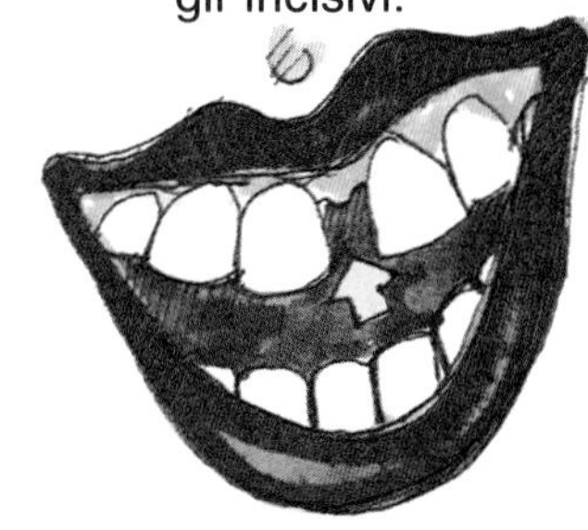

1101 gap

L'auto si tiene nell'**autorimessa**.

1102 garage

i rifiuti, **la spazzatura**

1103 garbage/rubbish*

il bidone dell'immondizia

1104 garbage can/rubbish bin*

Le verdure si coltivano nell'**orto**.

1105 vegetable **garden**

fare gargarismi

1106 to gargle

L'aglio ha un odore pungente.

1107 garlic

la giarrettiera

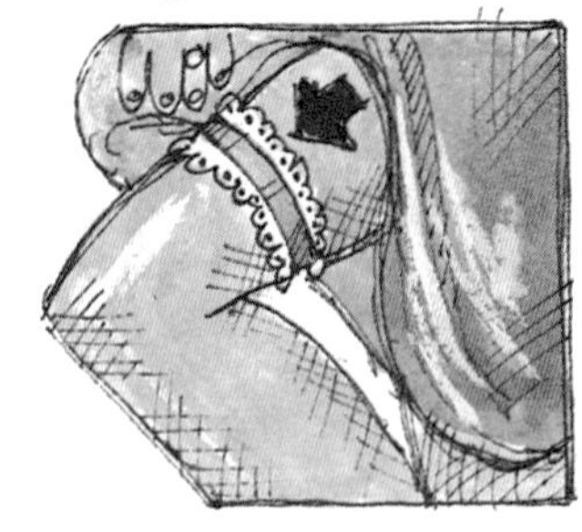

1108 garter

il gas

Il pallone era pieno di **gas**.
Alcuni **gas** sono più leggeri dell'aria.
La mamma cucina su una stufa a **gas**.

The balloon was filled with gas.
Some gases are lighter than air.
Mom cooks on a gas stove.

1109 gas

la benzina

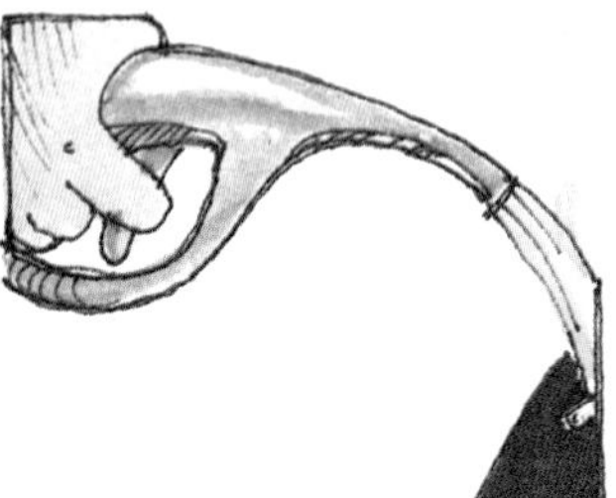

1110 gas/petrol*

il pedale dell'**acceleratore**

1111 gas pedal/accelerator*

una pompa della benzina

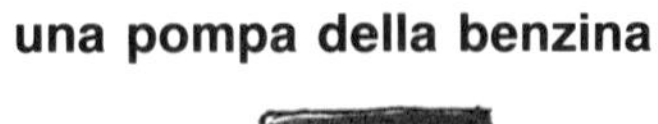

1112 gas/petrol pump*

un distributore di benzina

1113 gas/petrol station*

il portone
1114 gate

Luciana **raccoglie** i fiori.
1115 to gather

gli ingranaggi
1116 gears

Il diamante è **una pietra preziosa**.
1117 gem

il generale
1118 general

un amico **generoso**
1119 a generous friend

una persona **gentile**
1120 a gentle person

Papà è un vero **gentiluomo**.
1121 gentleman

un **vero** porco
1122 a genuine pig

Tutti **studiano** la geografia.
1123 geography

il geranio
1124 geranium

il gerbillo
1125 gerbil

I germi causano malattie.
1126 germ

Fufi, **acchiappa** il topo!
1127 Get that mouse!

Voglio **averlo** indietro.
1128 I want to get it back.

entrare nella piscina
1129 to get in the pool

Sabrina **scende dall'**autobus.
1130 to get off

Sabrina **monta sull'** autobus.
1131 to get on

Si libera della spazzatura.
1132 to get rid of

Al mattino **si alza** presto.
1133 to get up

Hai paura dei **fantasmi**?
1134 ghost
il gigante
1135 giant
il regalo
1136 gift
una balena **gigantesca**
1137 gigantic
ridacchiare
1138 to giggle
Il pesce usa **le branchie** per respirare.
1139 gills
Lo **zenzero** è una spezia.
1140 ginger
un pane di zenzero
1141 gingerbread
una carovana di **gitani** in viaggio
1142 gipsy
La giraffa ha il collo lungo.
1143 giraffe
Adriana è **una ragazza**.
1144 girl
Pia **ha dato** l'ombrello ad Anna.
1145 to give
il ghiacciaio
1148 glacier
Sono **contento**.
1149 I am glad.
un pannello di **vetro**
1150 glass
Anna glielo **ha restituito** quando è tornato il sole.
1146 to give back
Porti **gli occhiali**?
1152 glasses
scivolare
1153 to glide
un bicchiere d'acqua
1151 glass
Mi arrendo!
1147 I give up!

Un aliante è un aereo senza motore.
1154 glider
i guanti
1155 gloves
la colla
1156 glue
andare, **partire**
1157 to go
Il portiere difende **la porta**.
1161 goal
la capra
1162 goat
occhiali di protezione
1163 goggles
L'operaio **scende** a lavorare.
1158 to go down
il lingotto **d'oro**
1164 gold
il pesciolino rosso
1165 goldfish
Zio Gianni gioca a **golf**.
1166 golf
Fido **entra** nella cuccia per fare un pisolino.
1159 to go in
Ha un **buon** sapore.
1167 good
Ciao, mamma.
1168 Goodbye!
un'oca
1169 goose
Jack **sale** sulla pianta di fagioli.
1160 to go up
l'uva spina
1170 gooseberry
Lei pensa d'avere una pettinatura **stupenda**.
1171 gorgeous
il gorilla
1172 gorilla
governare
Il governo **governa** la nazione.
Governare una nazione non è cosi facile come sembra.
The government governs the country.
It is not as easy to govern a country as it seems.
1173 to govern

il governo

Il governo è eletto dalla popolazione.
Il papà di Sabrina, che è ammiraglio, lavora per **il governo**.

The government is elected by the people.
Sabrina's dad, the admiral, works for the government.

1174 government

Sarà punito per aver **afferrato** il gelato di Pia.

1175 to grab

E' molto **compito**.

1176 He is very gracious.

Frequento la prima **classe.**

1177 grade / form*

Raccogliamo **il grano** per ottenerne farina.

1178 grain

1000 **grammi** = 1 chilogrammo

1179 gram

i nonni e il loro **nipote**

1180 grandchild

il nonno

1181 grandfather

Alla nonna di Sabrina piace cucinare.

1182 grandmother

Il granito è una pietra dura.

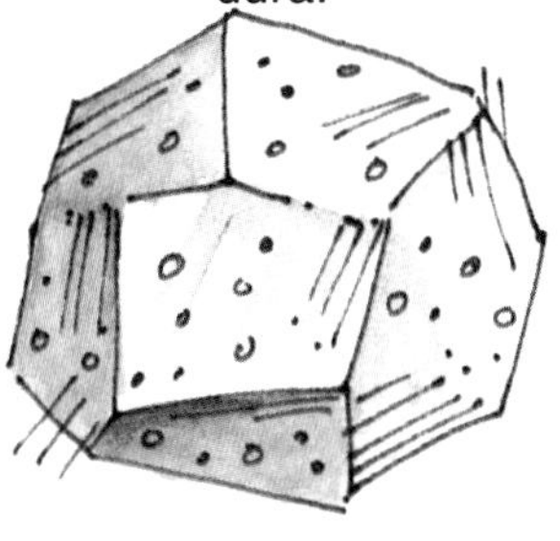

1183 granite

concedere, esaudire

Ti **concedo** una licenza di dieci giorni.
La buona fata **esaudirà** tre dei tuoi desideri.

I grant you ten days' leave of absence.
The good fairy will grant you three wishes.

1184 to grant

un grappolo d'**uva**

1185 grapes

il pompelmo

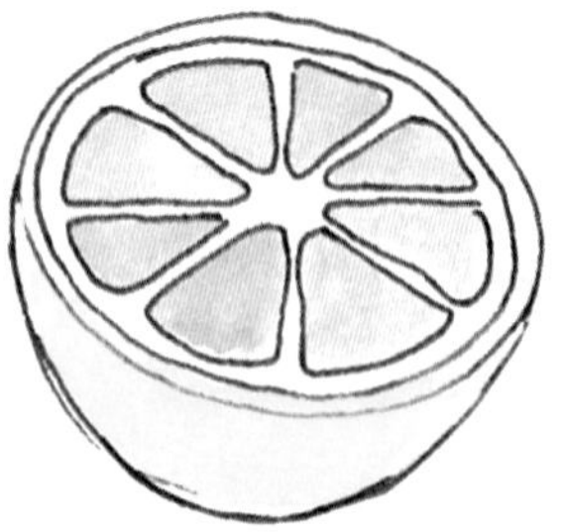

1186 grapefruit

il grafico

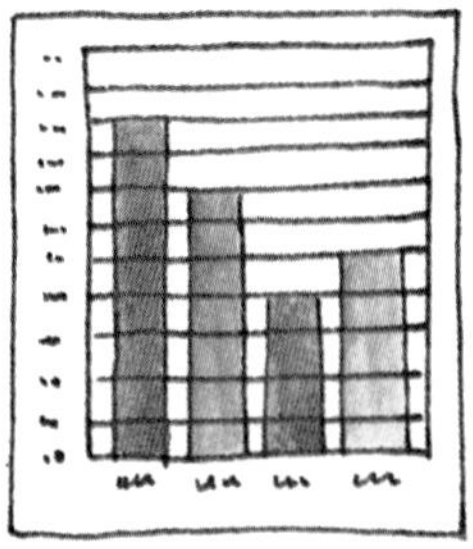

1187 graph

L'erba è verde.

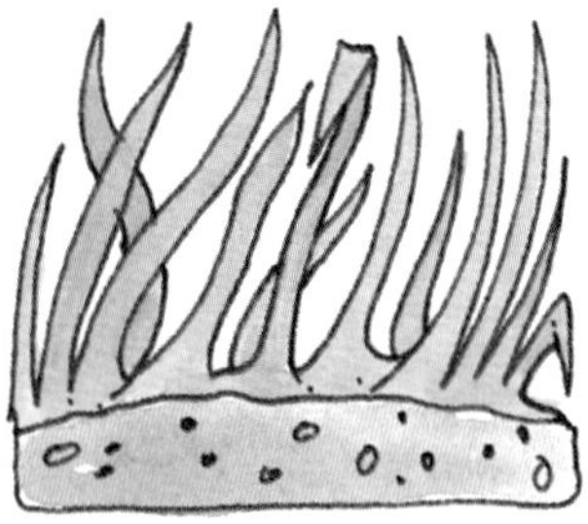

1188 grass

la cavalletta

1189 grasshopper

la grattugia

1190 grater

la tomba

1191 grave

la ghiaia lungo la strada

1192 gravel

La gravità fa cadere la mela.

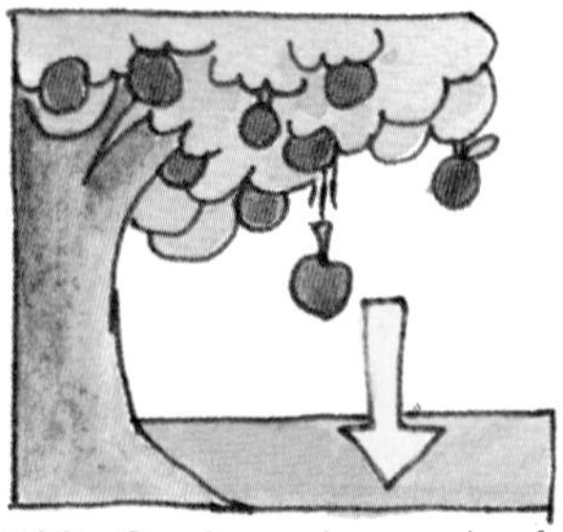

1193 Gravity makes apples fall.

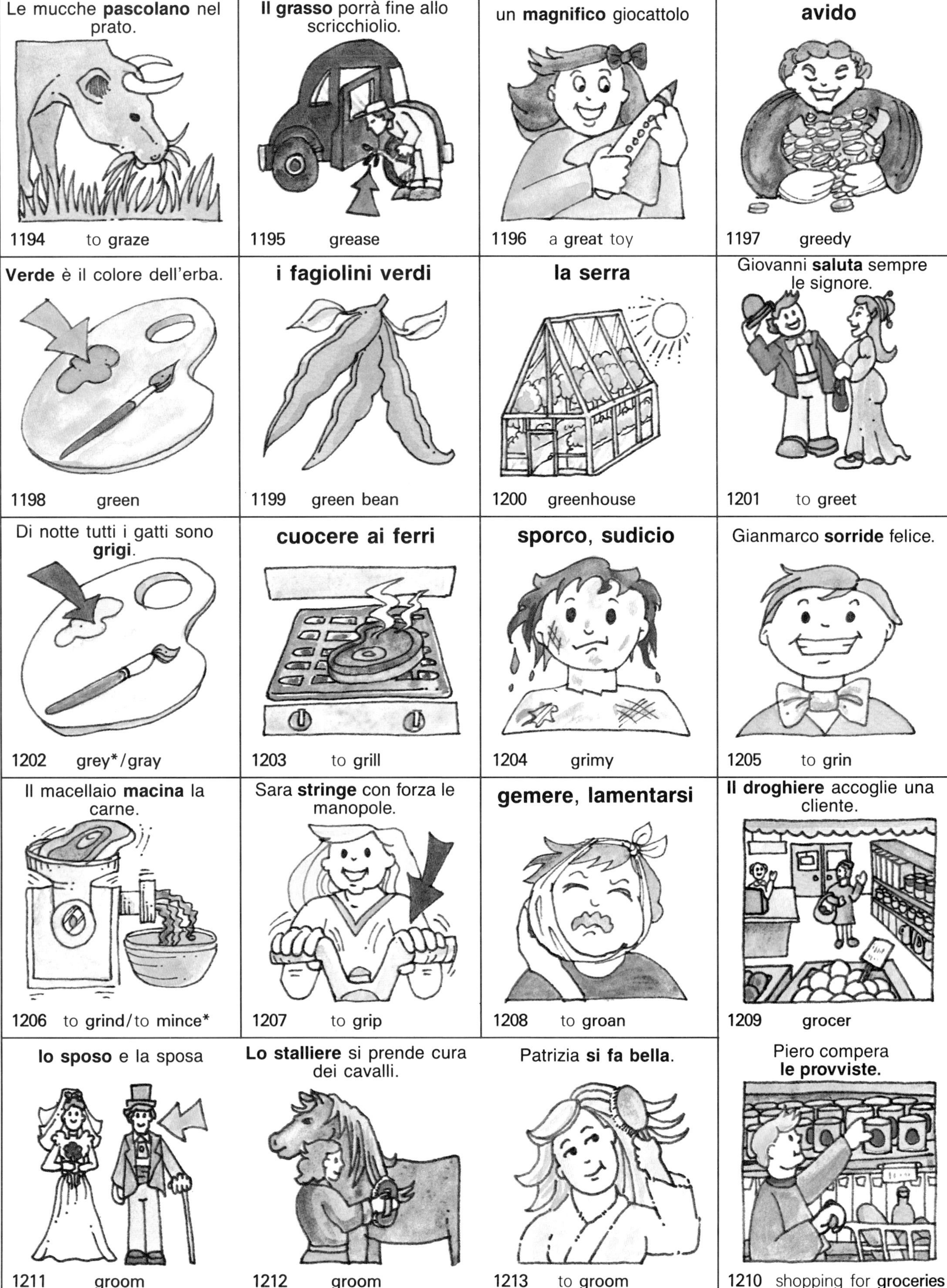
Le mucche **pascolano** nel prato.
1194 to graze
Il grasso porrà fine allo scricchiolio.
1195 grease
un **magnifico** giocattolo
1196 a great toy
avido
1197 greedy
Verde è il colore dell'erba.
1198 green
i fagiolini verdi
1199 green bean
la serra
1200 greenhouse
Giovanni **saluta** sempre le signore.
1201 to greet
Di notte tutti i gatti sono **grigi**.
1202 grey*/gray
cuocere ai ferri
1203 to grill
sporco, sudicio
1204 grimy
Gianmarco **sorride** felice.
1205 to grin
Il macellaio **macina** la carne.
1206 to grind/to mince*
Sara **stringe** con forza le manopole.
1207 to grip
gemere, lamentarsi
1208 to groan
Il droghiere accoglie una cliente.
1209 grocer
lo sposo e la sposa
1211 groom
Lo stalliere si prende cura dei cavalli.
1212 groom
Patrizia **si fa bella**.
1213 to groom
Piero compera **le provviste.**
1210 shopping for groceries

la scanalatura
1214 groove

Questo essere è **disgustoso.**
1215 gross/disgusting*

il terreno
1216 ground

la marmotta
1217 groundhog

un gruppo di persone
1218 group

crescere
1219 to grow

ringhiare
1220 to growl

un adulto
1221 grown-up

fare la guardia
1222 to guard

Aspetta! Lasciami **indovinare**.
1223 to guess

Il monaco accoglie **l'ospite.**
1224 guest

Lo **conduce** nella sua stanza.
1225 to guide

colpevole

Sabrina dice che non è **colpevole.**
E' **colpevole** colui che ha preso il barattolo delle caramelle.

Sabrina says she is not guilty. Whoever took the candy jar is guilty.

1226 guilty

un porcellino d'India, una cavia
1227 guinea pig

Pablo suona **la chitarra**.
1228 guitar

il **Golfo** del Messico
1229 Gulf of Mexico

I gabbiani vivono vicino all'acqua.
1230 gull

Le gengive coprono le radici dei denti.
1231 gum

Masticare **gomma** non è proprio la miglior abitudine.
1232 gum/chewing gum*

L'acqua scola nella **cunetta**.
1233 gutter

H
Fumare è **una** cattiva **abitudine**.
1234 bad **habit**
un aglefino
1235 haddock
una tempesta di **grandine**
1236 hail
La sorella di Sabrina ha tantissimi **capelli.**
1237 hair
la spazzola per capelli
1238 hairbrush
il parrucchiere
1239 hairdresser
Che grosso **asciugacapelli**!
1240 hairdryer
Vuoi l'altra **metà**?
1241 half
l'entrata, l'atrio
1242 hall
L'Halloween è la notte delle streghe.
1243 Halloween/Hallowe'en*
il corridoio
1244 hallway/corridor*
Il soldato **si fermò** fuori dalla porta.
1245 to **halt**
il martello
1246 hammer
martellare un pezzo di legno
1247 to hammer
l'amaca
1248 hammock
il criceto
1249 hamster
Una mano ha cinque dita.
1250 hand
dar via, distribuire
1251 to hand out
il freno a mano
1252 hand brake

le manette

1253 handcuffs

handicap, svantaggio

Essere ciechi è un **handicap,** ma si può superare qualsisi **svantaggio.**

Being blind is a handicap, but people can overcome any handicap.

1254 handicap

la maniglia

1255 handle

il corrimano

1256 handrail

Maurizio è convinto d'essere **bello**.

1257 handsome

una persona **capace** di fare di tutto

1258 handy person

Appendere il quadro diritto.

1259 to hang

tenere duro

1260 to hang on

aviorimessa

1262 hangar

Appendi il cappotto sull' **appendiabiti**.

1263 hanger

il fazzoletto da naso

1264 handkerchief

appendere una maglietta

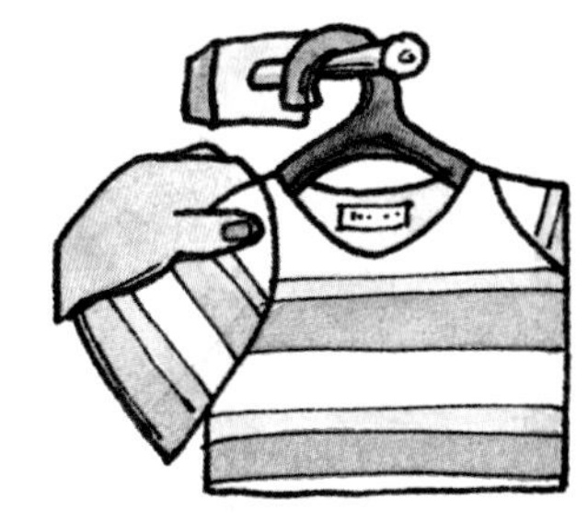

1261 to hang up

Gli incidenti possono **capitare**.

1265 Accidents **happen**.

Lui è **felice**.

1266 He is **happy**.

Le barche sono nel **porto**.

1267 harbor/harbour*

Troppo **duri** da rompere.

1268 hard

la lepre

1269 hare

Non si deve **fare del male** agli animali!

1270 to harm

un'armonica

1271 harmonica

La briglia fa parte dei **finimenti** del cavallo.

1272 harness

un'arpa
1273 harp
un inverno rigido
1274 a harsh winter
Giuseppe miete il grano.
1275 to harvest
il cappello
1276 hat
E' bello veder schiudere i pulcini.
1277 to hatch
un'accetta
1278 hatchet
Il pirata trasporta un sacco pesante.
1279 to haul
una casa infestata dagli spettri
1280 haunted house
Maria ha la bambola che Gina vuole.
1281 to have
Il falco è un uccello da preda.
1282 hawk
il fieno per i cavalli
1283 hay
La foschia rende le figure indistinte.
1284 Haze makes for a hazy day.
il nocciolo
1285 hazel
La nocciola è il frutto del nocciolo.
1286 hazelnut
la testa
1287 head
Ho mal di testa.
1288 I have a headache.
il poggiacapo
1289 headrest
La gamba rotta sta guarendo.
1290 to heal
un fiore sano
1291 healthy flower
un mucchio di spazzatura
1292 heap/pile*

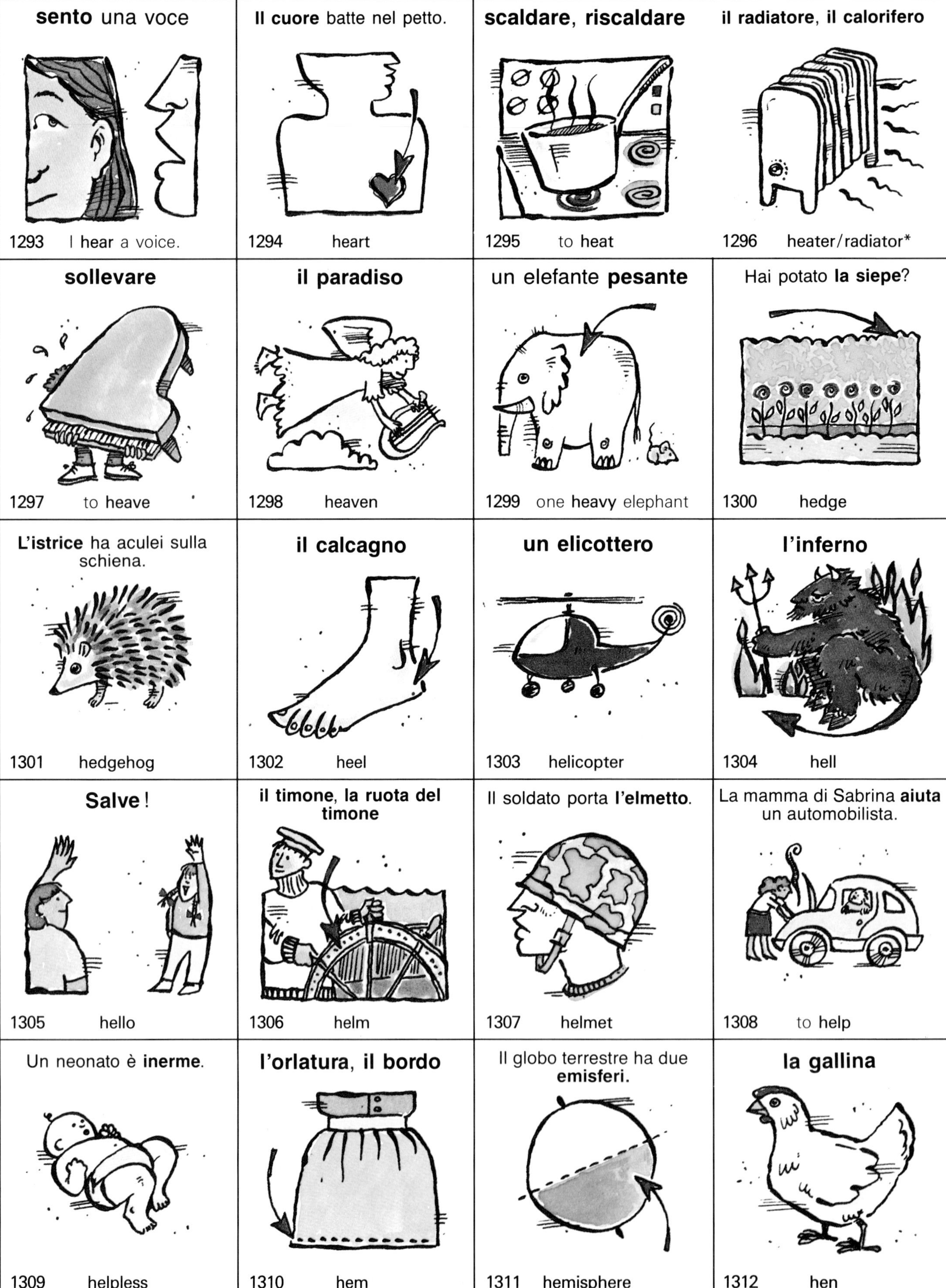
sento una voce
1293 I **hear** a voice.
Il cuore batte nel petto.
1294 heart
scaldare, **riscaldare**
1295 to heat
il radiatore, **il calorifero**
1296 heater/radiator*
sollevare
1297 to heave
il paradiso
1298 heaven
un elefante **pesante**
1299 one **heavy** elephant
Hai potato **la siepe**?
1300 hedge
L'istrice ha aculei sulla schiena.
1301 hedgehog
il calcagno
1302 heel
un elicottero
1303 helicopter
l'inferno
1304 hell
Salve!
1305 hello
il timone, **la ruota del timone**
1306 helm
Il soldato porta **l'elmetto**.
1307 helmet
La mamma di Sabrina **aiuta** un automobilista.
1308 to **help**
Un neonato è **inerme**.
1309 helpless
l'orlatura, **il bordo**
1310 hem
Il globo terrestre ha due **emisferi**.
1311 hemisphere
la gallina
1312 hen

Un ettagono ha sette lati.
1 2 3 4 5 6 7
1313 heptagon
le erbe
1314 herbs
una mandria di buoi
1315 herd
Vieni **qui**!
1316 Come here!
L'eremita vive da solo.
1317 hermit
un eroe
1318 hero
un'eroina
1319 heroine
un'aringa
1320 herring
Paolo **esita** a tuffarsi.
1321 to hesitate
Un esagono ha sei lati.
1 2 3 4 5 6
1322 hexagon
Gli orsi **vanno in letargo** d'inverno.
1323 to hibernate
avere il singhiozzo
1324 to hiccup/hiccough*
Il cuoio è la pelle di un animale.
1325 hide
Olga **si nasconde**.
1326 to hide
il nascondiglio
1327 hiding-place
una montagna molto **alta**
1328 a high mountain
un edificio alto
1329 highrise/tower block*
una scuola secondaria
1330 high school/secondary school*
una strada maestra, un'autostrada
1331 highway/motorway*
sequestrare un aereo
1332 to hijack a plane

Una collina con un albero in cima.
1333 hill

la cerniera
1334 hinge

le gambe **posteriori**
1335 hind legs

la mano sull'**anca**
1336 hand on hip

un ippopotamo
1337 hippopotamus

Studio **la storia**.
1338 I study history.

battere, **colpire**
1339 to hit

Le api vivono in **un alveare**.
1340 hive

accaparrare
1341 to hoard

una voce **roca**
1342 hoarse voice

Lavorare a maglia è **un passatempo** per la mamma.
1343 hobby

Mio fratello gioca a **hockey**.
1344 hockey/ice hockey*

la zappa
1347 hoe

Sabrina **tiene stretto** Tigre, il gatto.
1348 to hold

Sabrina non dovrebbe **tenerlo giù a terra**.
1349 to hold down

un dischetto da hockey
1345 hockey puck

il buco
1350 hole

Zio Dario ha lavorato sodo per andare in **vacanza.**
1351 holiday

Gli scoiattoli abitano in questo albero **cavo**.
1352 hollow tree

un bastone da hockey
1346 hockey stick

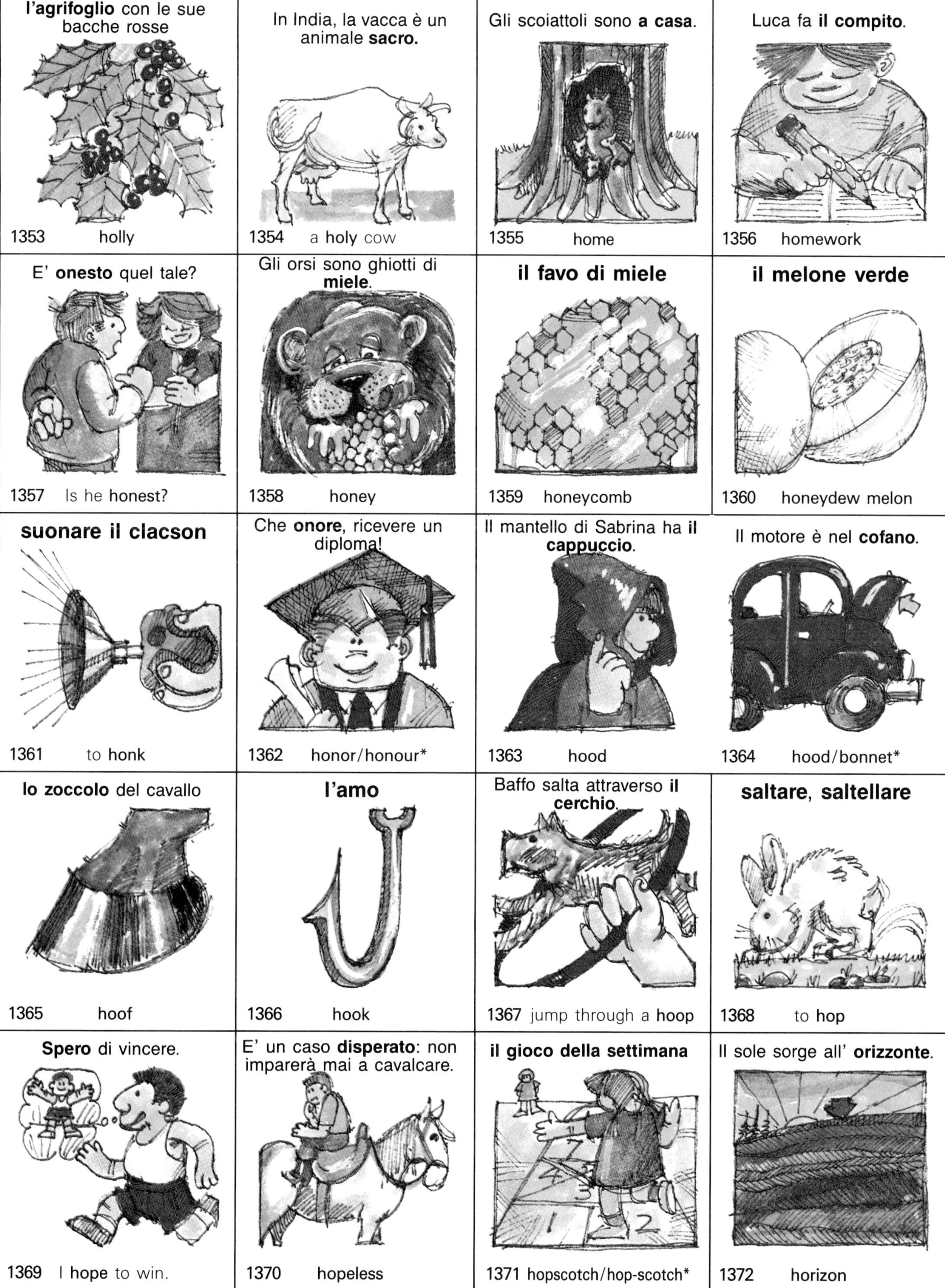
l'agrifoglio con le sue bacche rosse
1353 holly
In India, la vacca è un animale **sacro.**
1354 a holy cow
Gli scoiattoli sono **a casa**.
1355 home
Luca fa **il compito**.
1356 homework
E' **onesto** quel tale?
1357 Is he honest?
Gli orsi sono ghiotti di **miele**.
1358 honey
il favo di miele
1359 honeycomb
il melone verde
1360 honeydew melon
suonare il clacson
1361 to honk
Che **onore**, ricevere un diploma!
1362 honor/honour*
Il mantello di Sabrina ha **il cappuccio**.
1363 hood
Il motore è nel **cofano**.
1364 hood/bonnet*
lo zoccolo del cavallo
1365 hoof
l'amo
1366 hook
Baffo salta attraverso **il cerchio**.
1367 jump through a hoop
saltare, saltellare
1368 to hop
Spero di vincere.
1369 I hope to win.
E' un caso **disperato**: non imparerà mai a cavalcare.
1370 hopeless
il gioco della settimana
1371 hopscotch/hop-scotch*
Il sole sorge all' **orizzonte**.
1372 horizon

in posizione **orizzontale**

1373 horizontal

la tromba, **il clacson**

1374 horn

il corno inglese

1375 French **horn**

il corno

1376 horn

Il calabrone punge col suo pungiglione.

1377 hornet

il cavallo

1378 horse

il rafano

1379 horseradish

un ferro di cavallo

1380 horseshoe

un tubo di gomma

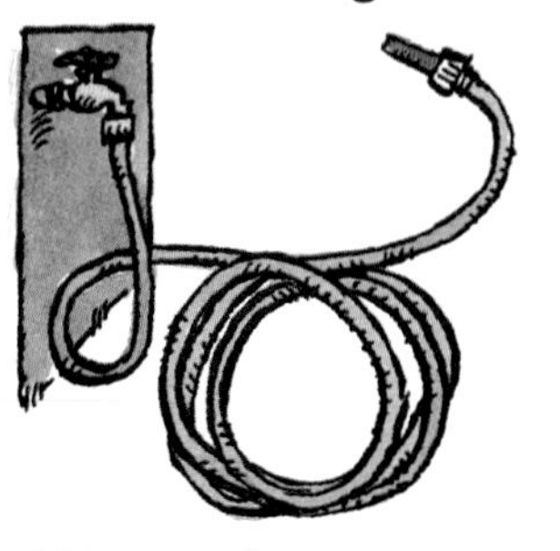

1381 hose

un ospedale

1382 hospital

Fa veramente **caldo**.

1383 hot

E' talmente **piccante** che mi brucia la lingua.

1384 hot

Quando viaggiamo, stiamo in **albergo**.

1386 hotel

Vi sono 60 minuti in **un'ora**.

1387 hour

la clessidra

1388 hourglass

il peperoncino piccante

1385 hot pepper

la casa

1389 house

uno hovercraft

1390 hovercraft

Ti insegno **come** fare.

1391 I will show you **how**.

Il cane **ulula** nella notte.

1392 to **howl**

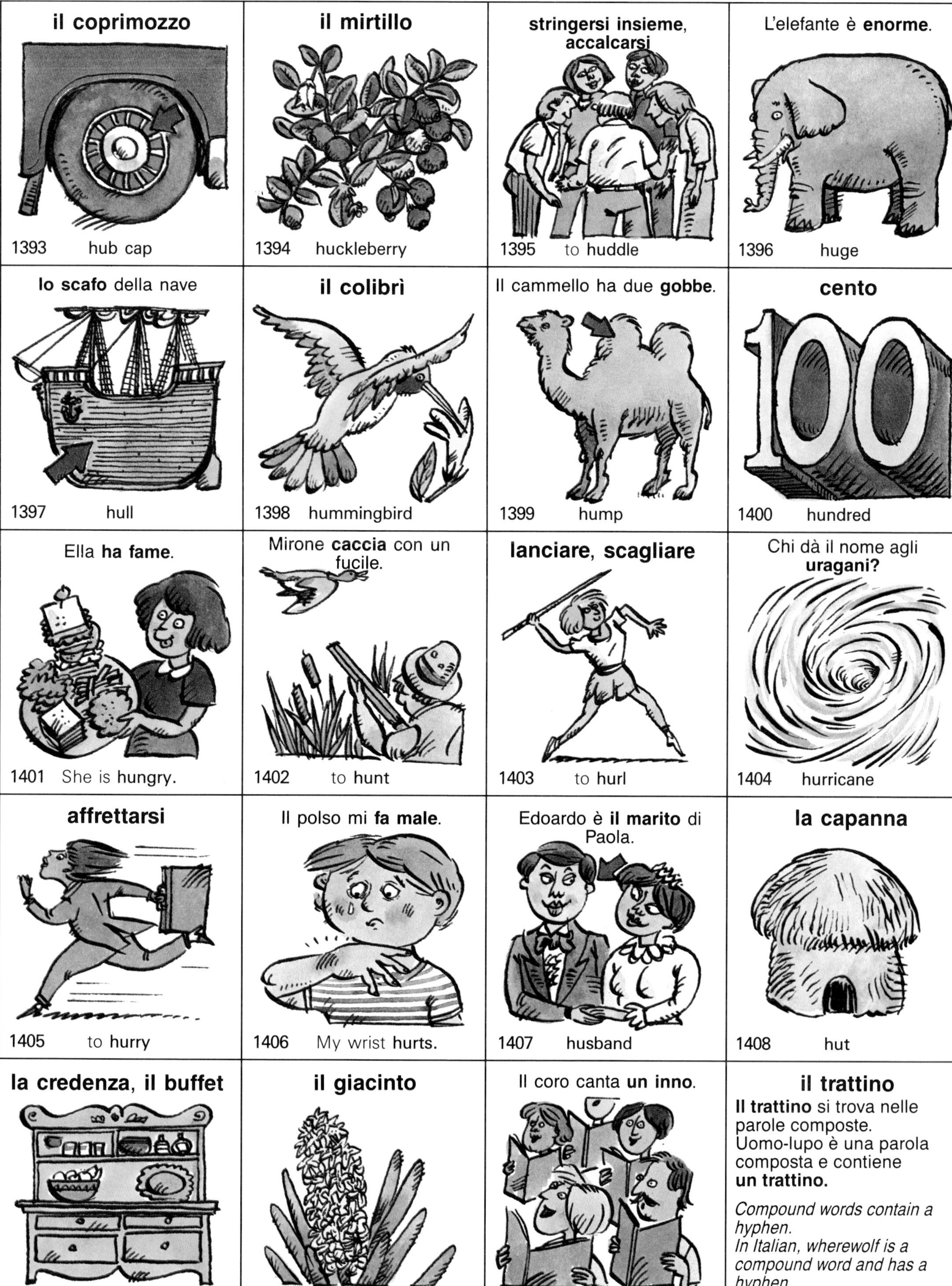
il coprimozzo
1393 hub cap
il mirtillo
1394 huckleberry
stringersi insieme, accalcarsi
1395 to huddle
L'elefante è enorme.
1396 huge
lo scafo della nave
1397 hull
il colibrì
1398 hummingbird
Il cammello ha due gobbe.
1399 hump
cento
100
1400 hundred
Ella ha fame.
1401 She is hungry.
Mirone caccia con un fucile.
1402 to hunt
lanciare, scagliare
1403 to hurl
Chi dà il nome agli uragani?
1404 hurricane
affrettarsi
1405 to hurry
Il polso mi fa male.
1406 My wrist hurts.
Edoardo è il marito di Paola.
1407 husband
la capanna
1408 hut
la credenza, il buffet
1409 hutch/sideboard*
il giacinto
1410 hyacinth
Il coro canta un inno.
1411 hymn
il trattino
Il trattino si trova nelle parole composte. Uomo-lupo è una parola composta e contiene un trattino.
Compound words contain a hyphen. In Italian, wherewolf is a compound word and has a hyphen.
1412 hyphen

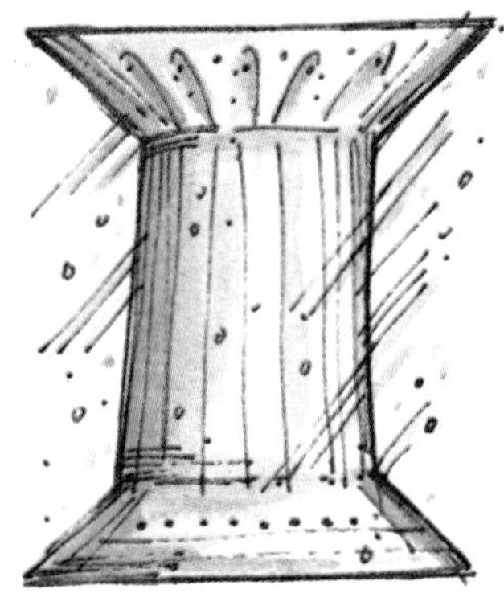

Il ghiaccio galleggia nel bicchiere.

1413 ice

il gelato

1414 ice cream

Gli **iceberg** possono far affondare le navi.

1415 iceberg

I ghiaccioli pendono dal tetto.

1416 icicle

La torta viene decorata con **zucchero a velo.**

1417 icing

Ha avuto **un'idea** luminosa.

1418 idea

due gemelli **identici**

1419 identical twins

un idiota

1420 idiot

ozioso, pigro

1421 idle

se

Se avessi un martello, lo userei solo quando nessuno dorme.
Te lo comprerei, **se** potessi.

If I had a hammer, I would only hammer when no one is sleeping.
I would buy it for you if I could.

1422 if

un iglù

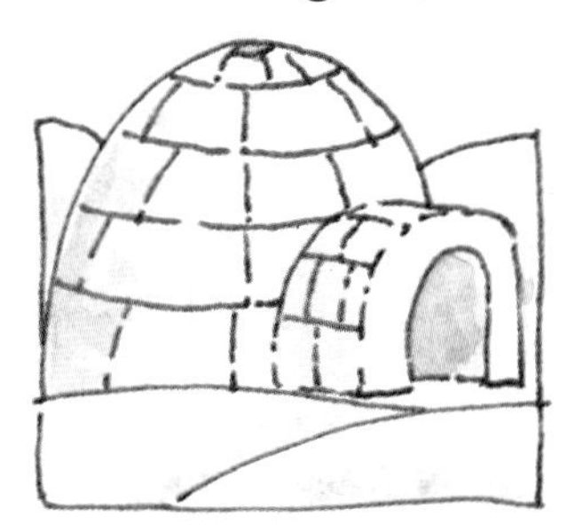

1423 igloo

la chiave dell'accensione

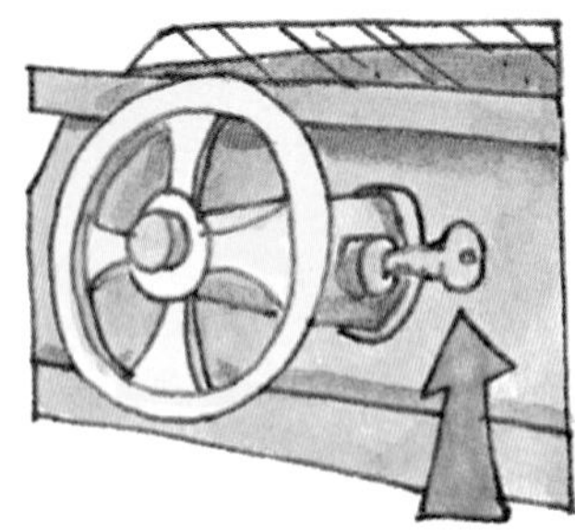

1424 ignition key

Paolo è **malato** da vari giorni.

1425 ill

illuminare

1426 to illuminate

una illustrazione

Le figure nei libri si chiamano **illustrazioni**.
Questo libro ha molte **illustrazioni**.

Pictures in books are called illustrations.
This dictionary has many illustrations.

1427 illustration

importante

Quel che è **importante** per Sabrina, non è forse molto **importante** per Luca.
Leggere e scrivere sono cose **importanti**.

What is important to Sabrina may not be important to Luca.
Reading and writing are important matters.

1428 important

in, nel (nella, nelle, negli)

La famiglia Rossi sta progettando un picnic **nel** parco.
Porteranno anche Baffo **in** macchina con loro.

The Rossi family is planning a picnic in the park.
They will take Baffo along in the car.

1429 in

L'incenso si brucia in chiesa.

1430 incense

Per fare un piede ci vogliono dodici **pollici**.

1431 inch

indice

C'è **un indice** alla fine di questo libro.
L'indice contiene tutte le parole del dizionario.

There is an index at the back of this book.
The index contains all the words in this dictionary.

1432 index

il color **indaco**

1433 indigo

all'interno

1434 indoors

il neonato, il bebè

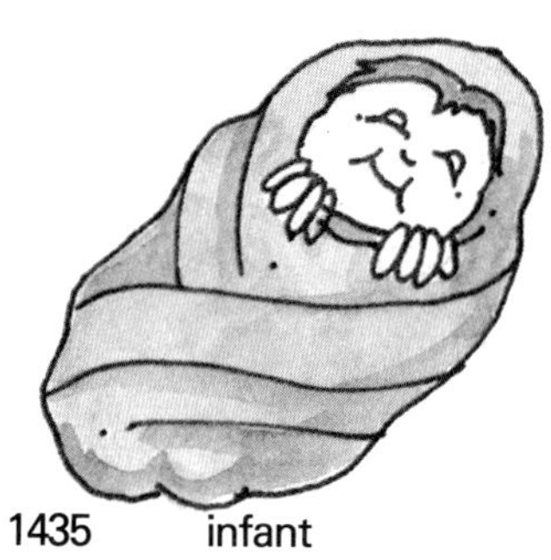

1435 infant

Zia Silvia ha **un'infezione**.

1436 infection

infettivo, contagioso

La sua malattia è **infettiva**.
La risata di papà è **contagiosa**.

Her condition is infectious.
Dad has an infectious laugh.

1437 infectious

Anna **informa** Lucia che traslocherà.

1438 to inform

L'orso **abita** nella caverna.

1439 The bear **inhabits** a cave.

le iniziali

1440 initials

un'iniezione nel braccio

1441 injection

una ferita al dito

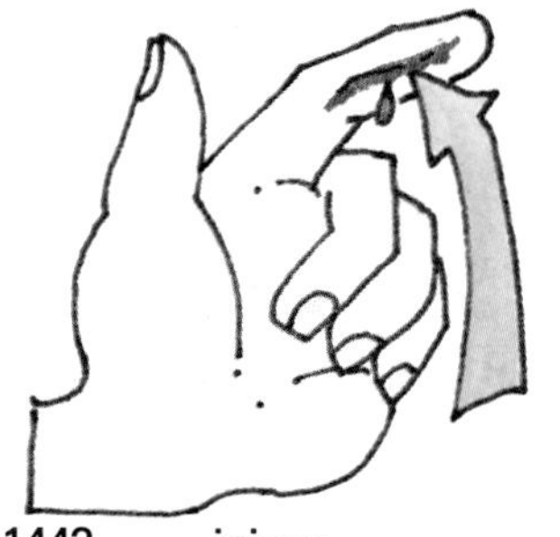

1442 injury

L'inchiostro è nel calamaio.

1443 ink

Vi sono molti tipi di **insetti.**

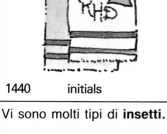

1444 insect

dentro la scatola

1445 inside

Insisto che tu faccia il bagno!

1446 to insist

ispezionare, esaminare

1447 to inspect

Usa un cucchiaio **invece di** una forchetta.

1449 Use a spoon **instead** of a fork!

le istruzioni per l'uso

1450 instruction

un istruttore

1451 instructor

un ispettore

1448 inspector

l'isolamento, **il materiale isolante**

L'isolamento dei fili elettrici serve a prevenire le scosse elettriche.
C'è **materiale isolante** nei muri della casa.

The insulation of electric wires prevents shocks.
There is insulation in the walls of the house.

1452 insulation

un incrocio

1453 intersection/crossroads*

un'intervista, **il colloquio**

1454 interview

Daniele entra **nella** stanza.

1455 **into** the room

Mamma **presenta** Dino a Fausto.

1456 to **introduce**

I Vichingi **invasero** altre nazioni.

1457 to **invade**

Alcuni divennero **invalidi.**

1458 **invalid**

Non ricordo di aver **inventato** quest'albero!

1459 to **invent**

un uomo **invisibile**

1460 **invisible**

Ha ricevuto **un invito** alla nostra festa.

1461 **invitation**

E' lui che l'**ha invitata.**

1462 He is **inviting** her.

un giaggiolo, **un iris**

1463 **iris**

Antonio si **stira** i pantaloni.

1464 to **iron**

il ferro da stiro

1465 **iron**

la maschera di **ferro**

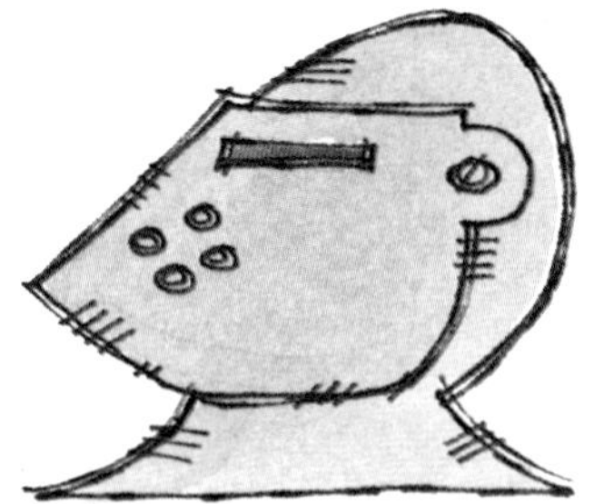

1466 **iron** mask

un'isola

1467 **island**

il prurito

Roberto ha **un** forte **prurito,** causato dall'edera del Canada.
Il prurito passerà, se lui non si gratta.

Roberto has a bad itch from poison ivy.
The itch will go away if he does not scratch.

1468 **itch**

avere il prurito

1469 to **itch**

La pelle mi **prude**.

1470 My skin is **itchy.**

L'edera si arrampica sui muri.

1471 **ivy**

colpire con un diretto sinistro
1472 to jab
La giacca non è della misura giusta.
1473 jacket
la sopraccoperta di un libro
1474 dust jacket
un bordo frastagliato
1475 jagged edge
dietro le sbarre della prigione
1476 jail/gaol*
la marmellata
1477 jam
bloccare la porta
1478 to jam
Gennaio è il primo mese dell'anno.
1479 January
il vasetto
1480 jar
Questo squalo ha fauci spaventose!
1481 jaw
i jeans
1482 jeans
la jeep, la camionetta
1483 jeep
la gelatina di frutta
1484 jelly
un motore a reazione
1485 jet engine
un aereo a reazione
1486 jet plane
il gioiello
1488 jewel
il gioco delle composizioni
1489 jigsaw puzzle
fare un lavoro
1490 doing a job
il getto d'acqua
1487 jet of water

Il fantino monta un cavallo da corsa.
1491 jockey
correre
1492 to jog
congiungere le due parti
1493 to join
l'articolazione del gomito
1494 joint
Zio Pierino pensa che sia proprio **un** bello **scherzo!**
1495 joke
Il giudice deciderà.
1496 judge
il giocoliere
1497 juggler
A Nina piace **il succo** d'arancia fresco.
1498 juice
Luglio è un buon mese per nuotare.
1499 July
La rana **salta**.
1500 to jump
Essa **salta dentro** l'acqua...
1501 to jump in
...poi **salta sopra** una pietra.
1502 to jump on
Antonio è un buon **saltatore**.
1503 jumper
lo scamiciato
1504 jumper/pinafore*
i cavi d'emergenza
1505 jumper cables/jump leads*
Giugno è un buon mese per il tennis.
1506 June
Ci sono tigri nella **giungla**.
1507 jungle
La giunca è una barca cinese.
1508 junk
i rottami, i rifiuti
1509 junk
appena, giusto
Sabrina è **appena** arrivata a casa.
Il giudice è **giusto**.
Sabrina just got home.
The judge is a just person.
1510 just

il caleidoscopio
1511 kaleidoscope
il canguro
1512 kangaroo
la chiglia di una barca a vela
1513 keel
Fido è contento del suo canile.
1514 kennel
un chicco di granturco
1515 kernel
il bollitore
1516 kettle
la chiave
1517 key
calciare
1518 to kick
il ragazzino
1519 kid
Anche le capre hanno dei piccoli.
1520 kid
Solo i criminali sequestrano le persone.
1521 to kidnap
un rene
1522 kidney
Il cacciatore ha ucciso il leone.
1523 to kill
I vasi d'argilla cuociono nel forno.
1524 kiln
1 chilogrammo = 1000 grammi
1525 kilogram
1 chilometro = 1000 metri
1526 kilometer/kilometre*
il kilt, il gonnellino scozzese
1527 kilt
Il vestito è una specie di indumento.
1528 A dress is a kind of garment.
una bambina gentile
1529 kind girl

Il re porta la corona.
1530 king
il martin pescatore
1531 kingfisher
l'edicola dei giornali
1532 kiosk
un'aringa affumicata
1533 kippers
baciare
1534 to kiss
Dammi **un bacio**.
1535 kiss
la cucina
1536 kitchen
L'aquilone vola alto nel cielo.
1537 kite
Il micino diventerà un gatto.
1538 kitten
il kiwi
1539 kiwi
il ginocchio
1540 knee
inginocchiarsi
1541 to kneel
il coltello
1542 knife
Sai **lavorare a maglia**?
1543 to knit
la maniglia della porta
1544 knob
bussare alla porta
1545 to knock
il nodo
1546 knot
sapere, **conoscere**
Sai che cosa significa?
Sabrina **sa** il francese.
Conosco quell'uomo.
Do you know what it means?
Sabrina knows French.
I know that man.
1547 to know
la nocca, **l'articolazione**
1548 knuckle
Il koala vive in Australia.
1549 koala bear

L
L'etichetta avverte del pericolo.
1550 label
il laboratorio
1551 laboratory
un colletto di **trine**
1552 lace
la scala
1554 ladder
il mestolo
1555 ladle
la signora
1556 lady
Marco **si allaccia** le scarpe.
1553 to lace
la coccinella
1557 ladybug/ladybird*
le lingue di gatto
1558 ladyfingers
Il mostro è nella sua **tana**.
1559 lair
Il lago è circondato dalla terra.
1560 lake
un agnello
1561 lamb
L'asino è **zoppo**.
1562 lame
la lampada
1563 lamp
un lampione
1564 lamp-post
la lancia del fante
1565 lance
la terra
1566 land
L'aereo **atterra**.
1567 to land
il pianerottolo
1568 landing

il padrone di casa

L'appartamento in cui viviamo appartiene al nostro **padrone di casa.** Ogni mese noi paghiamo l'affitto al **padrone di casa.**

The apartment in which we live belongs to the landlord. Every month we pay rent to the landlord.

1569 landlord

Le autostrade hanno parecchie **corsie**.

1570 lane

la lingua

Quante **lingue** parli? L'italiano è **la lingua** materna di Sabrina.

How many languages can you speak? Italian is Sabrina's first language.

1571 language

la lanterna

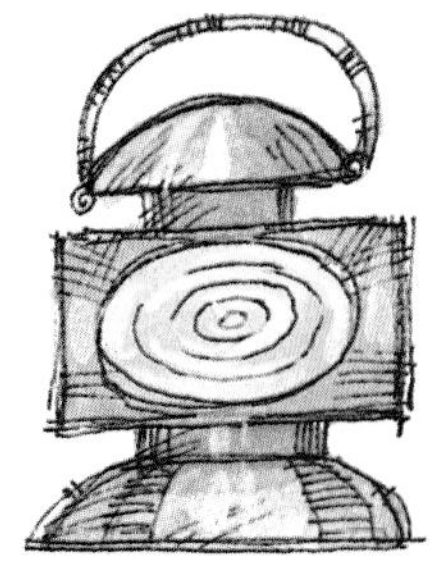

1572 lantern

La balia tiene il bimbo in **grembo**.

1573 lap

il larice

1574 larch

Il lardo fonde nella padella.

1575 lard

grande, grosso

1576 large

un'allodola

1577 lark

le ciglia

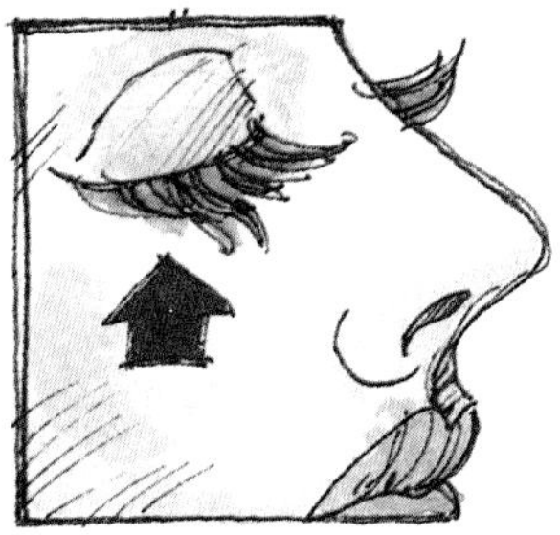

1578 lash

l'**ultimo** pezzo

1579 the **last** piece

Certe cose **durano** a lungo.

1580 Some things do **last.**

Metti il chiavistello, per favore!

1581 to latch

Sei **in ritardo**.

1582 You are **late.**

la schiuma di sapone, la saponata

1583 lather

ridere

1584 to laugh

La scialuppa li porta a riva.

1585 launch

lanciare un missile

1586 to launch

la piattaforma di lancio

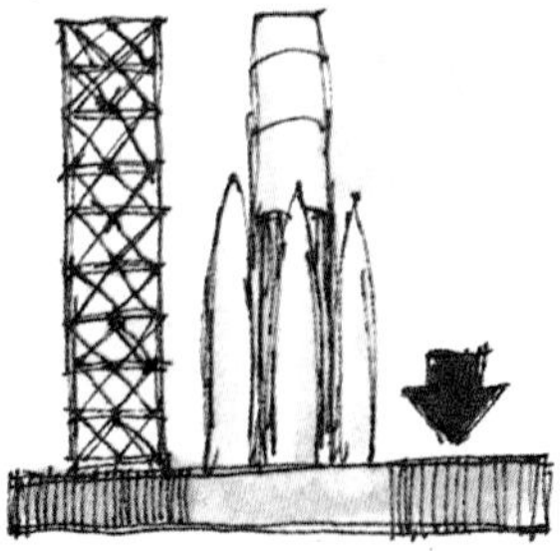

1587 launchpad

i panni sporchi

1588 laundry/washing*

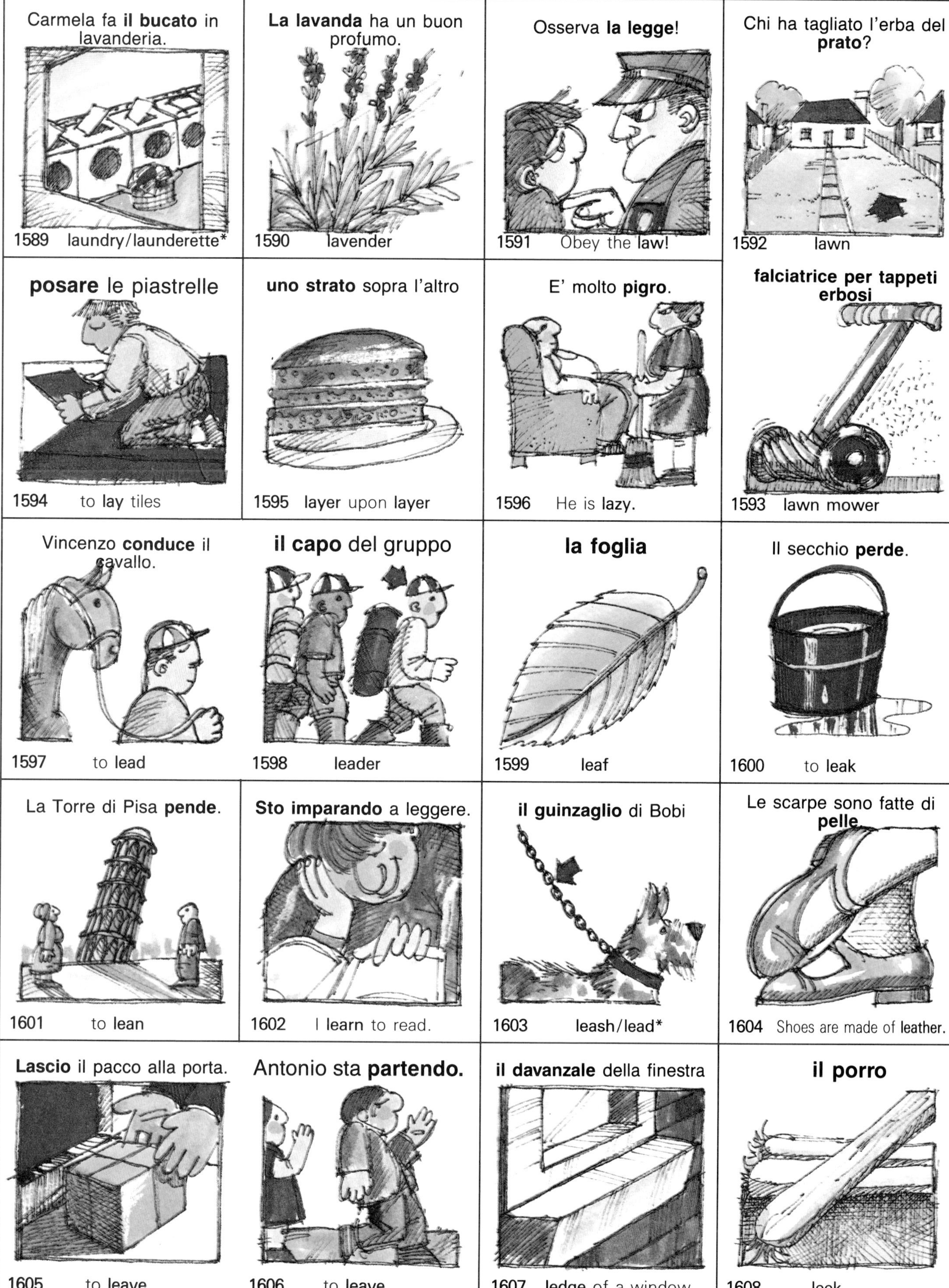

Carmela fa **il bucato** in lavanderia.
1589 laundry/launderette*

La lavanda ha un buon profumo.
1590 lavender

Osserva **la legge**!
1591 Obey the law!

Chi ha tagliato l'erba del **prato**?
1592 lawn

posare le piastrelle
1594 to lay tiles

uno strato sopra l'altro
1595 layer upon layer

E' molto **pigro**.
1596 He is lazy.

falciatrice per tappeti erbosi
1593 lawn mower

Vincenzo **conduce** il cavallo.
1597 to lead

il capo del gruppo
1598 leader

la foglia
1599 leaf

Il secchio **perde**.
1600 to leak

La Torre di Pisa **pende**.
1601 to lean

Sto imparando a leggere.
1602 I learn to read.

il guinzaglio di Bobi
1603 leash/lead*

Le scarpe sono fatte di **pelle**.
1604 Shoes are made of leather.

Lascio il pacco alla porta.
1605 to leave

Antonio sta **partendo.**
1606 to leave

il davanzale della finestra
1607 ledge of a window

il porro
1608 leek

Gira a **sinistra**!
1609 left

E' **mancino**.
1610 He is left-handed.

la gamba
1611 leg

la leggenda del ciclope
1612 legend

il limone
1613 lemon

la limonata
1614 lemonade

Ti posso **prestare** questo libro.
1615 to lend

la lente degli occhiali
1616 lens

Il leopardo sta in agguato.
1617 leopard

la calzamaglia
1618 leotard

Ce ne sono **di meno** in questa pila.
1619 There is less here.

la lezione del saggio
1620 lesson

Lasciami andare!
1621 Let me go!

una lettera dell'alfabeto
1622 letter of the alphabet

Sabrina ha scritto **una lettera**.
1623 letter

La lattuga cresce nell'orto.
1624 lettuce

una superficie **piana**
1625 level surface

la leva
1626 lever

Il bugiardo è stato punito.
1627 liar

In **biblioteca** si fa silenzio.
1628 library

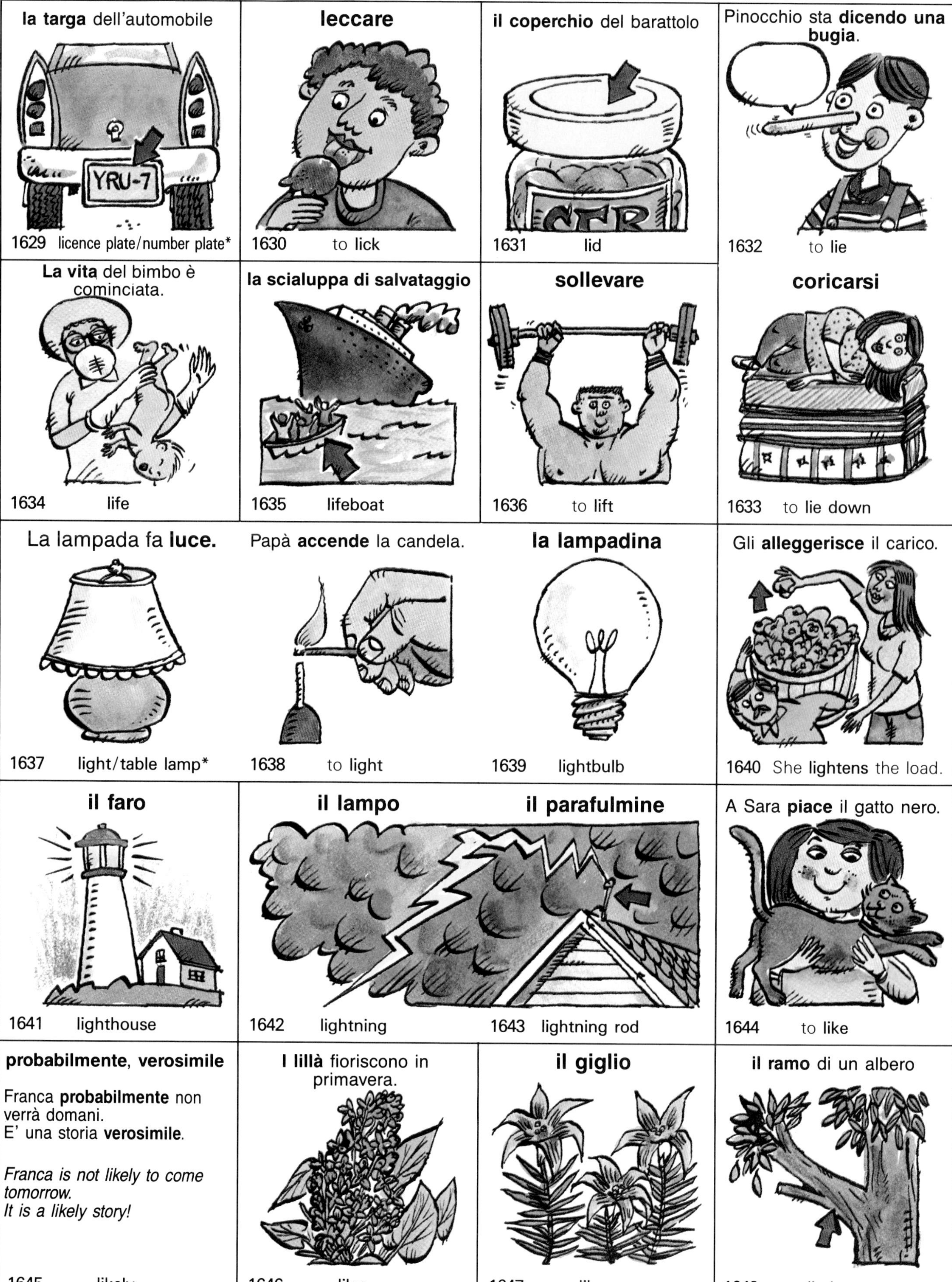
la targa dell'automobile
YRU-7
1629 licence plate/number plate*
leccare
1630 to lick
il coperchio del barattolo
1631 lid
Pinocchio sta **dicendo una bugia**.
1632 to lie
La vita del bimbo è cominciata.
1634 life
la scialuppa di salvataggio
1635 lifeboat
sollevare
1636 to lift
coricarsi
1633 to lie down
La lampada fa **luce.**
1637 light/table lamp*
Papà **accende** la candela.
1638 to light
la lampadina
1639 lightbulb
Gli **alleggerisce** il carico.
1640 She **lightens** the load.
il faro
1641 lighthouse
il lampo
1642 lightning
il parafulmine
1643 lightning rod
A Sara **piace** il gatto nero.
1644 to like
probabilmente, **verosimile**
Franca **probabilmente** non verrà domani.
E' una storia **verosimile**.
Franca is not likely to come tomorrow.
It is a likely story!
1645 likely
I lillà fioriscono in primavera.
1646 lilac
il giglio
1647 lily
il ramo di un albero
1648 limb

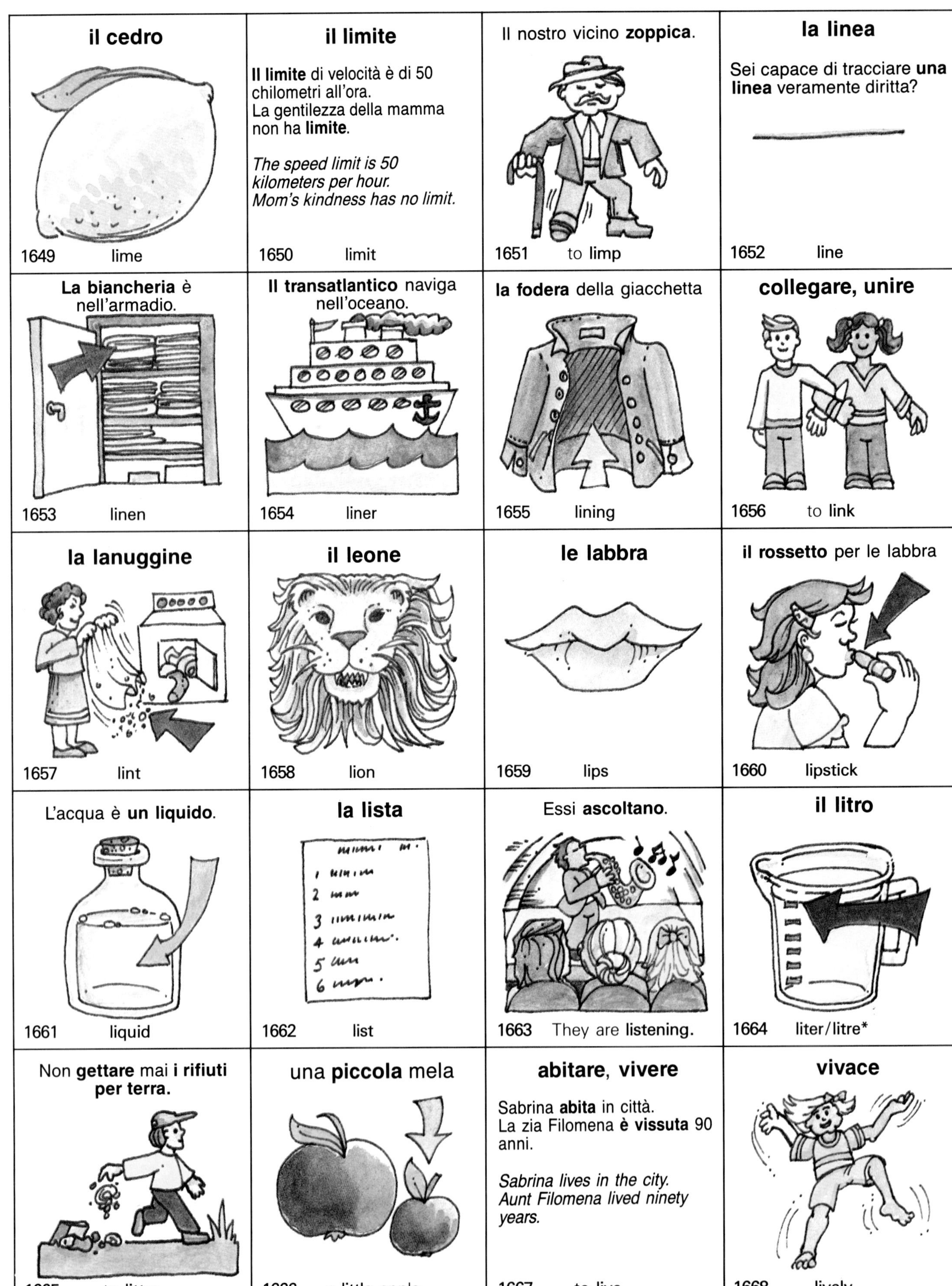

il cedro
1649 lime

il limite
Il limite di velocità è di 50 chilometri all'ora.
La gentilezza della mamma non ha **limite**.
The speed limit is 50 kilometers per hour.
Mom's kindness has no limit.
1650 limit

Il nostro vicino **zoppica**.
1651 to **limp**

la linea
Sei capace di tracciare **una linea** veramente diritta?
1652 line

La biancheria è nell'armadio.
1653 linen

Il transatlantico naviga nell'oceano.
1654 liner

la fodera della giacchetta
1655 lining

collegare, unire
1656 to link

la lanuggine
1657 lint

il leone
1658 lion

le labbra
1659 lips

il rossetto per le labbra
1660 lipstick

L'acqua è **un liquido**.
1661 liquid

la lista
1662 list

Essi **ascoltano**.
1663 They are **listening**.

il litro
1664 liter/litre*

Non **gettare** mai **i rifiuti per terra.**
1665 to **litter**

una **piccola** mela
1666 a **little** apple

abitare, **vivere**
Sabrina **abita** in città.
La zia Filomena **è vissuta** 90 anni.
Sabrina lives in the city.
Aunt Filomena lived ninety years.
1667 to **live**

vivace
1668 lively

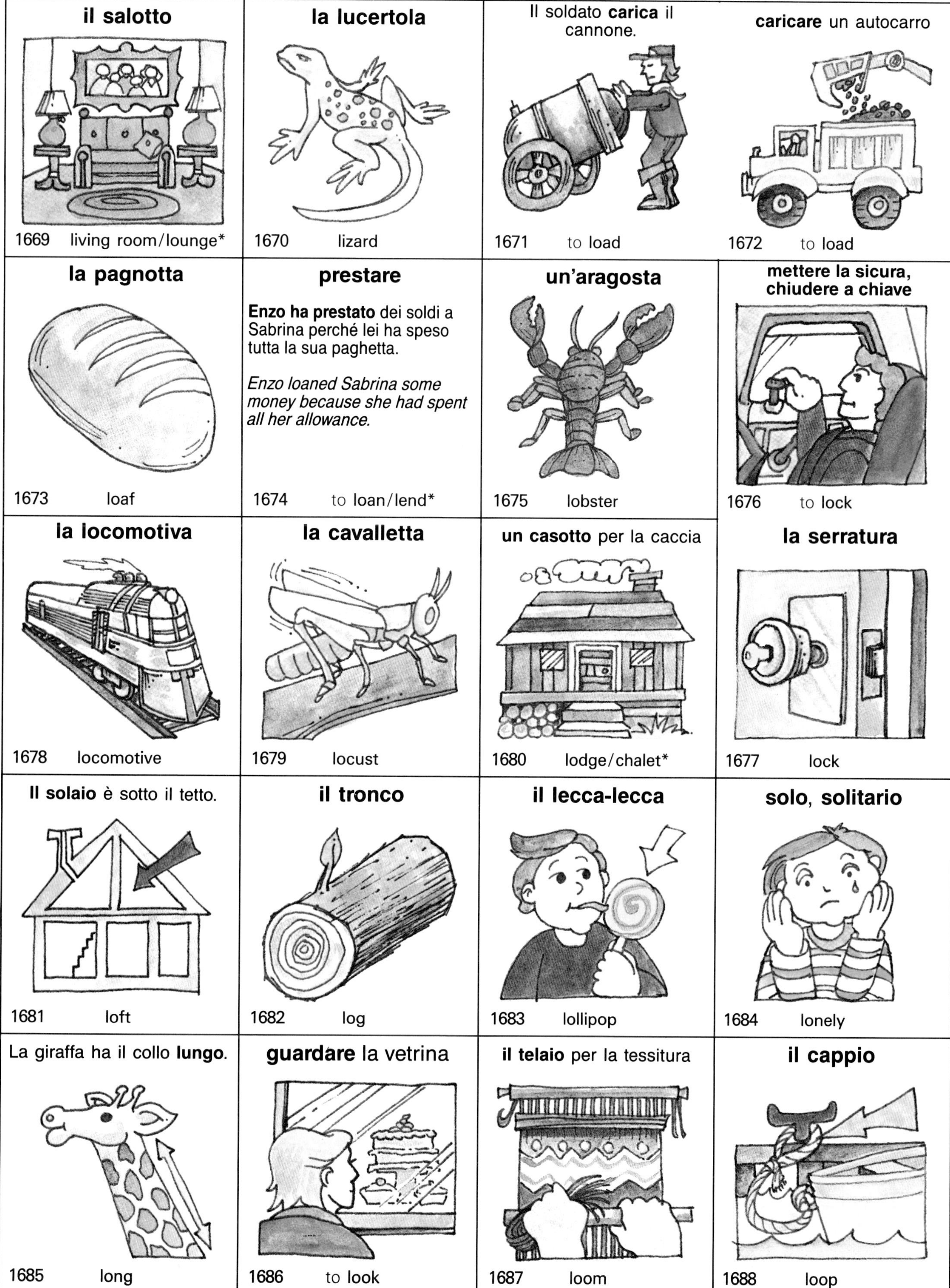
il salotto
1669 living room/lounge*
la lucertola
1670 lizard
Il soldato carica il cannone.
1671 to load
caricare un autocarro
1672 to load
la pagnotta
1673 loaf
prestare
Enzo ha prestato dei soldi a Sabrina perché lei ha speso tutta la sua paghetta.
Enzo loaned Sabrina some money because she had spent all her allowance.
1674 to loan/lend*
un'aragosta
1675 lobster
mettere la sicura, chiudere a chiave
1676 to lock
la locomotiva
1678 locomotive
la cavalletta
1679 locust
un casotto per la caccia
1680 lodge/chalet*
la serratura
1677 lock
Il solaio è sotto il tetto.
1681 loft
il tronco
1682 log
il lecca-lecca
1683 lollipop
solo, solitario
1684 lonely
La giraffa ha il collo lungo.
1685 long
guardare la vetrina
1686 to look
il telaio per la tessitura
1687 loom
il cappio
1688 loop

Il braccialetto è troppo **allentato.**
1689 loose

Bruno **ha perso** una manopola.
1690 to lose

la lozione per la pelle
1691 lotion

La musica è troppo **forte**.
1692 loud

il megafono
1693 loudspeaker

oziare, poltrire
1694 to lounge

l'amore

L'amore è una cosa molto importante.
Sabrina dice che quando si ha **l'amore**, si ha tutto.

Love is very important.
Sabrina says that if you have love you have everything.

1695 love

Si amano.
1696 to love

graziosa, attraente
1697 lovely

un ramo **basso**
1698 low branch

abbassare, calare
1699 to lower

fortunato

Luca è stato **fortunato** perché è andato al campeggio.
Sabrina è **fortunata** ad avere un fratello così simpatico.

Luca was very lucky to be sent to camp.
Sabrina is lucky to have such a cute brother.

1700 lucky

i bagagli
1701 luggage

L'acqua **tiepida** non è né calda, né fredda.
1702 lukewarm water

Mamma canta **la ninna nanna** al suo bambino.
1703 lullaby

il legname da costruzione
1704 lumber/timber*

il gonfiore, il bernoccolo
1705 lump

la seconda colazione
1706 lunch

il cestino della colazione
1707 lunchbox

E' importante avere **i polmoni** sani.
1708 lung

M
la rivista illustrata
1709 magazine
Le larve non sono molto belle.
1710 maggot
una strana **magia** ...
1711 magic
La calamita attira i chiodi.
1713 magnet
un **magnifico** leone
1714 magnificent
La lente ingrandisce l'insetto.
1715 magnifying glass
Il mago fa comparire un coniglietto.
1712 magician
la gazza
1716 magpie
spedire per posta, imbucare
1717 to mail/post*
Il postino consegna la posta.
1718 mail carrier/postman*
Che cosa **fa** Marco?
1719 to make
il trucco di Milena
1720 makeup
il maschio e la femmina
1721 male
il maglio, **il mazzuolo**
1722 mallet
un uomo
1723 man
Il mandarino è un frutto delizioso.
1724 mandarin
Suona **il mandolino**.
1725 mandolin
la criniera del cavallo
1726 mane
Il mango è un frutto dolcissimo.
1727 mango

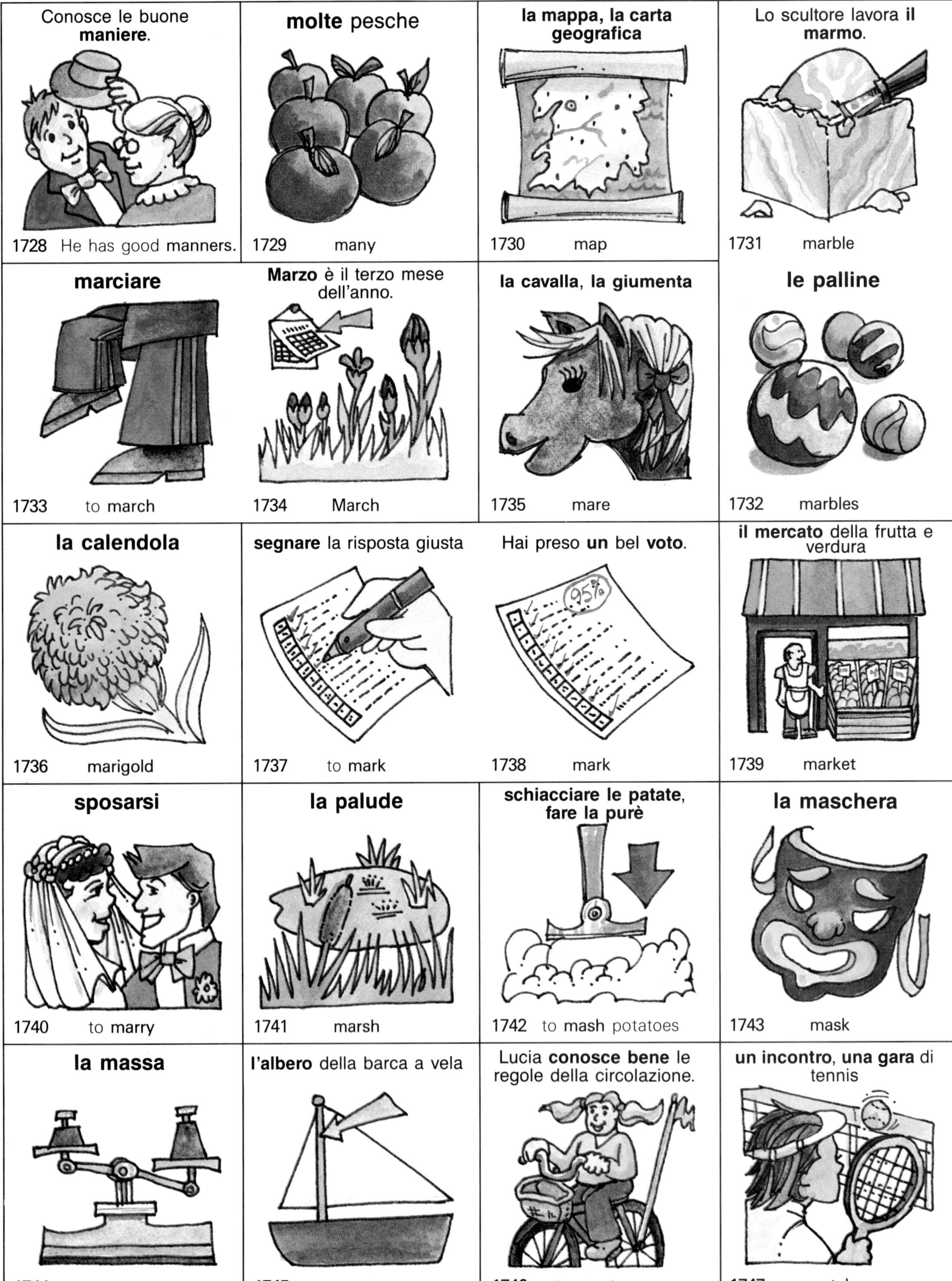
Conosce le buone **maniere**.
1728 He has good manners.
molte pesche
1729 many
la mappa, la carta geografica
1730 map
Lo scultore lavora **il marmo**.
1731 marble
marciare
1733 to march
Marzo è il terzo mese dell'anno.
1734 March
la cavalla, la giumenta
1735 mare
le palline
1732 marbles
la calendola
1736 marigold
segnare la risposta giusta
1737 to mark
Hai preso **un** bel **voto**.
95%
1738 mark
il mercato della frutta e verdura
1739 market
sposarsi
1740 to marry
la palude
1741 marsh
schiacciare le patate, fare la purè
1742 to mash potatoes
la maschera
1743 mask
la massa
1744 mass
l'albero della barca a vela
1745 mast
Lucia **conosce bene** le regole della circolazione.
1746 to master
un incontro, una gara di tennis
1747 match

Non bisogna giocare con **i fiammiferi**. 1748 match	**la matematica** 2 + 2 = 4 1749 mathematics	**la cosa, la faccenda** Copiare a scuola è **una cosa** grave. Questa è **una faccenda** che non capisco. *To cheat in school is a serious matter.* *This is a matter I do not understand.* 1750 matter	**Il materasso** è vecchio. 1751 mattress
Maggio è il quinto mese dell'anno. 1752 May	**forse** **Forse** Sabrina dovrebbe restare a casa. La risposta non è né sì né no: è **forse**. *Maybe Sabrina should stay home.* *The answer is not yes, and it is not no: it is maybe.* 1753 maybe	**il sindaco** della città 1754 mayor	Non perderti nel **labirinto**! 1755 maze
il prato 1756 meadow	**lo stornello americano** 1757 meadowlark	**il pasto** 1758 meal	un ragazzo **cattivo** 1759 mean person
Marianna ha **il morbillo**. 1760 measles	**misurare** 1 2 3 4 5 6 1761 to measure	**la carne** 1762 meat	**il meccanico** 1763 mechanic
Sara ha vinto **una medaglia** per il suo coraggio. 1764 medal	**Una medicina** prescritta dal dottore. 1765 medicine	**medio** 1766 medium	**incontrare** 1767 to meet

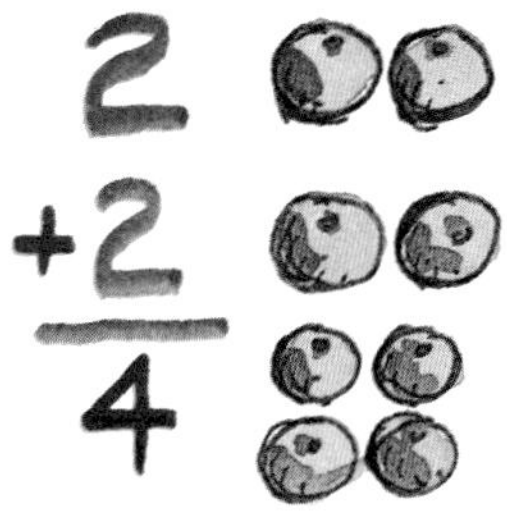

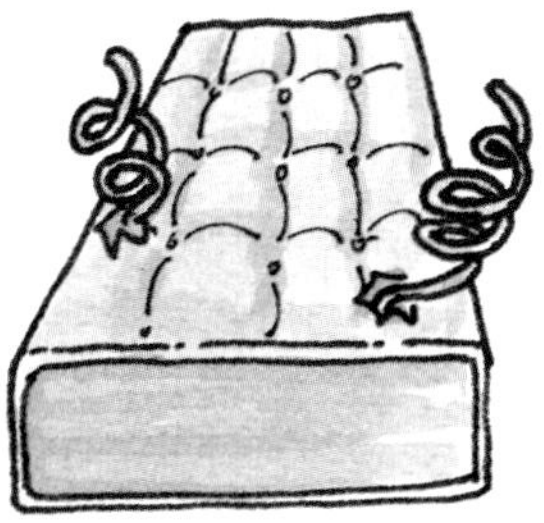

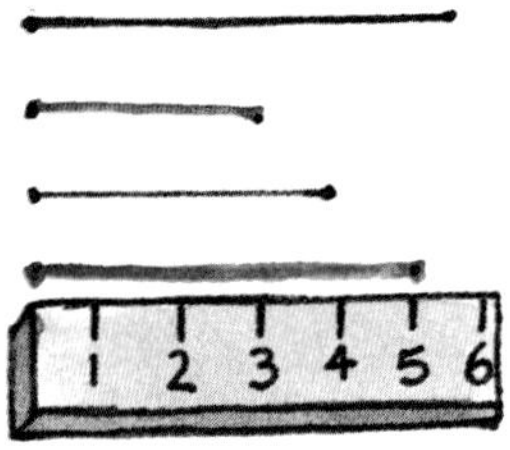

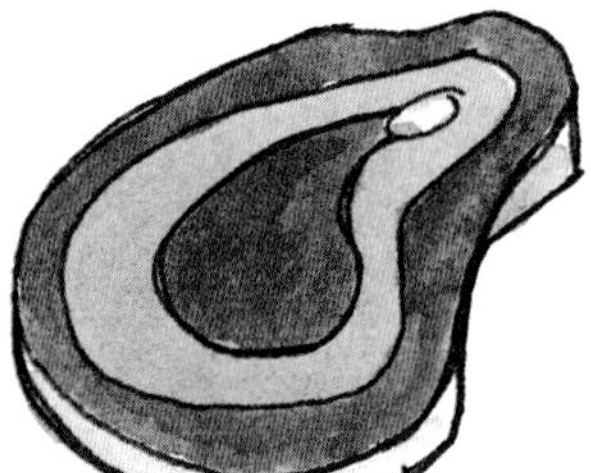

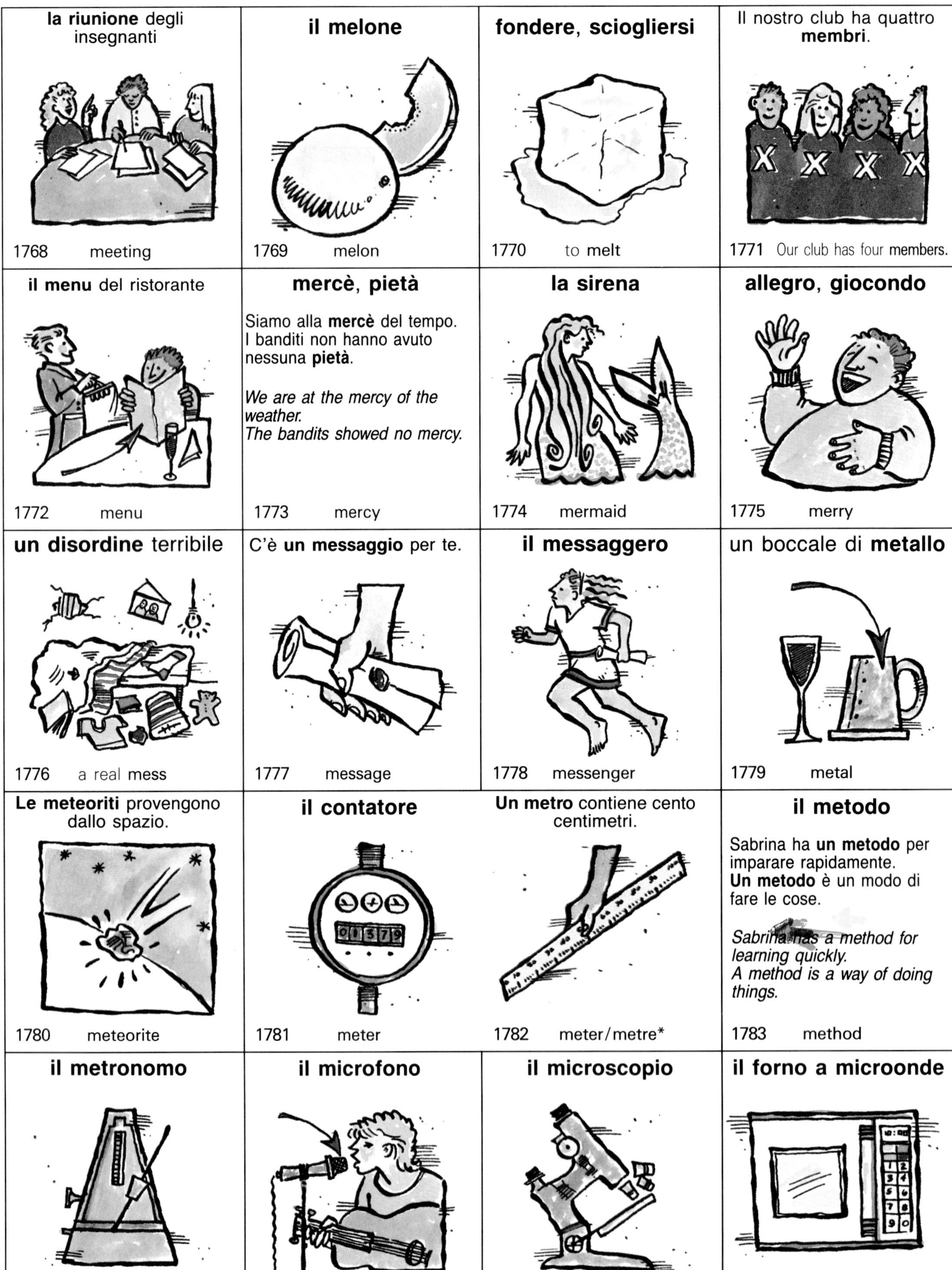

la riunione degli insegnanti
1768 meeting
il melone
1769 melon
fondere, sciogliersi
1770 to melt
Il nostro club ha quattro membri.
1771 Our club has four members.
il menu del ristorante
1772 menu
mercè, pietà
Siamo alla mercè del tempo.
I banditi non hanno avuto nessuna pietà.
We are at the mercy of the weather.
The bandits showed no mercy.
1773 mercy
la sirena
1774 mermaid
allegro, giocondo
1775 merry
un disordine terribile
1776 a real mess
C'è un messaggio per te.
1777 message
il messaggero
1778 messenger
un boccale di metallo
1779 metal
Le meteoriti provengono dallo spazio.
1780 meteorite
il contatore
01379
1781 meter
Un metro contiene cento centimetri.
1782 meter/metre*
il metodo
Sabrina ha un metodo per imparare rapidamente.
Un metodo è un modo di fare le cose.
Sabrina has a method for learning quickly.
A method is a way of doing things.
1783 method
il metronomo
1784 metronome
il microfono
1785 microphone
il microscopio
1786 microscope
il forno a microonde
1787 microwave oven

mezzogiorno 1788 midday	nel **mezzo** 1789 in the middle	**il nano** 1790 midget	**mezzanotte** 1791 midnight
il miglio **Un miglio** equivale a 1,6 chilometri. Il limite di velocità è di 30 **miglia all'ora.** *One mile equals 1.6 kilometers. The speed limit is 30 miles per hour.* 1792 mile	**il latte** di mucca 1793 milk	**Il mulino** è sulla riva del fiume. 1794 mill	**la mente**, **l'intelligenza** E=MC² 1795 mind
La miniera è sotto terra. 1796 mine	**Il minatore** lavora nella miniera. 1797 miner	**i minerali** 1798 minerals	**il pesciolino** 1799 minnow
La menta è una pianta aromatica. 1800 mint	Sette **meno** cinque, uguale due. 7-5=2 1801 minus	Vi sono 60 **minuti** in un'ora. 1802 minute	**uno** strano **miracolo** 1803 miracle
il miraggio nel deserto 1804 mirage	**lo specchio** 1805 mirror	**L'avaro** tiene tutto per sè. 1806 miser	**Sento la mancanza** della mia famiglia. 1807 to miss

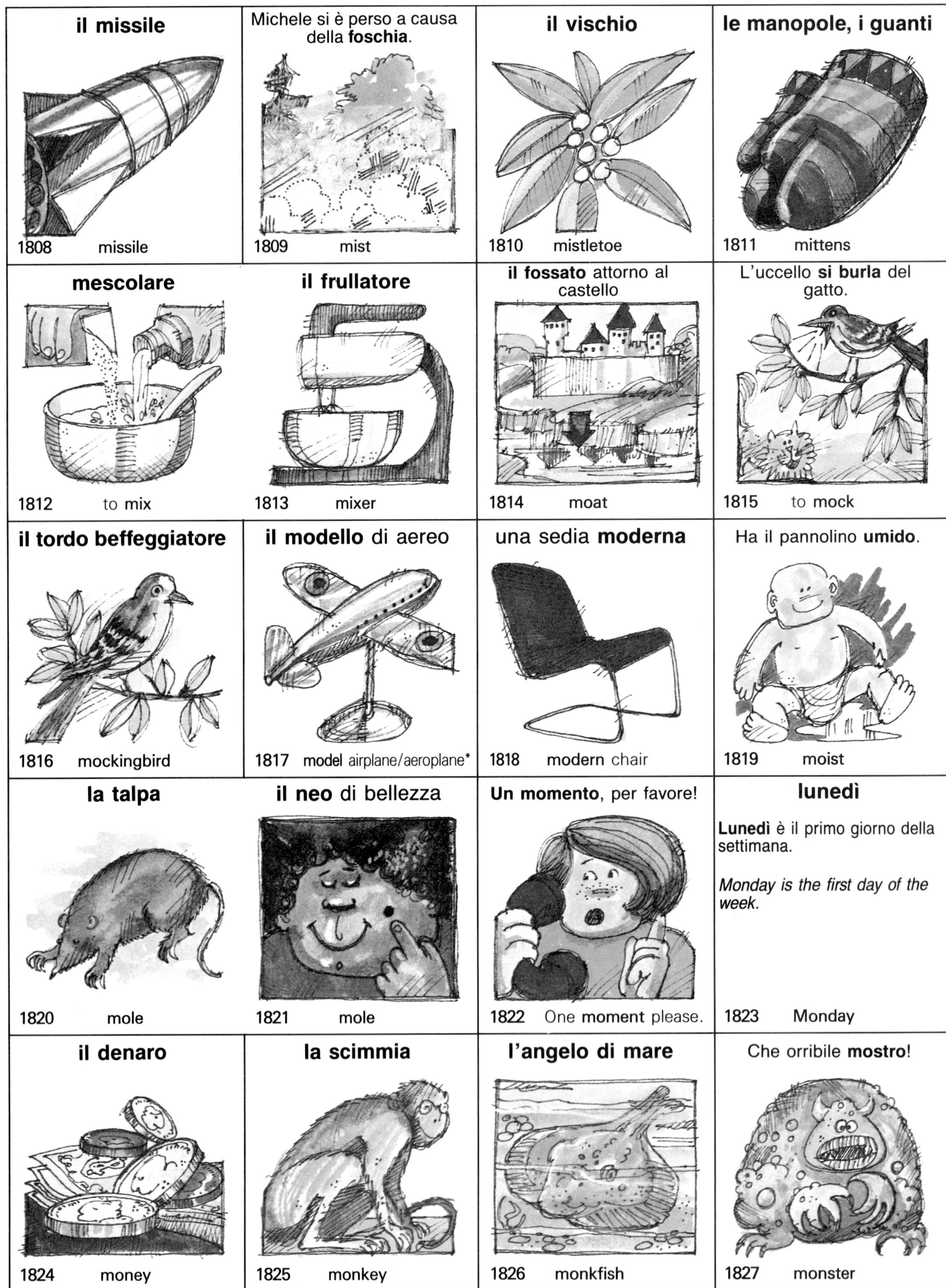
il missile
1808 missile
Michele si è perso a causa della **foschia**.
1809 mist
il vischio
1810 mistletoe
le manopole, i guanti
1811 mittens
mescolare
1812 to mix
il frullatore
1813 mixer
il fossato attorno al castello
1814 moat
L'uccello **si burla** del gatto.
1815 to mock
il tordo beffeggiatore
1816 mockingbird
il modello di aereo
1817 model airplane/aeroplane*
una sedia **moderna**
1818 modern chair
Ha il pannolino **umido**.
1819 moist
la talpa
1820 mole
il neo di bellezza
1821 mole
Un momento, per favore!
1822 One moment please.
lunedì
Lunedì è il primo giorno della settimana.
Monday is the first day of the week.
1823 Monday
il denaro
1824 money
la scimmia
1825 monkey
l'angelo di mare
1826 monkfish
Che orribile **mostro**!
1827 monster

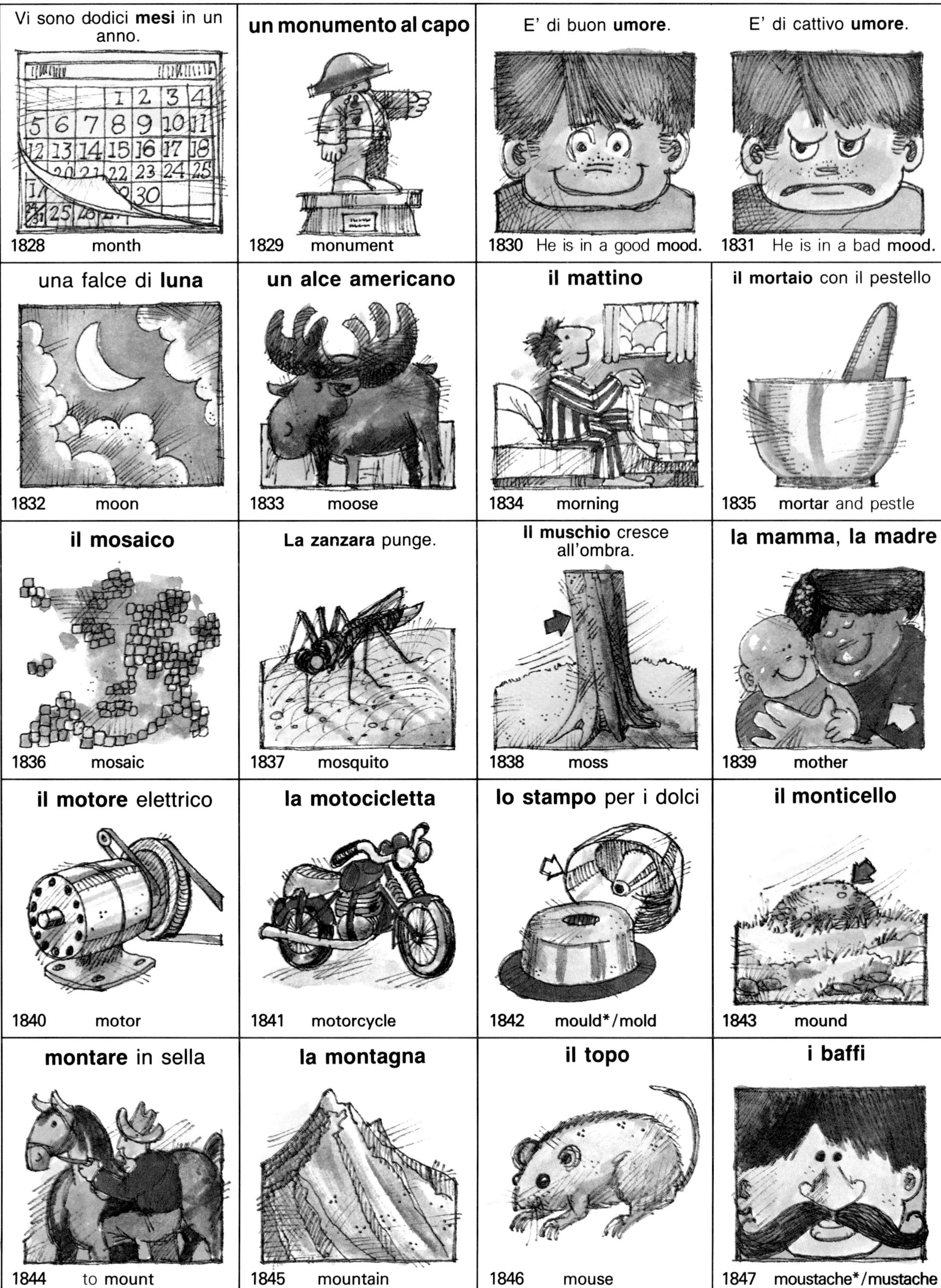

Vi sono dodici **mesi** in un anno.
1828 month

un monumento al capo
1829 monument

E' di buon **umore**.
1830 He is in a good **mood**.

E' di cattivo **umore**.
1831 He is in a bad **mood**.

una falce di **luna**
1832 moon

un alce americano
1833 moose

il mattino
1834 morning

il mortaio con il pestello
1835 **mortar** and pestle

il mosaico
1836 mosaic

La zanzara punge.
1837 mosquito

Il muschio cresce all'ombra.
1838 moss

la mamma, la madre
1839 mother

il motore elettrico
1840 motor

la motocicletta
1841 motorcycle

lo stampo per i dolci
1842 mould*/mold

il monticello
1843 mound

montare in sella
1844 to mount

la montagna
1845 mountain

il topo
1846 mouse

i baffi
1847 moustache*/mustache

la bocca
1848 mouth
La lumaca **si muove** lentamente.
1849 to move
il **movimento** del pendolo
1850 movement
il cinema, la sala cinematografica
1851 movie/film*
falciare l'erba del prato
1852 to mow the lawn
E' **troppo** per me.
1853 too much for me
Perché è seduto nel **fango**?
1854 mud
il mulo
1855 mule
moltiplicare
1856 multiply
Maurizio ha **gli orecchioni**.
1857 mumps
Uccidere qualcuno è un crimine terribile.
1858 to murder
il muscolo
1859 muscle
il museo
1860 museum
Alcuni **funghi** sono velenosi.
1861 mushroom
A Sabrina piace **la musica**.
1862 music
La mamma di Sabrina è **una musicista**.
1863 musician
Le cozze vivono nel mare.
1864 mussel
Devi saltare.
1865 You must jump.
la mostarda, la salsa di senape
1866 mustard
Ha **la museruola** sul **muso**.
1867 muzzle

N
il chiodo
1868 nail
un'unghia
1869 fingernail
forbicine per le unghie
1870 nail clipper
Sono ambedue nudi.
1872 naked
Il mio nome è. . .
ANN
1873 My name is...
il tovagliolo, la salvietta
1874 napkin/serviette*
inchiodare
1871 to nail
troppo stretto per passarvi
1875 too narrow to pass
L'Islanda è una nazione.
1876 nation
naturale
Gli alimenti naturali fanno bene alla salute.
La frutta contiene zucchero naturale.
It is healthy to eat natural foods.
Fruit contains natural sugar.
1877 natural
La natura è meravigliosa.
1878 nature
La ragazzina è cattiva.
1879 She is naughty.
navigare
1880 to navigate
sempre più vicino
1881 near
lindo, accurato
1882 neat
non piacevole, ma necessario
1883 Not pleasant, but necessary.
il collo
1884 neck
la collana
1885 necklace
Le api fanno il miele con il nettare.
1886 nectar

la pesca-noce

1887 nectarine

il bisogno, la necessità

Sabrina aiuta sempre gli amici nel **bisogno**.
Il cibo e l'abitazione sono **necessità** fondamentali.

Sabrina always helps her friends in need.
Food and shelter are basic needs.

1888 need

Ho bisogno di un bicchier d'acqua.

1889 I need water.

Sei capace di infilare **l'ago**?

1890 needle

Trascura il suo cane.

1891 He **neglects** his dog.

Il cavallo **nitrisce**.

1892 to neigh

i vicini

1893 neighbors/neighbours*

Né l'una, **né** l'altra mi va bene.

1894 **neither** one fits

un'insegna al **neon**

1895 neon sign

Mio nipote è figlio di mio fratello.

1896 My **nephew** is my brother's son.

Abbiamo molti **nervi** nel nostro corpo.

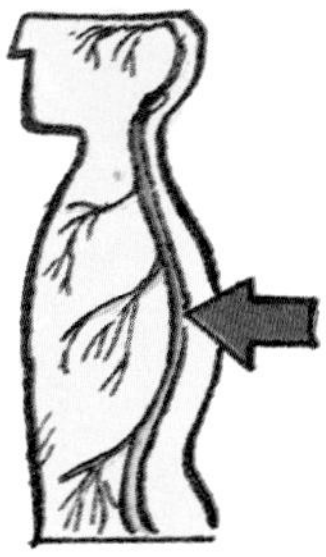

1897 nerve

Roberto è **nervoso**.

1898 nervous

due uova nel **nido**

1899 nest

Le ortiche pungono.

1900 nettle

Non giocare **mai** con il fuoco.

1901 **Never** play with fire!

un cappello **nuovo**

1902 new

le notizie

Mamma legge **le notizie**.
Ho buone **notizie** per te.
Hai **notizie** da casa?

Mom reads the news.
I have good news for you.
Any news from home?

1903 news

il giornale

1904 newspaper

Avanti **il prossimo**!

1905 Next !

Lo scoiattolo **rosicchia** una nocciuola.

1906 to nibble

Uno dei due è **beneducato**.
1907 nice
il nickel
1908 nickel
il soprannome
Si chiama Sabrina, ma **il** suo **soprannome** è Saby.
Her name is Sabrina but her nickname is Saby.
1909 nickname
Mia nipote è la figlia di mio fratello.
1910 My **niece** is my brother's daughter.
Le civette cacciano di **notte**.
1911 night
L'usignolo canta splendidamente.
1912 nightingale
Sebastiano ha **un incubo**.
1913 nightmare
nove
1914 nine
La risposta è **no**!
1916 no
nobile
Re Arturo era **nobile** e generoso.
Aiutare quella signora anziana ad attraversare la strada è stato un atto **nobile**.
King Arthur was noble and generous.
Helping that old lady across the street was a noble deed.
1917 noble
il nobiluomo
1918 nobleman
il nono quadratino
1915 ninth
Non c'è **nessuno** qui.
1919 nobody
il rumore
1920 noise
A **mezzogiorno** il sole è al suo punto più alto.
1921 noon
il nord
1922 north
Ho una mosca sul **naso**!
1923 nose
la noce
1924 nuts
lo schiaccianoci
1925 nutcracker
le calze di **nailon**
1926 nylon stockings/**tights***

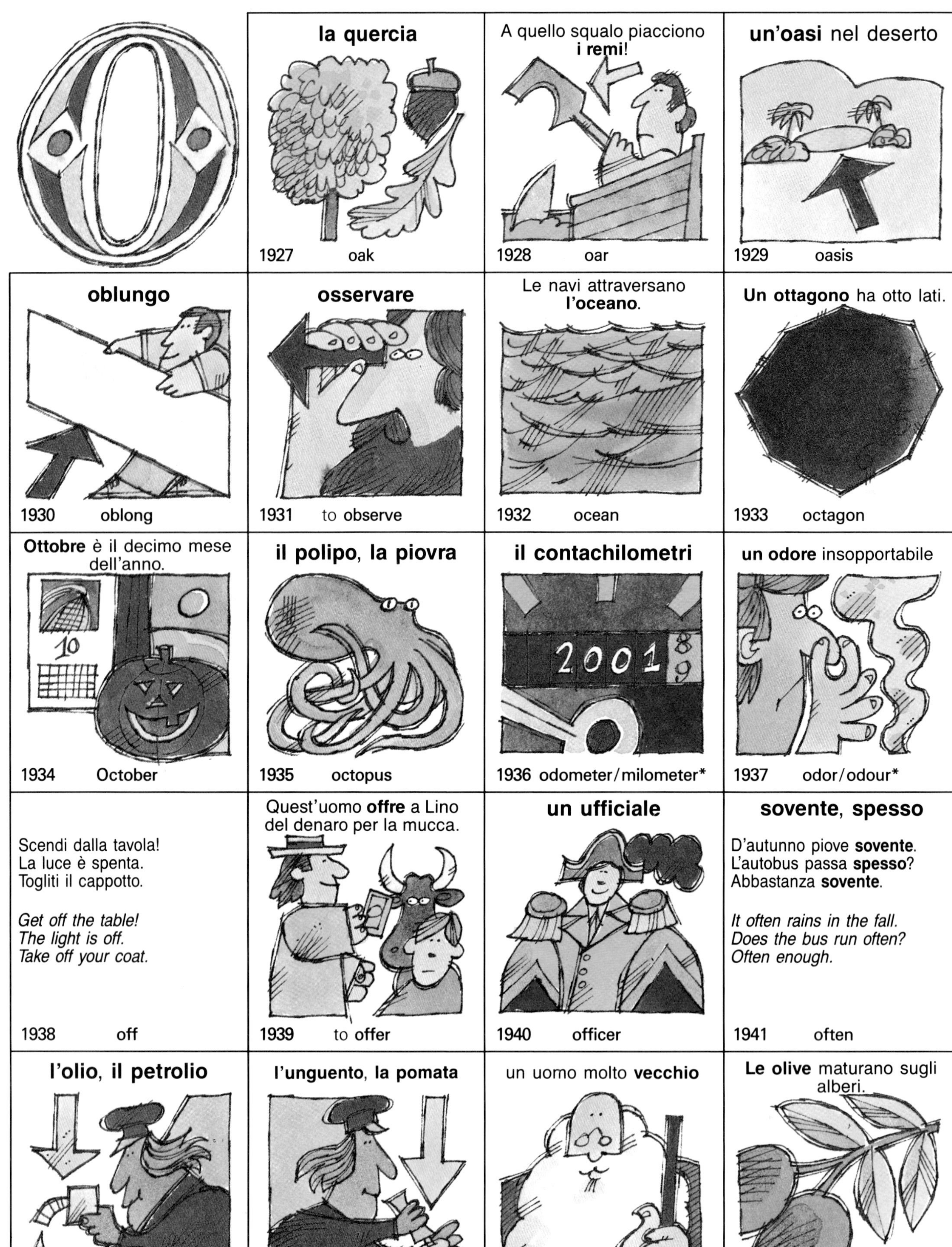
O
la quercia
1927 oak
A quello squalo piacciono i remi!
1928 oar
un'oasi nel deserto
1929 oasis
oblungo
1930 oblong
osservare
1931 to observe
Le navi attraversano l'oceano.
1932 ocean
Un ottagono ha otto lati.
1933 octagon
Ottobre è il decimo mese dell'anno.
10
1934 October
il polipo, la piovra
1935 octopus
il contachilometri
2001
1936 odometer/milometer*
un odore insopportabile
1937 odor/odour*
Scendi dalla tavola!
La luce è spenta.
Togliti il cappotto.
Get off the table!
The light is off.
Take off your coat.
1938 off
Quest'uomo offre a Lino del denaro per la mucca.
1939 to offer
un ufficiale
1940 officer
sovente, spesso
D'autunno piove sovente.
L'autobus passa spesso?
Abbastanza sovente.
It often rains in the fall.
Does the bus run often?
Often enough.
1941 often
l'olio, il petrolio
1942 oil
l'unguento, la pomata
1943 ointment
un uomo molto vecchio
1944 old
Le olive maturano sugli alberi.
1945 olive

Il cuoco fa **una frittata**. 1946 omelette	Il vaso di fiori è **sul** tavolo. 1947 on the table	**una volta** C'era **una volta** una bambina chiamata Sabrina... Mario è andato al campeggio solo **una volta**. *Once upon a time, there was a little girl called Sabrina...* *Mario has been to camp only once.* 1948 once	il numero **uno** 1949 one
la cipolla 1950 onion	mio **unico** amore 1951 my only love	Non lasciare la porta **aperta**. 1952 open	**aprire** 1953 to open
un'operazione 1954 operation	**un opossum** 1955 opossum	**opposto, dirimpetto** Il bene è **l'opposto** del male. Venivano dalla direzione **opposta**. I Rossi abitano **dirimpetto** a noi. *Good is the opposite of bad.* *They came from the opposite direction.* *The Rossis live opposite us.* 1956 opposite	**o, oppure** Vuoi una mela **o** una pera? Puoi fare il compito **oppure** lavare i piatti. *Do you prefer an apple or a pear?* *You can do your homework or wash the dishes.* 1957 or
Bisogna pelare **l'arancia**. 1958 orange	il color **arancione** 1959 orange	**Il frutteto** è pieno di alberi da frutta. 1960 orchard	**un'orchestra** 1961 orchestra
un'orchidea 1962 orchid	Il signor Edoardo **ordina** la cena. 1963 to order	**l'origano** 1964 oregano	Alberto suona **l'organo**. 1965 organ

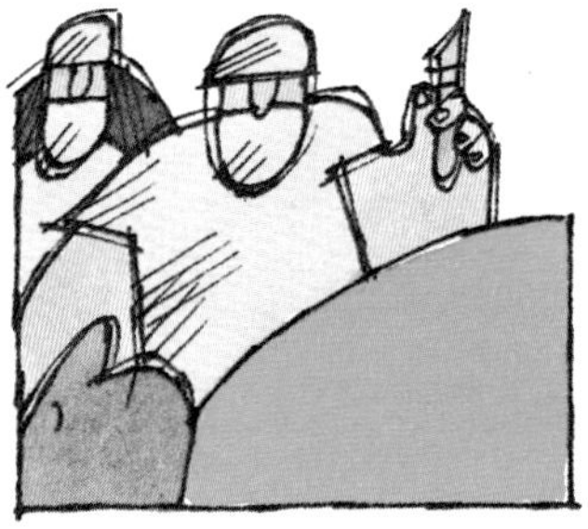

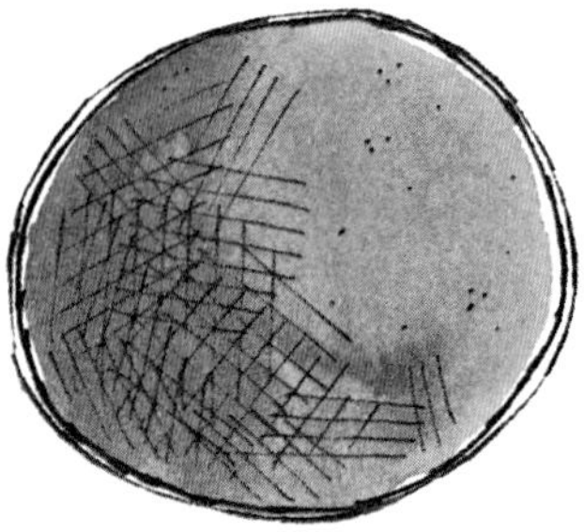

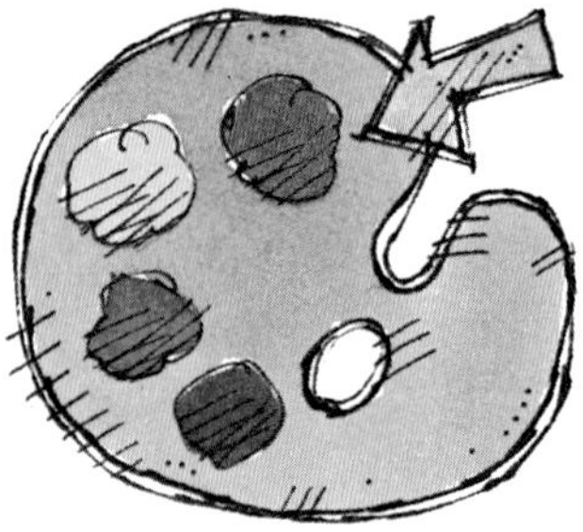

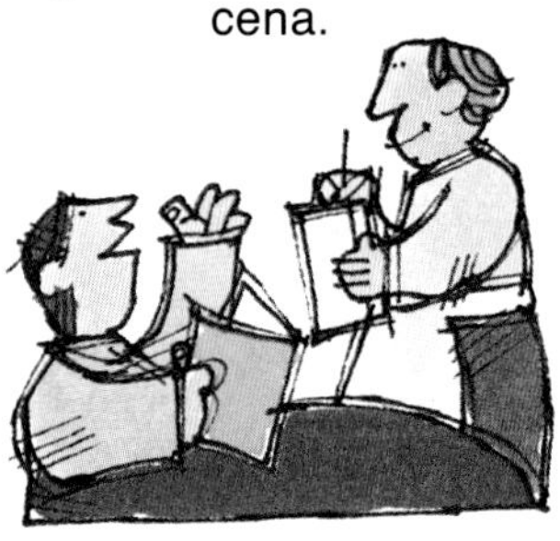

il rigogolo, **l'oriolo**
1966 oriole
Un orfano non ha genitori.
1967 orphan
Lo struzzo è un uccello che non vola.
1968 ostrich
La lontra è abilissima nel prendere i pesci.
1969 otter
Dodici **once** fanno una libbra.
1970 ounce
fuori, **all'aria aperta**
1971 outdoors
Ti piace **il** mio **vestito**?
1972 outfit
ovale
1973 oval
C'è una focaccia nel **forno**.
1974 oven
Uomo **in mare**!
1975 Man overboard!
il soprabito
1976 overcoat
Il secchio **trabocca**.
1977 to overflow
la soprascarpa, **la caloscia**
1978 overshoe
capovolgere, **rovesciarsi**
1979 to overturn
essere in debito, **dovere**
E' meglio non **essere in debito** con nessuno.
Dobbiamo molto ai nostri genitori.
It is best not to owe any money.
We owe a great deal to our parents.
1980 to owe
il gufo
1981 owl
avere, **possedere**
La famiglia Bianchi **ha** una villetta al mare.
Possediamo la casa in cui abitiamo.
The Bianchi family owns a house at the seaside.
We own the house we live in.
1982 to own
il bue
1983 ox
Il palombaro ha bisogno di **ossigeno**.
1984 oxygen
un'ostrica
1985 oyster

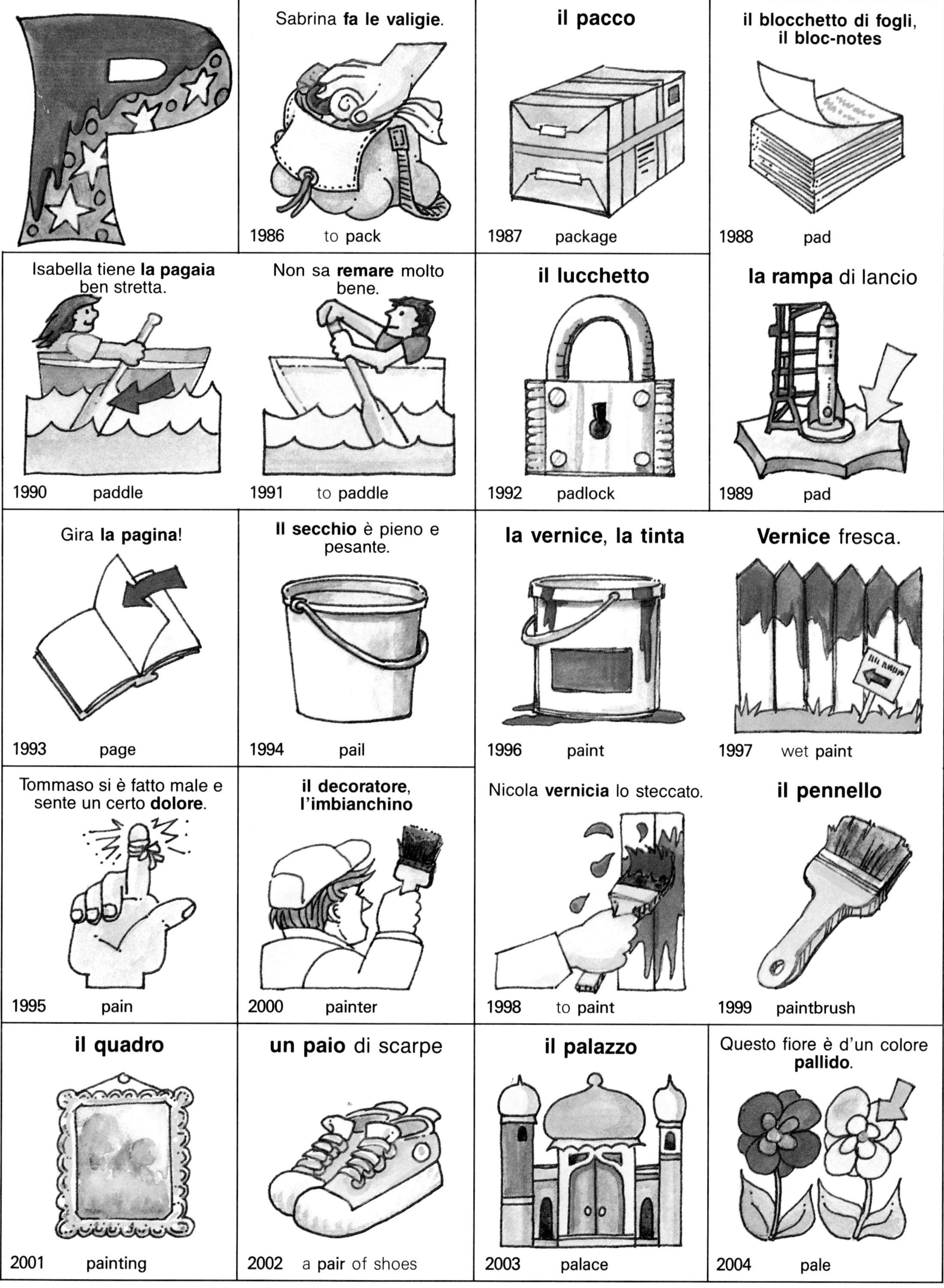
P
Sabrina **fa le valigie**.
1986 to pack
il pacco
1987 package
il blocchetto di fogli, il bloc-notes
1988 pad
Isabella tiene **la pagaia** ben stretta.
1990 paddle
Non sa **remare** molto bene.
1991 to paddle
il lucchetto
1992 padlock
la rampa di lancio
1989 pad
Gira **la pagina**!
1993 page
Il secchio è pieno e pesante.
1994 pail
la vernice, **la tinta**
1996 paint
Vernice fresca.
1997 wet paint
Tommaso si è fatto male e sente un certo **dolore**.
1995 pain
il decoratore, l'imbianchino
2000 painter
Nicola **vernicia** lo steccato.
1998 to paint
il pennello
1999 paintbrush
il quadro
2001 painting
un paio di scarpe
2002 a pair of shoes
il palazzo
2003 palace
Questo fiore è d'un colore **pallido**.
2004 pale

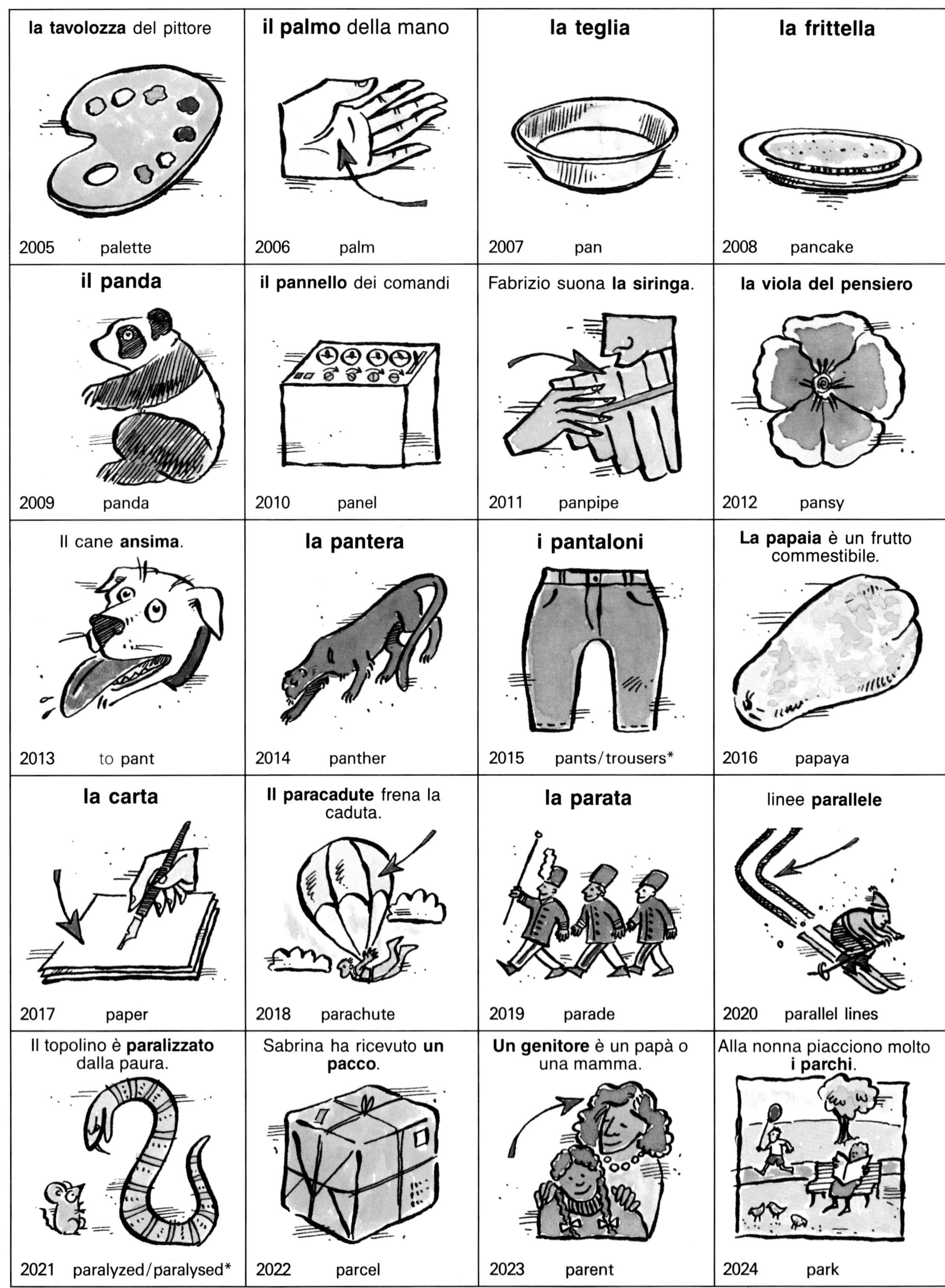
la tavolozza del pittore
2005 palette
il palmo della mano
2006 palm
la teglia
2007 pan
la frittella
2008 pancake
il panda
2009 panda
il pannello dei comandi
2010 panel
Fabrizio suona **la siringa**.
2011 panpipe
la viola del pensiero
2012 pansy
Il cane **ansima**.
2013 to pant
la pantera
2014 panther
i pantaloni
2015 pants/trousers*
La papaia è un frutto commestibile.
2016 papaya
la carta
2017 paper
Il paracadute frena la caduta.
2018 parachute
la parata
2019 parade
linee **parallele**
2020 parallel lines
Il topolino è **paralizzato** dalla paura.
2021 paralyzed/paralysed*
Sabrina ha ricevuto **un pacco**.
2022 parcel
Un genitore è un papà o una mamma.
2023 parent
Alla nonna piacciono molto **i parchi**.
2024 park

parcheggiare 2025 to park	**la giacca a vento** 2026 parka	**il parlamento** 2027 parliament	**Il pappagallo** ripete tutto quel che dico. 2028 parrot
il prezzemolo 2029 parsley	**La pastinaca** produce una radice commestibile. 2030 parsnip	Ci sono dei **granelli** di polvere nell'aria. 2031 particle	**il cavaliere**, **la dama** 2032 partner
la festa, **il ricevimento** 2033 party	Maria **passa** la palla . . . 2034 to pass	. . . e Felice **sviene** dal colpo. 2035 to pass out	**il corridoio** 2036 passage
Sabrina ama **le feste**. 2037 passenger	Per viaggiare all'estero occorre **il passaporto**. 2038 passport	**passato** Nel **passato** non v'erano né automobili né aeroplani. Ieri è il **passato**; domani è il futuro. *In the past, there were no planes or cars.* *Yesterday is the past; tomorrow is the future.* 2039 past	**la pasta**, **la pastasciutta** 2040 pasta
Il signor Bianchi **incolla** la carta da parati. 2041 to paste	Il ricamo è **il passatempo** preferito di Maria. 2042 pastime	**la pasticceria**, **le paste** 2043 pastry	Le pecore brucano l'erba nel **pascolo**. 2044 pasture

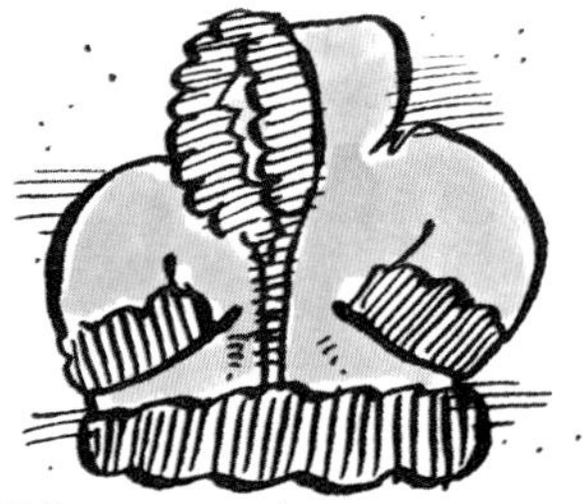

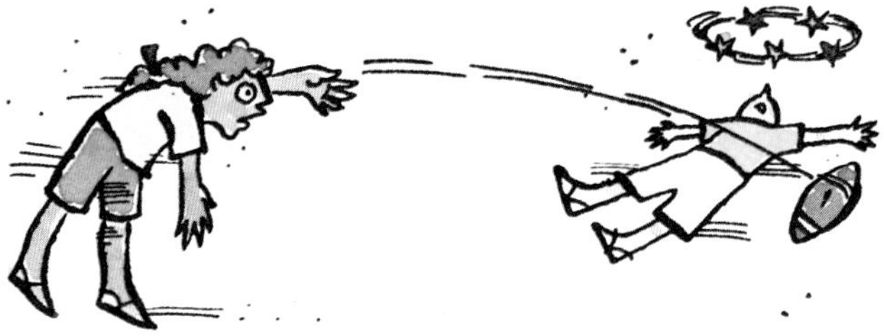

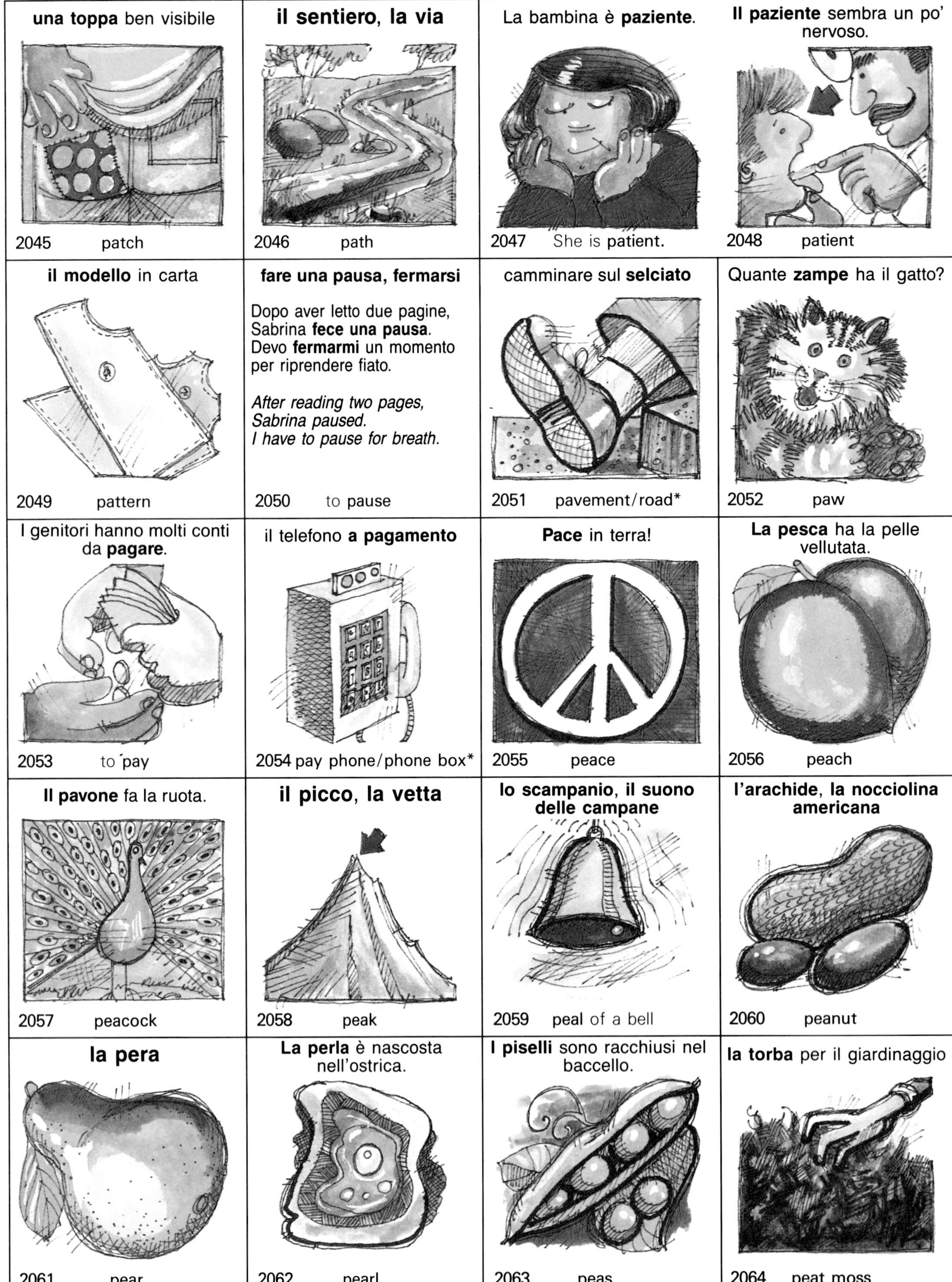
una toppa ben visibile
2045 patch
il sentiero, la via
2046 path
La bambina è paziente.
2047 She is patient.
Il paziente sembra un po' nervoso.
2048 patient
il modello in carta
2049 pattern
fare una pausa, fermarsi
Dopo aver letto due pagine, Sabrina fece una pausa.
Devo fermarmi un momento per riprendere fiato.
After reading two pages, Sabrina paused.
I have to pause for breath.
2050 to pause
camminare sul selciato
2051 pavement/road*
Quante zampe ha il gatto?
2052 paw
I genitori hanno molti conti da pagare.
2053 to pay
il telefono a pagamento
2054 pay phone/phone box*
Pace in terra!
2055 peace
La pesca ha la pelle vellutata.
2056 peach
Il pavone fa la ruota.
2057 peacock
il picco, la vetta
2058 peak
lo scampanio, il suono delle campane
2059 peal of a bell
l'arachide, la nocciolina americana
2060 peanut
la pera
2061 pear
La perla è nascosta nell'ostrica.
2062 pearl
I piselli sono racchiusi nel baccello.
2063 peas
la torba per il giardinaggio
2064 peat moss

i ciottoli, i sassolini
2065 pebbles

la noce americana
2066 pecan

beccare
2067 to peck

il pedale della bicicletta
2068 pedal

Il **pedone** cammina sul marciapiede.
2070 pedestrian

il passaggio pedonale
2071 pedestrian crossing

pelare, **sbucciare**
2072 to peel

pedalare
2069 to pedal

Il **pellicano** ha il becco molto lungo.
2073 pelican

la penna a sfera
2074 pen

la matita
2075 pencil

Il **pendolo** oscilla da destra a sinistra.
2076 pendulum

Il **pinguino** ha il piumaggio bianco e nero.
2077 penguin

il temperino
2078 penknife

Il **pentagono** ha cinque lati.
2079 pentagon

la gente
2080 people

I grani di **pepe** sono accanto al macinino.
2081 pepper

la menta peperita
2082 peppermint

il pesce persico
2083 perch

L'uccello ha trovato **un posatoio**.
2084 perch

un'ottima **prestazione**
2085 performance
il profumo
2086 perfume
Si mette **un punto fermo** alla fine di ogni periodo.
glurg!
2087 period/full stop*
La pervinca ha fiori violacei.
2088 periwinkle
la persona
2089 person
un insetto nocivo
2090 pest
Gaetano **importuna** suo padre.
2091 to pester
il suo **animale favorito**
2092 pet
Quanti **petali** ha questo fiore?
2094 petal
la petunia
2095 petunia
La farmacista vende medicinali.
2096 pharmacist/chemist*
coccolare, **accarezzare**
2093 to pet
la farmacia
2097 pharmacy/chemist's*
il fagiano
2098 pheasant
il telefono
2099 phone
la fotografia, **la foto**
2100 photograph
il pianoforte della mamma di Sabrina
2101 piano
Scegli una carta!
2102 to pick
prendere su, **sollevare**
2103 to pick up
il piccone
2104 pickaxe

i sottaceti
2105 pickles
mettere sotto aceto
2106 to pickle
scampagnata, **merenda all'aperto**
2107 picnic
Pablo dipinge **quadri** molto strani.
2108 picture
la torta di ciliegie
2109 pie
un pezzo di torta
2110 a piece/slice* of pie
Rosa **mette insieme** i pezzi della tazza.
2111 to piece together
il molo, **il pontile**
2112 pier
il maiale, **il porco**
2113 pig
il piccione, **il colombo**
2114 pigeon
Il maiale è nel **porcile**.
2115 pigsty
il mucchio, **il cumulo**
2116 pile
Le pillole possono essere pericolosissime.
2117 pill/tablet*
il pilastro, **la colonna**
2118 pillar
Si dorme bene su **un cuscino**.
2119 pillow
la federa del cuscino
2120 pillowcase
il pilota dell'aereo
2121 pilot
il foruncolo
2122 pimple
Il granchio ha due **chele**, o **pinze**.
2123 pincers
Non **pizzicare**, fa male!
2124 to pinch

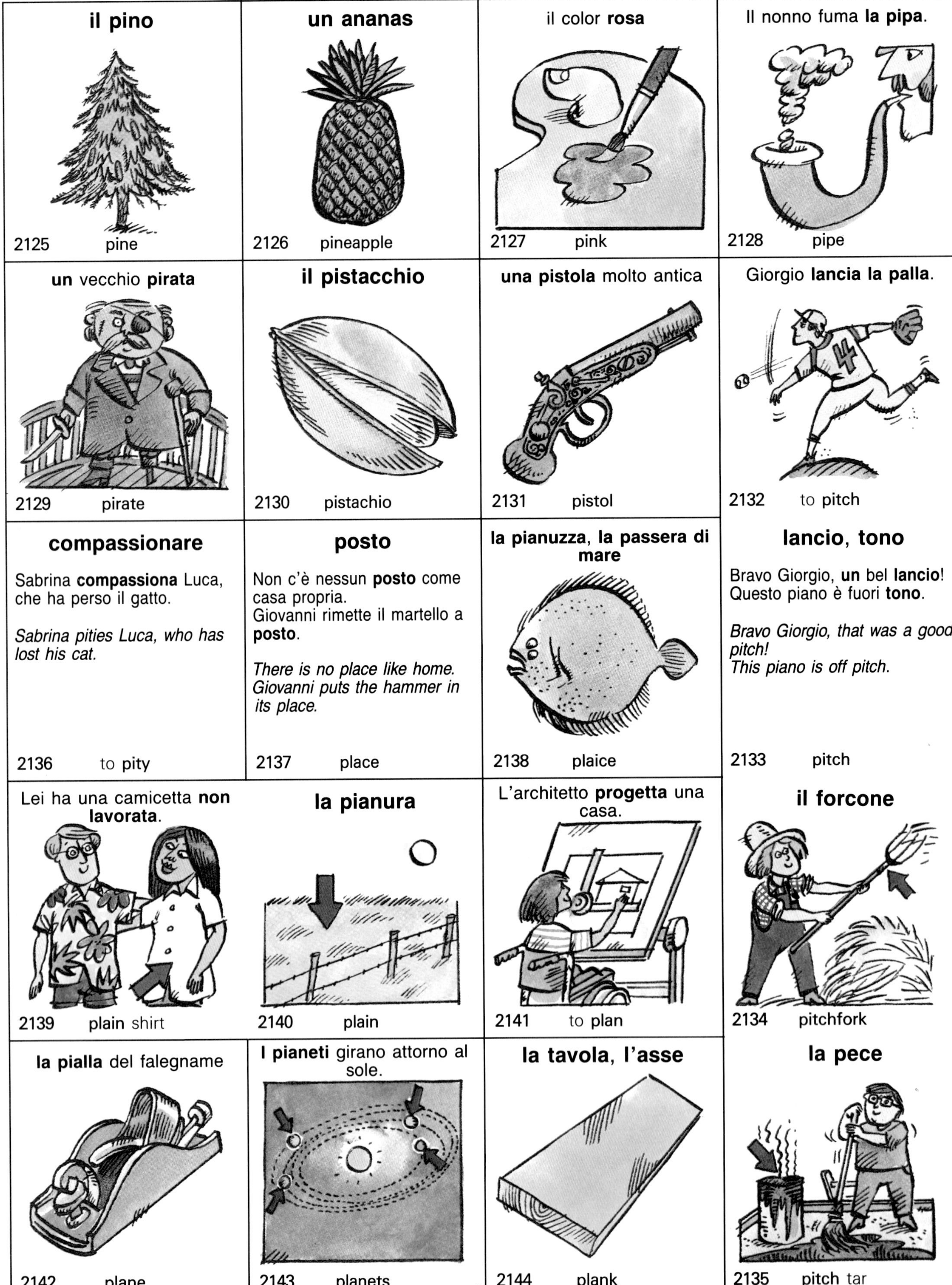

il pino
2125 pine

un ananas
2126 pineapple

il color **rosa**
2127 pink

Il nonno fuma **la pipa**.
2128 pipe

un vecchio **pirata**
2129 pirate

il pistacchio
2130 pistachio

una pistola molto antica
2131 pistol

Giorgio **lancia la palla**.
2132 to pitch

compassionare

Sabrina **compassiona** Luca, che ha perso il gatto.

Sabrina pities Luca, who has lost his cat.

2136 to pity

posto

Non c'è nessun **posto** come casa propria.
Giovanni rimette il martello a **posto**.

There is no place like home.
Giovanni puts the hammer in its place.

2137 place

la pianuzza, la passera di mare
2138 plaice

lancio, tono

Bravo Giorgio, **un** bel **lancio**!
Questo piano è fuori **tono**.

Bravo Giorgio, that was a good pitch!
This piano is off pitch.

2133 pitch

Lei ha una camicetta **non lavorata**.
2139 plain shirt

la pianura
2140 plain

L'architetto **progetta** una casa.
2141 to plan

il forcone
2134 pitchfork

la pialla del falegname
2142 plane

I pianeti girano attorno al sole.
2143 planets

la tavola, l'asse
2144 plank

la pece
2135 pitch tar

la pianta
piantare
2145 plants
2146 to plant
intonaco, stucco
L'operaia intonaca il muro.
2147 plaster
2148 to plaster
la plastica
2149 plastic
la plastilina
2150 plasticine
Questo è il piatto di Sabrina.
2151 plate
un altipiano
2152 plateau
la banchina della stazione
2153 platform
I bambini giocano nella sabbia.
2154 to play
un campo-giuochi
2155 playground
le carte da giuoco
2156 playing cards
supplicare il carnefice
2157 to plead
una giornata piacevole
2158 a pleasant day
Un bicchier di latte, per favore.
2159 A glass of milk, please.
le pieghe del gonnellino
2160 pleat
le pinze
2161 pliers
Il contadino ara la terra con un aratro.
2162 plow/plough*
spennare un volatile
2163 to pluck
inserire la spina nella presa
2164 plug

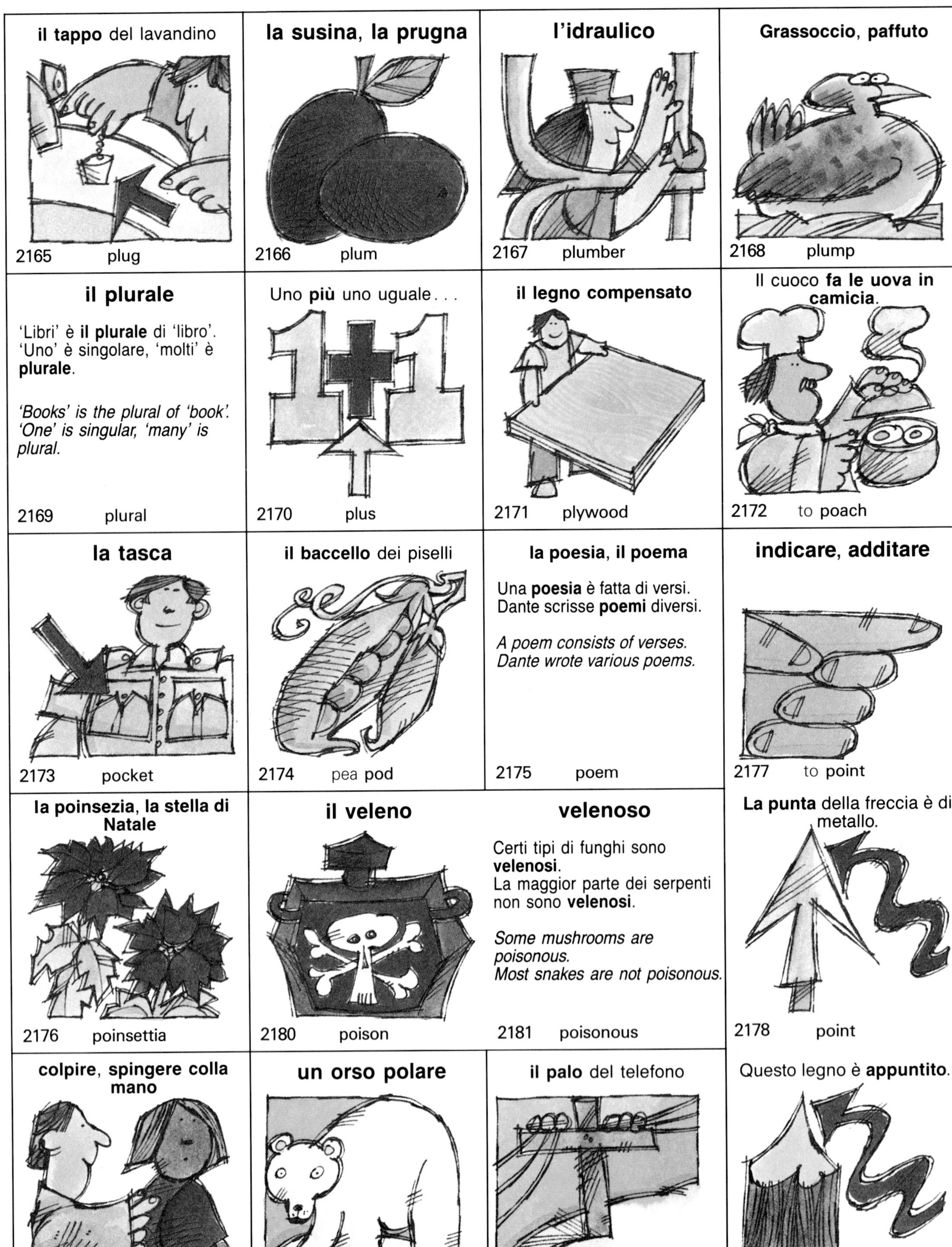

il tappo del lavandino
2165 plug

la susina, la prugna
2166 plum

l'idraulico
2167 plumber

Grassoccio, paffuto
2168 plump

il plurale
'Libri' è **il plurale** di 'libro'. 'Uno' è singolare, 'molti' è **plurale**.

'Books' is the plural of 'book'. 'One' is singular, 'many' is plural.
2169 plural

Uno **più** uno uguale. . .
2170 plus

il legno compensato
2171 plywood

Il cuoco **fa le uova in camicia**.
2172 to poach

la tasca
2173 pocket

il baccello dei piselli
2174 pea pod

la poesia, il poema
Una **poesia** è fatta di versi. Dante scrisse **poemi** diversi.

A poem consists of verses. Dante wrote various poems.
2175 poem

indicare, additare
2177 to point

la poinsezia, la stella di Natale
2176 poinsettia

il veleno
2180 poison

velenoso
Certi tipi di funghi sono **velenosi**. La maggior parte dei serpenti non sono **velenosi**.

Some mushrooms are poisonous. Most snakes are not poisonous.
2181 poisonous

La punta della freccia è di metallo.
2178 point

colpire, spingere colla mano
2182 to poke

un orso polare
2183 polar bear

il palo del telefono
2184 pole

Questo legno è **appuntito**.
2179 pointed

il poliziotto, l'agente di polizia
2185 policeman

la donna poliziotto
2186 policewoman

lucidare, levigare
2187 to polish

ben educato, cortese
Gridare non è da persona **ben educata**.
L'insegnante si aspetta una risposta **cortese**.
It is not polite to shout.
The teacher expects a polite answer.
2188 polite

il **polline** dei fiori
2189 pollen

La **melagrana** è un frutto.
2190 pomegranate

uno **stagno** in mezzo al bosco
2191 pond

il **pony** di Donatella
2192 pony

Nuotano nella **piscina**.
2193 pool

mettere in comune
2194 to pool

povero, scadente
La sua famiglia non è **povera**, ma non è neppure ricca.
Sabrina ha riportato voti **scandenti**, perché non ha studiato molto.
Her family is not poor, but it is not rich either.
Sabrina had poor results because she did not work hard.
2195 poor

far saltare il tappo
2196 to pop

il pioppo
2197 poplar

il papavero
2198 poppy

ben voluto, in voga
L'insegnante di Sabrina è **ben voluto** dai suoi alunni.
Questa canzone era **in voga** l'estate scorsa.
Sabrina's teacher is popular with his pupils.
This song was popular last summer.
2199 popular

la veranda
2200 porch

I pori sono piccoli fori nella pelle.
2201 Pores are little holes in the skin.

la pappa d'avena
2202 porridge

il porto
2203 port

portatile
Sabrina vorrebbe una radio **portatile**, ma non ha risparmiato abbastanza per comprarla.
Sabrina wants a portable radio but she has not saved up enough money.
2204 portable

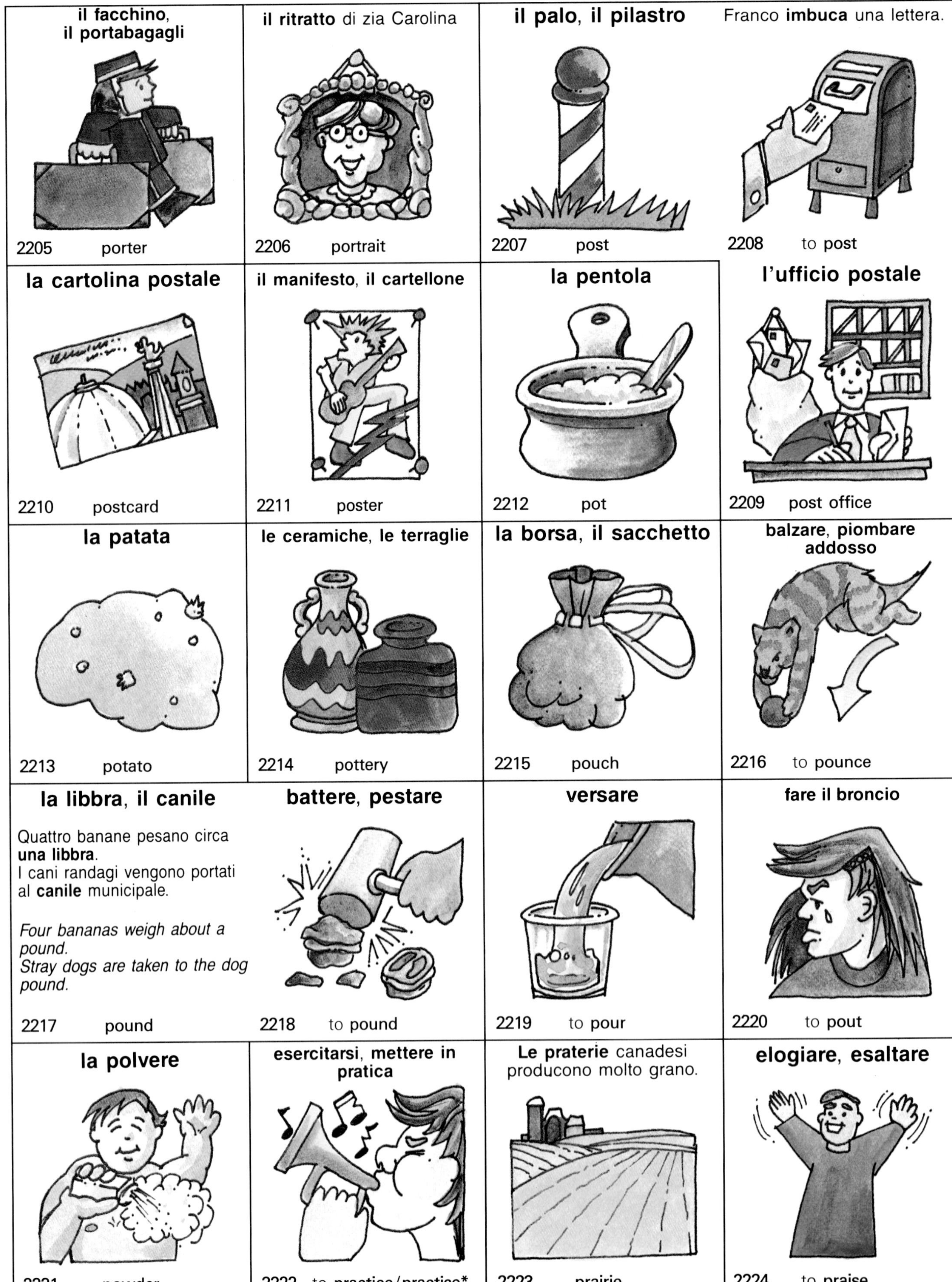

il facchino, il portabagagli
2205 porter

il ritratto di zia Carolina
2206 portrait

il palo, il pilastro
2207 post

Franco **imbuca** una lettera.
2208 to post

la cartolina postale
2210 postcard

il manifesto, il cartellone
2211 poster

la pentola
2212 pot

l'ufficio postale
2209 post office

la patata
2213 potato

le ceramiche, le terraglie
2214 pottery

la borsa, il sacchetto
2215 pouch

balzare, piombare addosso
2216 to pounce

la libbra, il canile

Quattro banane pesano circa **una libbra**.
I cani randagi vengono portati al **canile** municipale.

Four bananas weigh about a pound.
Stray dogs are taken to the dog pound.

2217 pound

battere, pestare
2218 to pound

versare
2219 to pour

fare il broncio
2220 to pout

la polvere
2221 powder

esercitarsi, mettere in pratica
2222 to practice/practise*

Le praterie canadesi producono molto grano.
2223 prairie

elogiare, esaltare
2224 to praise

Il cavallo **si impenna**. 2225 to prance	**pregare** 2226 to pray	Io **preferisco** questo. 2227 to prefer	La donna è **incinta**. 2228 She is pregnant.
Io sono **presente**. 2229 I am present.	**il regalo** per il compleanno 2230 birthday present	**presentare, consegnare** un premio 2231 to present	**la composta** di frutta 2232 preserved fruit
premere il bottone 2233 to press	**una bambina** graziosa 2234 pretty	La civetta ha **la preda** tra gli artigli. 2235 prey	**Il prezzo** è segnato sul cartellino. 2236 price
pungere 2237 to prick	un animale **munito di aculei** 2238 prickly animal	una scuola **elementare** 2239 primary school	**la primula** 2240 primrose
il principe 2241 prince	**la principessa** 2242 princess	**la preside** della scuola 2243 school principal/Head teacher*	**il principio, la teoria** **Il principio** fondamentale è quello di lavorare assiduamente. **In teoria**, sono d'accordo con te. *The first principle is to work hard.* *In principle, I agree with you.* 2244 principle

stampare

2245 to print

Il prisma separa i colori della luce.

2246 prism

Il ladro è in **prigione** per i crimini che ha commesso.

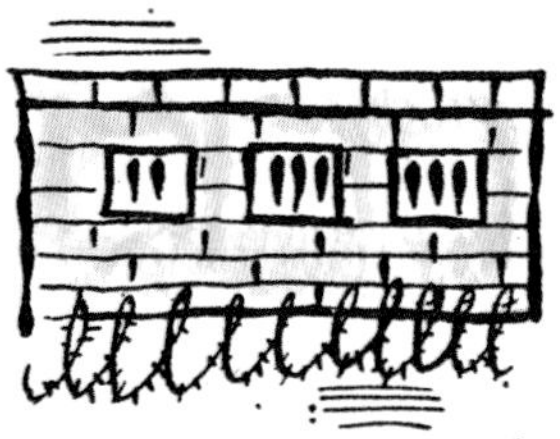

2247 prison

il detenuto

2248 prisoner

privato

Sabrina ed io siamo impegnate in una conversazione **privata**.
Questa è una proprietà **privata**.

Sabrina and I are having a private conversation.
This is private property.

2249 private

il premio

2250 prize

il problema

2251 problem

i prodotti agricoli

2252 produce

Sono pochi **i programmi** televisivi interessanti.

2254 program/programme*

vietato ai cani

2255 prohibited

il progetto

Debora sta lavorando a **un progetto** difficile.
Sabrina non ha avuto buoni risultati con il suo **progetto**.

Debora is working on a difficult project.
Sabrina did not do well on her project.

2256 project

Questa fabbrica **produce** automobili.

2253 This factory **produces** cars.

Lo prometto!

2257 I promise.

il dente del forcone

2258 prong

Pronuncia le parole chiaramente.

2259 to pronounce

la prova del delitto

2260 proof of guilt

puntellare, sostenere

2261 to prop

l'elica dell'aeroplano

2262 propeller

vestito **con proprietà**

2263 properly dressed

proprietà

Sabrina dice "E' mio" quando vuol dire "Questo è di mia **proprietà**".
La sua famiglia possiede **una proprietà** in campagna.

Sabrina says "This is mine" when she means "This is my property".
Her family owns property in the country.

2264 property

protestare 2265 to protest	La gatta è **fiera** dei suoi piccoli. 2266 I am a **proud** cat.	Lo posso **provare**. 2267 to prove	**il proverbio** Come dice **il proverbio**, can che abbaia non morde. *As the proverb goes, his bark is worse than his bite.* 2268 proverb
provvedere, mettere a disposizione 2269 to provide chairs	**La prugna** è il frutto del susino. 2270 prune	**potare** 2271 to prune	il telefono **pubblico** 2272 public telephone/phone box*
il budino 2273 pudding/afters*	**la pozzanghera** 2274 puddle	**sbuffare, tirar boccate di fumo** 2275 to puff	**la pulcinella di mare** 2276 puffin
tirare 2277 to pull	**la puleggia, la carrucola** 2278 pulley	**il maglione, il pullover** 2279 pullover/sweater*	Il medico controlla **il polso** a Sabrina. 2280 pulse
la pompa 2281 pump	**pompare, gonfiare** 2282 to pump	**la zucca** 2283 pumpkin	**colpire con un pugno** 2284 to punch

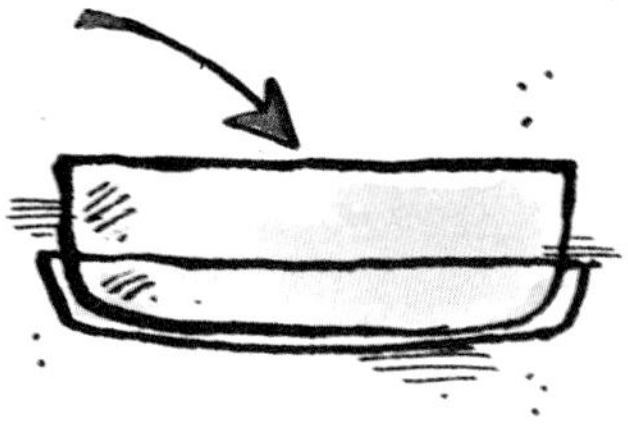

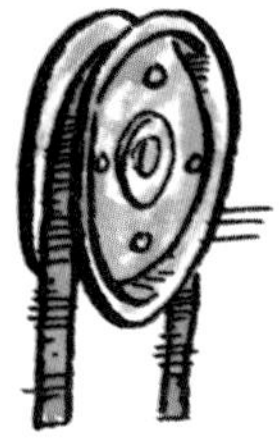

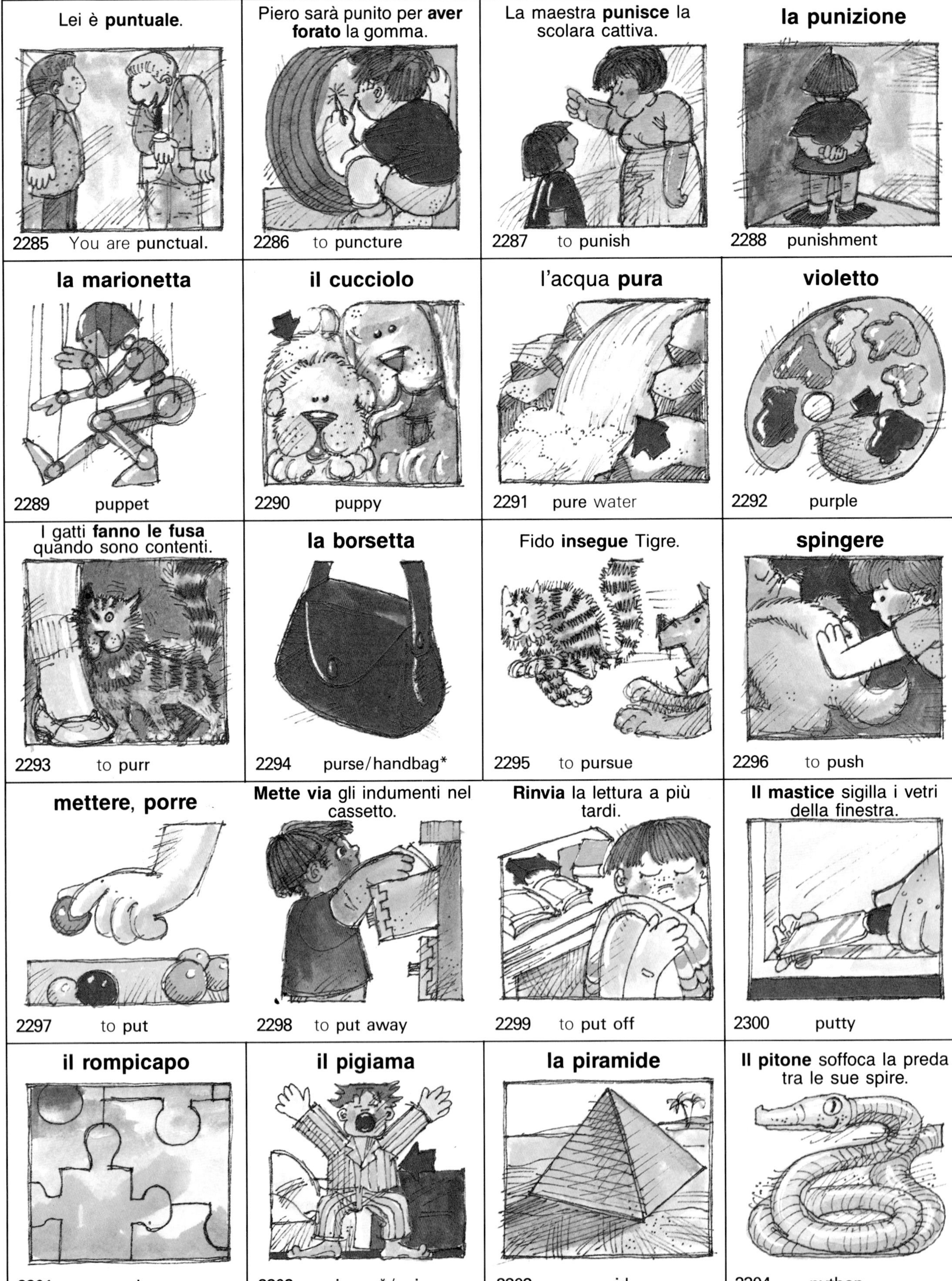

Lei è **puntuale**.
2285 You are punctual.

Piero sarà punito per **aver forato** la gomma.
2286 to puncture

La maestra **punisce** la scolara cattiva.
2287 to punish

la punizione
2288 punishment

la marionetta
2289 puppet

il cucciolo
2290 puppy

l'acqua **pura**
2291 pure water

violetto
2292 purple

I gatti **fanno le fusa** quando sono contenti.
2293 to purr

la borsetta
2294 purse/handbag*

Fido **insegue** Tigre.
2295 to pursue

spingere
2296 to push

mettere, porre
2297 to put

Mette via gli indumenti nel cassetto.
2298 to put away

Rinvia la lettura a più tardi.
2299 to put off

Il mastice sigilla i vetri della finestra.
2300 putty

il rompicapo
2301 puzzle

il pigiama
2302 pyjamas*/pajamas

la piramide
2303 pyramid

Il pitone soffoca la preda tra le sue spire.
2304 python

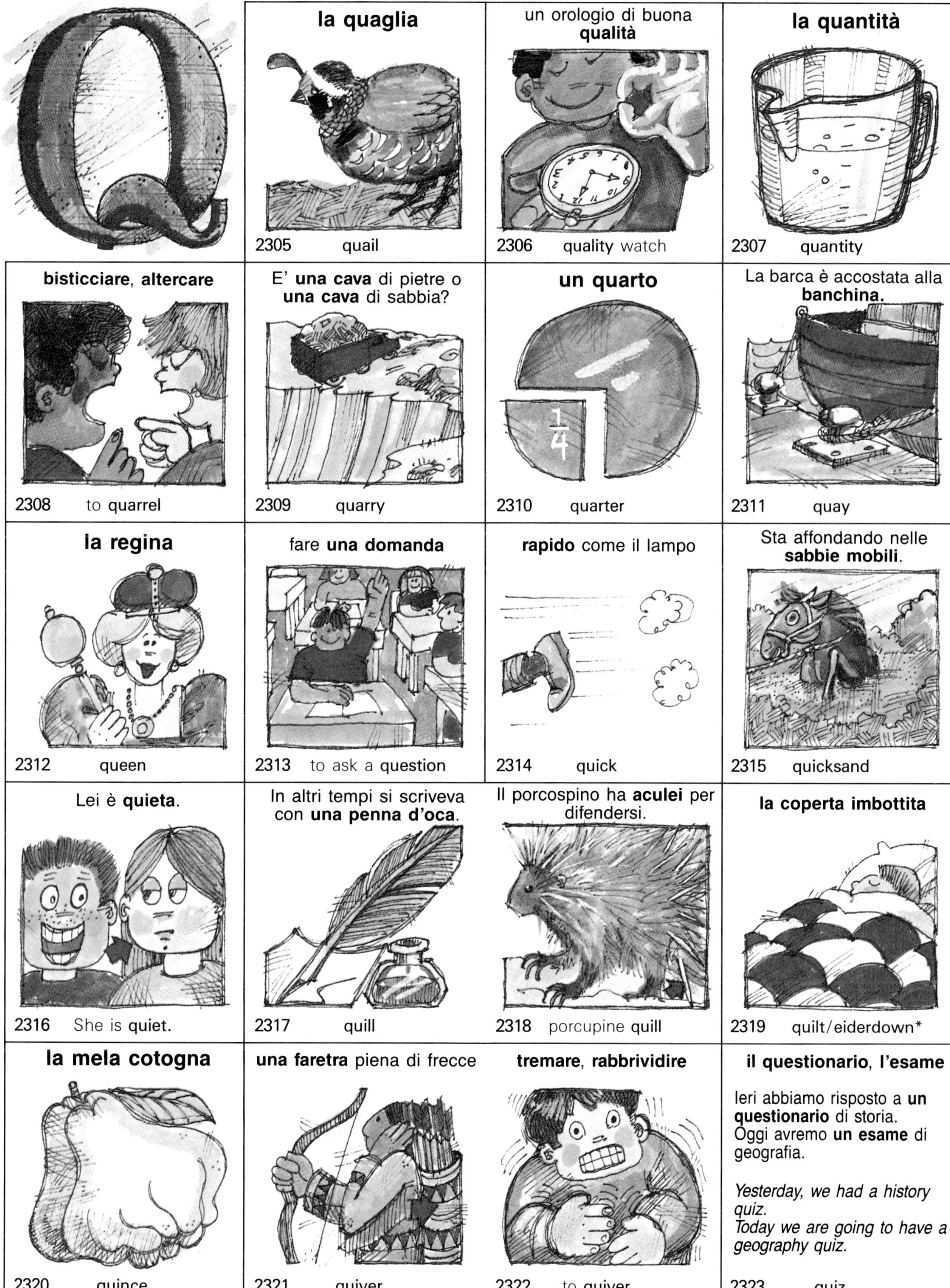
la quaglia
2305 quail
un orologio di buona **qualità**
2306 quality watch
la quantità
2307 quantity
bisticciare, **altercare**
2308 to quarrel
E' **una cava** di pietre o **una cava** di sabbia?
2309 quarry
un quarto
1/4
2310 quarter
La barca è accostata alla **banchina.**
2311 quay
la regina
2312 queen
fare **una domanda**
2313 to ask a question
rapido come il lampo
2314 quick
Sta affondando nelle **sabbie mobili**.
2315 quicksand
Lei è **quieta**.
2316 She is quiet.
In altri tempi si scriveva con **una penna d'oca**.
2317 quill
Il porcospino ha **aculei** per difendersi.
2318 porcupine quill
la coperta imbottita
2319 quilt/eiderdown*
la mela cotogna
2320 quince
una faretra piena di frecce
2321 quiver
tremare, **rabbrividire**
2322 to quiver
il questionario, **l'esame**
Ieri abbiamo risposto a **un questionario** di storia.
Oggi avremo **un esame** di geografia.
Yesterday, we had a history quiz.
Today we are going to have a geography quiz.
2323 quiz

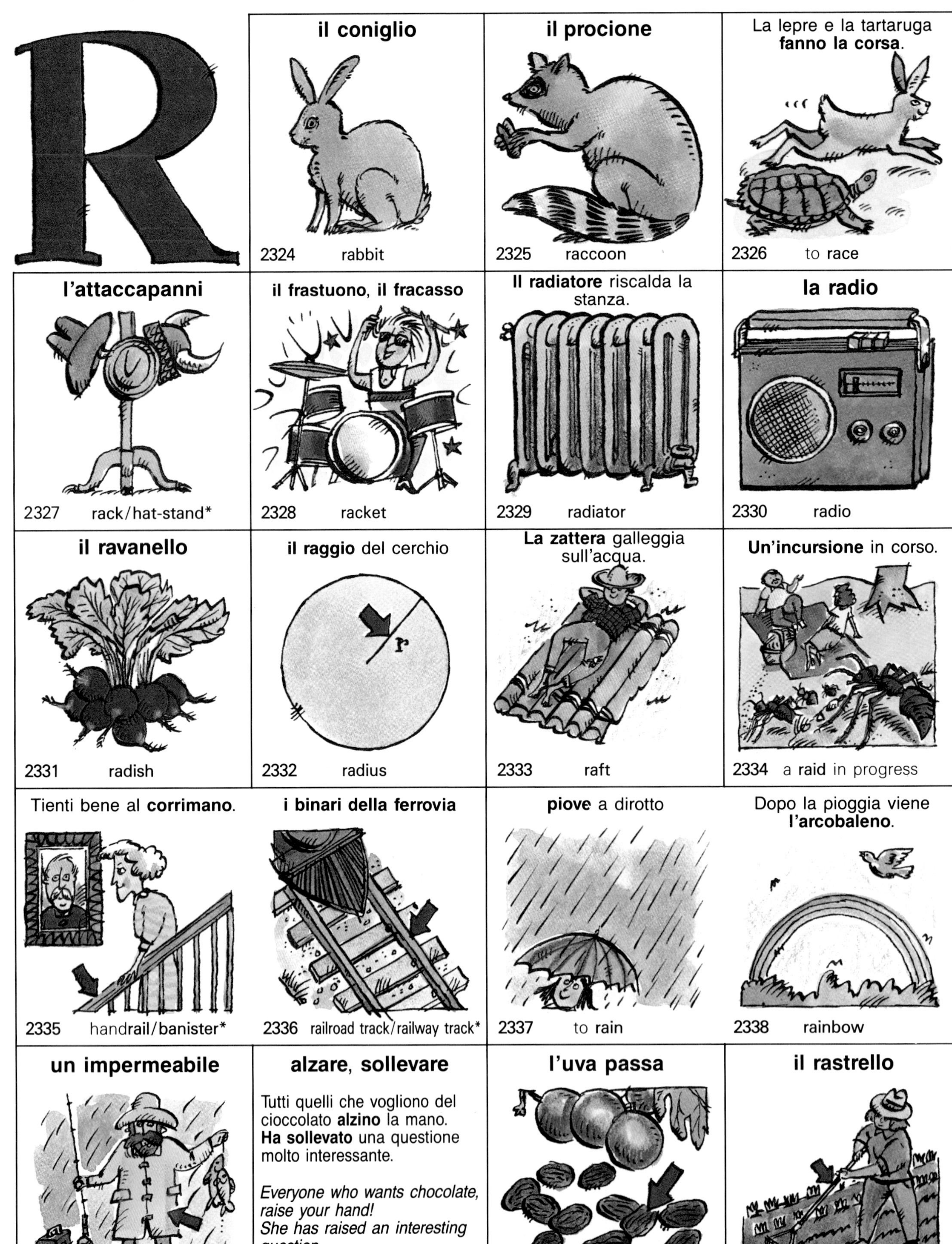
R
il coniglio
2324 rabbit
il procione
2325 raccoon
La lepre e la tartaruga **fanno la corsa**.
2326 to race
l'attaccapanni
2327 rack/hat-stand*
il frastuono, il fracasso
2328 racket
Il radiatore riscalda la stanza.
2329 radiator
la radio
2330 radio
il ravanello
2331 radish
il raggio del cerchio
r
2332 radius
La zattera galleggia sull'acqua.
2333 raft
Un'incursione in corso.
2334 a raid in progress
Tienti bene al corrimano.
2335 handrail/banister*
i binari della ferrovia
2336 railroad track/railway track*
piove a dirotto
2337 to rain
Dopo la pioggia viene l'arcobaleno.
2338 rainbow
un impermeabile
2339 raincoat
alzare, sollevare
Tutti quelli che vogliono del cioccolato alzino la mano.
Ha sollevato una questione molto interessante.
Everyone who wants chocolate, raise your hand!
She has raised an interesting question.
2340 to raise
l'uva passa
2341 raisin
il rastrello
2342 rake

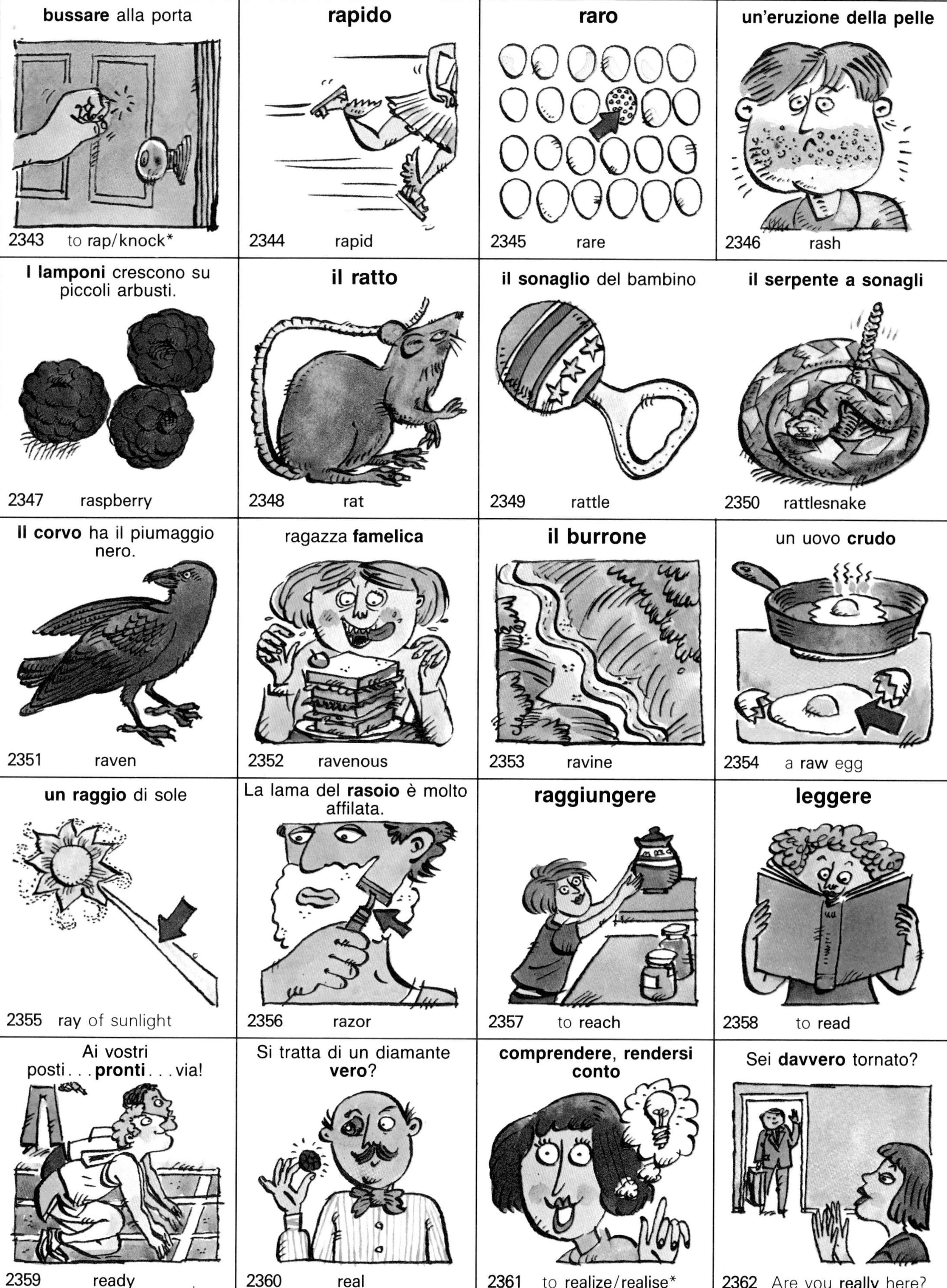
bussare alla porta
2343 to rap/knock*
rapido
2344 rapid
raro
2345 rare
un'eruzione della pelle
2346 rash
I lamponi crescono su piccoli arbusti.
2347 raspberry
il ratto
2348 rat
il sonaglio del bambino
2349 rattle
il serpente a sonagli
2350 rattlesnake
Il corvo ha il piumaggio nero.
2351 raven
ragazza famelica
2352 ravenous
il burrone
2353 ravine
un uovo crudo
2354 a raw egg
un raggio di sole
2355 ray of sunlight
La lama del rasoio è molto affilata.
2356 razor
raggiungere
2357 to reach
leggere
2358 to read
Ai vostri posti. . . pronti. . . via!
2359 ready
Si tratta di un diamante vero?
2360 real
comprendere, rendersi conto
2361 to realize/realise*
Sei davvero tornato?
2362 Are you really here?

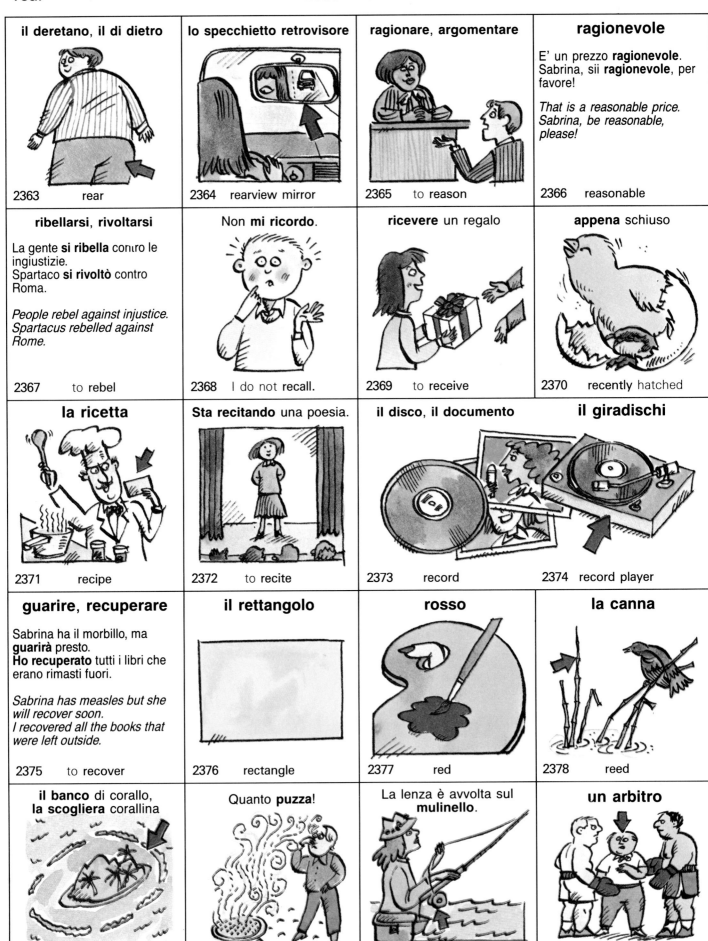

il deretano, il di dietro

2363 rear

lo specchietto retrovisore

2364 rearview mirror

ragionare, argomentare

2365 to reason

ragionevole

E' un prezzo **ragionevole**.
Sabrina, sii **ragionevole**, per favore!

That is a reasonable price.
Sabrina, be reasonable, please!

2366 reasonable

ribellarsi, rivoltarsi

La gente **si ribella** contro le ingiustizie.
Spartaco **si rivoltò** contro Roma.

People rebel against injustice.
Spartacus rebelled against Rome.

2367 to rebel

Non **mi ricordo**.

2368 I do not recall.

ricevere un regalo

2369 to receive

appena schiuso

2370 recently hatched

la ricetta

2371 recipe

Sta recitando una poesia.

2372 to recite

il disco, il documento

2373 record

il giradischi

2374 record player

guarire, recuperare

Sabrina ha il morbillo, ma **guarirà** presto.
Ho recuperato tutti i libri che erano rimasti fuori.

Sabrina has measles but she will recover soon.
I recovered all the books that were left outside.

2375 to recover

il rettangolo

2376 rectangle

rosso

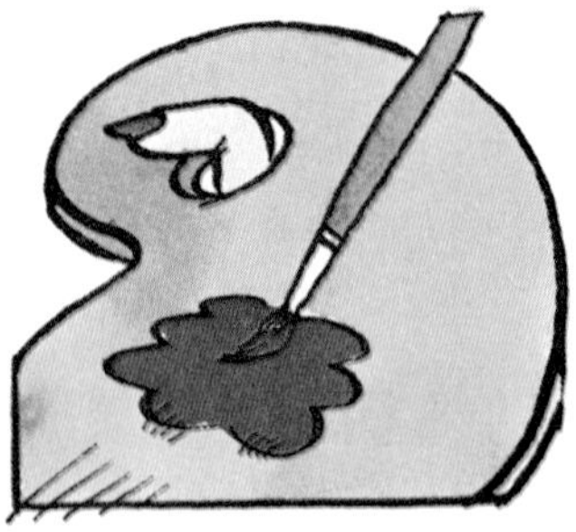

2377 red

la canna

2378 reed

il banco di corallo,
la scogliera corallina

2379 reef

Quanto **puzza**!

2380 to reek

La lenza è avvolta sul **mulinello**.

2381 reel

un arbitro

2382 referee

il riflesso, **l'immagine riflessa** 2383 reflection	Non lasciare **il frigorifero** aperto! 2384 refrigerator	**rifiutare** 2385 to refuse	**la regione** 2386 region
iscriversi 2387 to register	**rimpiangere** 2388 to regret	Gli attori **fanno le prove**. 2389 Actors **rehearse** a play.	**la renna** 2390 reindeer
le redini del cavallo 2391 reins	**i parenti** 2392 relatives	**riposare**, **rilassarsi** 2393 to relax	**rilasciare**, **liberare** 2394 to release
Ricordati di lavarti i denti! 2395 **Remember** to brush your teeth.	un'isoletta **remota** 2396 **remote** island	Filippo **si toglie** il cappello. 2397 to remove	**affittare** **Affittiamo** un appartamento. Se non hai la macchina, ne puoi **affittare** una. *We rent an apartment. If you do not have a car, you can rent one.* 2398 to rent
Annamaria si **ripara** la bicicletta. 2399 to repair	Il pappagallo **ripete** tutto. 2400 to repeat	Giovanna **sostituisce** la lampadina. 2401 to replace	Lui domanda, lei **risponde**. 2402 to reply

il rettile 2403 reptile	**salvare, soccorrere** 2404 to rescue	**il serbatoio** 2405 reservoir	**responsabile** Sabrina, sei **responsabile** di tuo fratello. Papà vide il latte versato e chiese: "Chi è **il responsabile**?" *Sabrina, you are responsible for your little brother.* *Dad saw the spilled milk and asked: "Who is responsible for this?"* 2406 responsible
Paolo **si riposa** nella sua poltrona. 2407 to rest	**il ristorante** 2408 restaurant	**restituire, ritornare** Sabrina **restituisce** sempre i libri della biblioteca. Giovanni è in viaggio, ma **ritornerà** presto. *Sabrina always returns her library books.* *Giavonni is travelling but he will return soon.* 2409 to return	Battista **fa marcia indietro**. 2410 reverse
il rinoceronte 2411 rhinoceros	**il rabarbaro** 2412 rhubarb	**la rima** Cuore fa **rima** con amore. Cerca una parola che fa **rima** con . . . *'Cuore' rhymes with 'amore'.* *Find a word that rhymes with . . .* 2413 rhyme	**la costola** 2414 rib
Sei capace di fare un fiocco con **un nastro**? 2415 ribbon	**il riso** 2416 rice	**ricco** **I ricchi** devono aiutare i poveri. Le arance sono **ricche** di vitamine. *The rich must help the poor.* *Oranges are rich in vitamins.* 2417 rich	Non sanno risolvere questo **enigma**. 2418 riddle
andare a cavallo 2419 to **ride** a horse	**la cresta, la catena di monti** 2420 ridge	la mano **destra** 2421 my **right** hand	**destra, giusto** All'angolo, gira a **destra**. Rubare non è **giusto**. *Turn right at the corner.* *It is not right to steal.* 2422 right

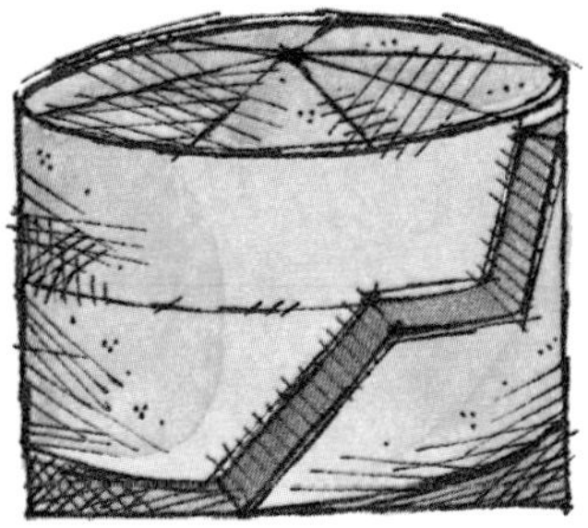

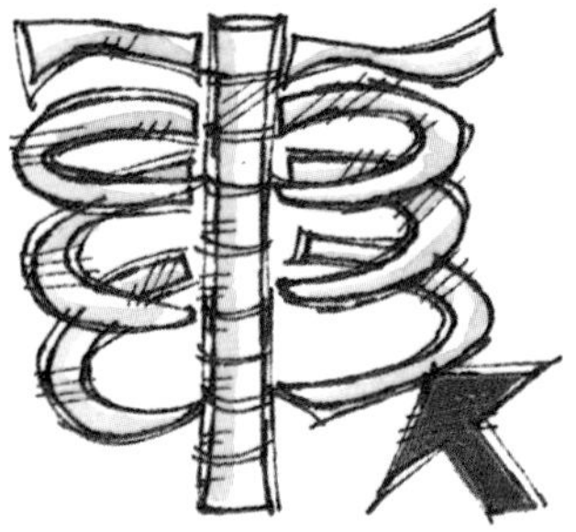

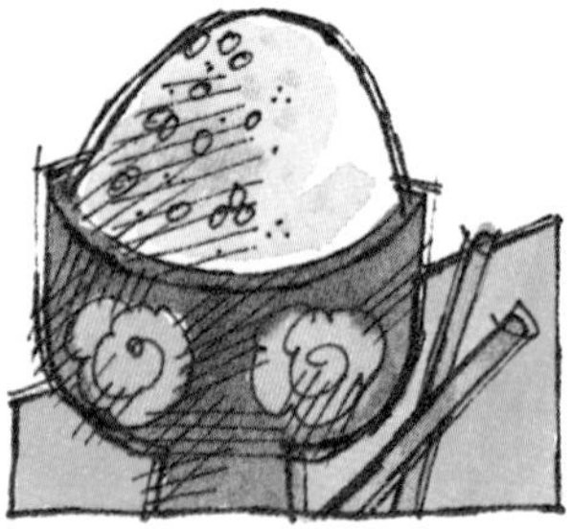

destro, persona che si serve della destra
2423 right-handed

la scorza
2424 rind

l'anello
2425 ring

Lo zio Sam **suona il campanello**.
2426 to ring

la pista di pattinaggio
2427 rink

Papà **sciacqua** le stoviglie.
2428 to rinse

un'insurrezione, un tumulto
2429 riot

Ha lacerato i pantaloni.
2430 to rip

Le mela è **matura**.
2431 ripe

un'increspatura, una piccola onda
2432 ripple

Il sole **sorge**.
2433 The sun rises.

il rischio

Il meteorologo disse che c'era **il rischio** di una brinata.
Si prudente quando decidi di correre **un rischio**!

The weatherman said there was risk of frost.
Be careful when taking a risk!

2434 risk

i rivali
2435 rivals

Il fiume serpeggia.
2436 river

la strada tortuosa
2437 road

Il leone **ruggisce**.
2438 to roar

Ha tolto **l'arrosto** dal forno.
2439 roast

il ladro
2440 robber

il pettirosso
2441 robin

una roccia, un masso
2442 rock

dondolare
2443 to rock
il razzo
2444 rocket
la sedia a dondolo
2445 rocking chair
la canna da pesca
2446 rod
il rotolo di carta
2447 roll
rotolare
2448 to roll
un pattino a rotelle
2449 roller skate
il mattarello
2450 rolling pin
Il tetto è fatto di tegole.
2451 roof
la stanza, la camera
2452 room
Il gallo si appollaia per la notte.
2453 to roost
la radice
2454 root
la corda
2455 rope
La rosa ha delle spine.
2456 rose
il rosmarino
2457 rosemary
Simona ha le guance rosee.
2458 rosy
La mela è marcia.
2459 rotten apple
ruvido
2460 rough
Il bottone è rotondo.
2461 round
una fila di quattro bottoni
2462 4 buttons in a row

Rema meglio di Luca.
2463 to **row**

regale
2464 **royal**

Il pneumatico e la palla sono di **gomma**.
2465 **rubber**

i rifiuti, **le immondizie**
2466 **rubbish**

Il rubino è una pietra rossa.
2467 **ruby**

il timone
2468 **rudder**

E' **maleducato**.
2469 He is **rude**.

un terreno **accidentato**
2470 **rugged** terrain

le rovine di un antico castello
2471 **ruin**

la regola, **il dominio**

Mamma e papà stabiliscono **le regole** di condotta in casa. Certi paesi sono sotto **il dominio** di un re.

Mom and Dad make the rules in this house. Some countries are under the rule of a king.
2472 **rule**

il sovrano
2473 **ruler**

Sente **un brontolio** lontano.
2474 I hear a **rumble**.

correre
2475 to **run**

scappare, **scampare**
2476 to **run away**

investire
2477 to **run over**

esaurire le proprie energie
2478 to **run out** of energy

precipitarsi
2479 to **rush**

Il robot è coperto di **ruggine**.
2480 **rust**

un solco nella strada
2481 **rut**

La segale è una pianta simile al grano.
2482 **rye**

il sacco di farina
2483 sack
La verità è un principio **sacro**.
2484 Truth is a sacred principle.
triste
2485 sad
la sella
2486 saddle
Che cosa c'è nella **cassaforte**?
2487 safe
Il vento gonfia **la vela**.
2488 sail
il sailboard
2489 sailboard
La barca a vela scivola sul lago.
2490 sailboat/sailing boat*
il marinaio
2491 sailor
l'insalata
2492 salad
la svendita
2493 sale
il salmone
2494 salmon
il sale e il pepe
2495 salt
salutare, **fare il saluto**
2496 to salute
stesso, **identico**
2497 same
la sabbia
2498 sand
il sandalo
2499 sandal
Sabrina si è preparata **un panino**.
2500 sandwich
la linfa dell'albero
2501 sap

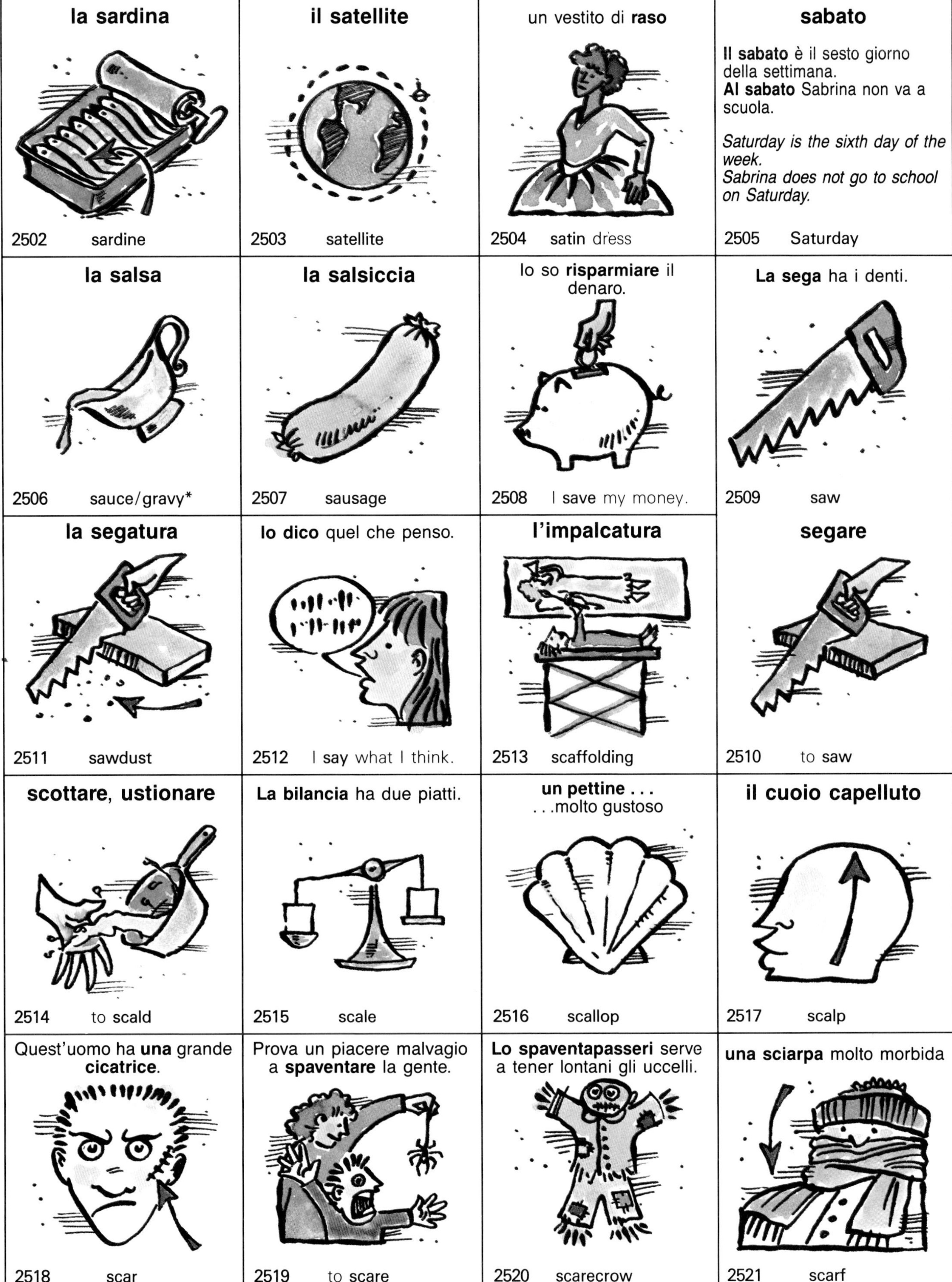
la sardina
2502 sardine
il satellite
2503 satellite
un vestito di raso
2504 satin dress
sabato
Il sabato è il sesto giorno della settimana.
Al sabato Sabrina non va a scuola.
Saturday is the sixth day of the week.
Sabrina does not go to school on Saturday.
2505 Saturday
la salsa
2506 sauce/gravy*
la salsiccia
2507 sausage
Io so risparmiare il denaro.
2508 I save my money.
La sega ha i denti.
2509 saw
la segatura
2511 sawdust
Io dico quel che penso.
2512 I say what I think.
l'impalcatura
2513 scaffolding
segare
2510 to saw
scottare, ustionare
2514 to scald
La bilancia ha due piatti.
2515 scale
un pettine . . .
. . .molto gustoso
2516 scallop
il cuoio capelluto
2517 scalp
Quest'uomo ha una grande cicatrice.
2518 scar
Prova un piacere malvagio a spaventare la gente.
2519 to scare
Lo spaventapasseri serve a tener lontani gli uccelli.
2520 scarecrow
una sciarpa molto morbida
2521 scarf

scarlatto
2522 scarlet
la scena del delitto
2523 scene of a crime
il paesaggio
2524 scenery
l'erudizione, la borsa di studio
2525 scholarship
la scuola del villaggio
2526 school
la goletta
2527 schooner
le forbici
2528 scissors
raccogliere, prendere con la paletta
2529 to scoop
la motoretta
2530 scooter
La carta è bruciacchiata dalla fiamma.
2531 scorched paper
segnare una rete
2532 to score
un esploratore
2533 scout
i pezzi di carta
2534 scraps of paper
una scorticatura, una lacerazione
2535 scrape
il raschietto
2536 scraper
il graffio, la graffiatura
2537 scratch
la zanzariera
2538 screen
la vite
2539 screw
il cacciavite
2540 screwdriver
lavare, fregare
2541 to scrub

Lo scultore lavora il marmo.
2542 sculptor

il cavalluccio marino
2543 seahorse

il **Mare** Adriatico
2544 Adriatic sea

il gabbiano
2545 seagull

la foca
2546 seal

la cucitura
2547 seam

Che cosa **cerca** nell'erba?
2548 to search

il riflettore
2549 searchlight

le stagioni

Le quattro **stagioni** dell'anno sono la primavera, l'estate, l'autunno e l'inverno.

The four seasons are: spring, summer, autumn and winter.

2550 seasons

il sedile
2551 seat

Sabrina ha allacciato **la cintura di sicurezza**.
2552 seatbelt

l'alga marina
2553 seaweed

il secondo
2554 second

Ho **un segreto**.
2555 I have a secret.

vedere
2556 to see

l'altalena
2557 see-saw

il seme
2558 seed

Sembra morto.
2559 It seems to be dead.

afferrare
2560 to seize

Sei **un egoista**.
2561 You are selfish.

Rebecca **vende** frutta. 2562 to sell	**il semicerchio** 2563 semicircle	**mandare, spedire** 2564 to send	**una pelle delicata** 2565 sensitive skin
la frase, la sentenza Sei capace di fare **una frase** completa? Il giudice ha pronunciato **la sentenza**: due anni di carcere. *Can you make a full sentence? The judge has issued the sentence: two years in jail.* 2566 sentence	**la sentinella** 2567 sentry	In **settembre** maturano molte frutta. 2568 September	**servire** un pasto 2569 to serve
sette 2570 seven	**la settima** foca 2571 seventh	**parecchi, vari** 2572 several	Ella **cuce** con filo e ago. 2573 to sew
la macchina da cucire 2574 sewing machine	**consunto, sciupato** 2575 shabby	**la baracca** 2576 shack	**un'ombra** 2577 shadow
un cane **dal pelo lungo** 2578 shaggy	**scuotere, agitare** 2579 to shake	l'acqua **poco profonda** 2580 shallow water	Mamma si lava i capelli con **lo shampoo**. 2581 shampoo

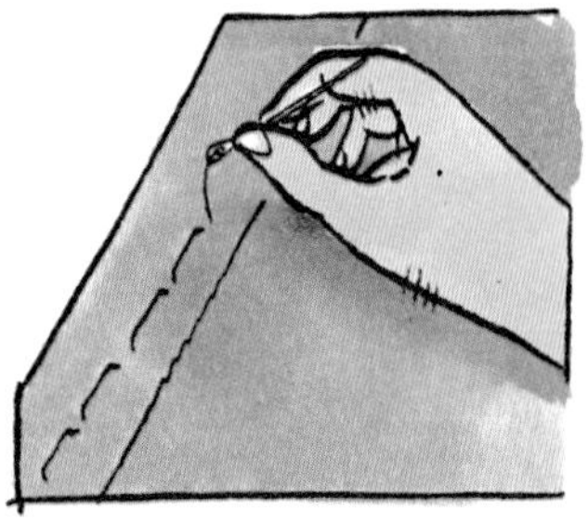

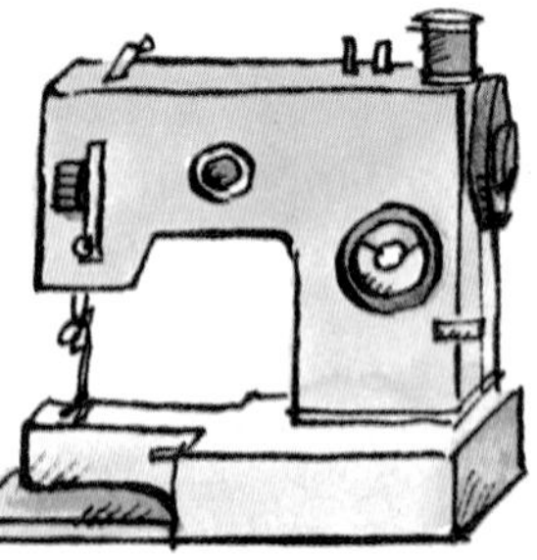

Possiamo **spartirla**.
2582 to share
Pensi che **lo squalo** stia imparando a volare?
2583 shark
affilato, tagliente
2584 sharp
L'affilatoio serve ad affilare i coltelli.
2585 knife sharpener
frantumare, rompere
2588 to shatter
rasarsi, farsi la barba
2589 to shave
le cesoie
2590 shears
l'affilatrice per i pattini
2586 skate sharpener
il fodero, la guaina
2591 sheath
Sabrina conta **le pecore** per addormentarsi.
2592 sheep
il lenzuolo del letto
2593 sheet
il temperamatite
2587 pencil sharpener
la mensola
2594 shelf
la conchiglia
2595 shell
L'insetto ha trovato **un rifugio**.
2596 shelter
Il pastore custodisce le pecore.
2597 shepherd
Lo scudo protegge il guerriero.
2598 shield
lo stinco
2599 shin
Il sole **risplende** nel cielo azzurro.
2600 to shine
l'assicella
2601 shingle

Il fuoco di Sant'Antonio è un male doloroso.
2602 shingles

I diamanti della corona sono **splendenti**.
2603 shiny

la nave
2604 ship

Robinson ha fatto **naufragio**.
2605 shipwreck

la camicia
2606 shirt

rabbrividire
2607 to shiver

Attenzione alle **scosse** elettriche!
2608 shock

le scarpe, **le calzature**
2609 shoes

Sei capace ad annodare **i legacci** delle scarpe?
2610 shoelace

il calzolaio, **il ciabattino**
2611 shoemaker

sparare, **tirare**
2612 to shoot

la bottega, **il negozio**
2613 shop

il bottegaio, **il negoziante**
2614 shopkeeper

la vetrina
2615 shop window

la spiaggia
2616 shore

piccolo di statura
2617 short

i calzoncini
2618 shorts

la spalla
2619 shoulder

urlare, **strillare**
2620 to shout

Non bisogna **urtare** la gente.
2621 to shove

la pala da neve
2622 shovel

mostrare
2623 to show

mettersi in mostra, pavoneggiarsi
2624 to show off

Finalmente **è comparso**.
2625 to show up/appear*

Remo sta facendo **la doccia**.
2626 shower

strillare, gridare
2627 to shriek

il gamberetto
2628 shrimp

La camicetta **si è accorciata**.
2629 to shrink

un arbusto, un cespuglio
2630 shrub

mescolare le carte
2631 shuffle

Di notte si chiudono **le imposte**.
2632 shutters

timido
2633 shy

ammalato
2634 sick

il fianco della casa
2635 side

Sabrina cammina sempre sul **marciapiede**.
2636 sidewalk/pavement*

sospirare di sollievo
2637 to sigh

il cartello
2638 sign

segnalare, fare segnali
2639 to signal

la firma
2640 signature

silenzioso

Non capita spesso che Sabrina sia **silenziosa**.
Una notte **silenziosa** è una notte tranquilla.

Sabrina is not silent very often.
A silent night is a quiet night.

2641 silent

il davanzale della finestra

2642 sill

sciocco, **stupido**

Gregorio pensa che Sabrina sia assolutamente **sciocca**. Sabrina pensa che Gregorio faccia cose **stupide**.

Gregorio thinks Sabrina is utterly silly. Sabrina thinks Gregorio does silly things.

2643 silly

l'argento

2644 silver

semplice

E' la verità pura e **semplice**. C'è una soluzione molto **semplice**.

That is the pure and simple truth. There is a very simple solution.

2645 simple

cantare

2646 to sing

singolare

'Uomo' è il **singolare** di 'uomini'. 'Uomo' è **singolare**, 'uomini' è plurale.

'Man' is the singular of 'men'. 'Man' is singular, 'men' is plural.

2647 singular

il lavandino della cucina

2648 sink

Aiuto! La barca **affonda**.

2649 to sink

centellinare, **sorseggiare**

2650 to sip

la sirena

2651 siren

Paola **è la sorella** di Osvaldo.

2652 sister

sedere, **essere seduto**

2653 to sit

sei

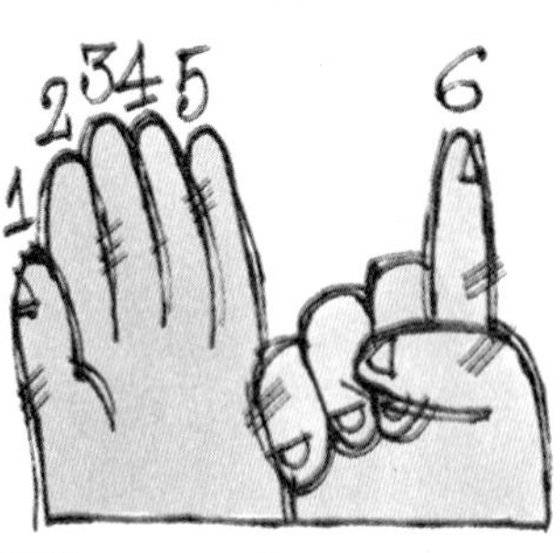

2654 six

la sesta

2655 sixth

Questo è della mia **taglia**!

2656 size

pattinare

2657 to skate

lo skateboard

2658 skateboard

Che cosa fa **uno scheletro** nel mio armadio?

2659 skeleton

L'artista **abbozza** una figura.

2660 to sketch

gli sci

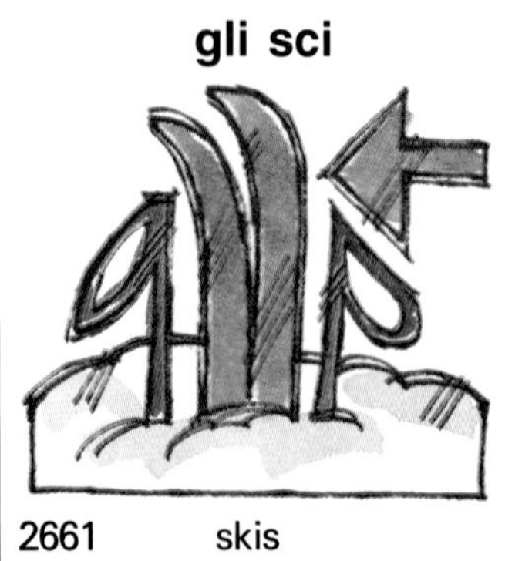

2661 skis

sciare
2662 to ski
slittare
2663 to skid
la pelle
2664 skin
saltare alla corda
2665 to skip
Il capitano regge il timone.
2666 skipper/captain*
la gonna
2667 skirt
il cranio, il teschio
2668 skull
Il cielo è nuvoloso.
2669 sky
un'allodola
2670 skylark
il grattacielo
2671 skyscraper
Ha sbattuto la porta.
2672 to slam
un pavimento inclinato
2673 slanting floor
schiaffeggiare
2674 to slap
Zorro ha ripreso a sfregiare.
2675 to slash
la lavagnetta
2676 slate
La slitta scivola giù per la china.
2677 sled/sleigh*
Zorro che dorme
2678 to sleep
il sacco a pelo
2679 sleeping bag
Paolo è assonnato.
2680 sleepy
il nevischio
2681 sleet

la manica
2682 sleeve
lo scivolo
2683 slide
Una è snella, l'altra è grassa.
2684 slim
Il verme ha un corpo viscido.
2685 slimy
Ha il braccio al collo in una benda.
2686 sling
la fionda
2687 slingshot/catapult*
scivolare
2688 to slip
la pantofola
2689 slipper
viscido
2690 slippery
Quant' è trascurato!
2691 slob
il pendio del monte
2692 slope
la fessura
2693 slot
Il ragazzo cammina dinoccolato.
2694 to slouch
rallentare
Rallenta, papà! Vai troppo forte.
La macchina rallenta all'angolo della strada.
Slow down, Dad! You are going too fast.
The car slows down at the corner.
2695 to slow down
la poltiglia, la neve sciolta
2696 slush
Uno è piccolo, l'altro è grande.
2697 small
intelligente, elegante
Sabrina si crede molto intelligente, perché ha superato l'esame.
Ella indossa un abito molto elegante.
Sabrina thinks she is very smart because she passed her exam.
She is wearing a very smart dress.
2698 smart/clever*
Non fracassare l'orologio.
2699 to smash
imbrattare, macchiare
2700 to smear
Ernesto odora il fiore rosso.
2701 to smell

La puzzola emette un liquido **nauseabondo**.
2702 smelly
fumare
2703 to smoke
liscio, **senza scosse**
Il ghiaccio su cui Sabrina pattina è molto **liscio**.
Un buon pilota di aereo atterra **senza scosse**.
The ice Sabrina is skating on is very smooth.
A good airplane pilot makes smooth landings.
2704 smooth
A Noemi piace **fare spuntini** tra i pasti.
2705 to have a snack
la lumaca
2706 snail
il serpente
2707 snake
spezzarsi d'un colpo
2708 to snap
le scarpe da tennis
2709 sneakers/trainers*
starnutire
2710 to sneeze
la maschera e **il boccaglio**
2711 snorkel
La neve scende a larghe falde.
2712 snow
il fiocco di neve
2713 snowflake
le racchette da neve
2714 snowshoes
Lavati le mani col **sapone**.
2715 soap
il calcio
2716 soccer
il calzino
2717 sock
la presa di corrente
2718 socket
il divano, **il sofà**
2719 sofa/couch*
Batuffo ha il pelo **soffice**.
2720 soft
il soldato
2721 soldier

2722	**la sogliola**	sole
2723	Ella **risolve** il problema.	She **solves** the problem.
2724	**fare un salto mortale, fare una capriola**	to **somersault**
2725	il padre e **il figlio**	son
2726	**il canto, la canzone**	song
2727	**presto, tra poco** Sarà **presto** notte. Sabrina tornerà **tra poco**. *Soon it will be dark.* *Sabrina will be home soon.*	soon
2728	**Il mago** fa un incantesimo.	sorcerer
2729	Il mio braccio è **dolorante**.	My arm is **sore**.
2730	**l'acetosella**	sorrel
2731	Maciste è davvero **spiacente**.	sorry
2732	Alfio **separa** le uova chiare da quelle scure.	to **sort**
2733	**la minestra, la zuppa**	soup
2734	Il limone ha un sapore **agro**.	sour
2735	**il sud**	south
2736	**La scrofa** è la madre dei porcellini.	sow
2737	**seminare**	to **sow**
2738	**la nave spaziale**	spaceship
2739	**La vanga** serve per il giardinaggio.	spade
2740	**sculacciare**	to **spank**
2741	**la ruota di scorta**	**spare** tire/tyre*

la scintilla, **la favilla** 2742 spark	Gli anelli **scintillano** al sole. 2743 to sparkle	**il passero** 2744 sparrow	Che lingua **parlano**? 2745 to speak
la lancia 2746 spear	La tartaruga ha difficoltà ad **accelerare**. 2747 to speed up	Annalisa **scrive** il suo nome **lettera per lettera**. 2748 to spell	**spendere** del denaro 2749 to spend
La sfera è rotonda. 2750 sphere	**piccante** 2751 spicy	**Il ragno** tesse la sua ragnatela. 2752 spider	**un aculeo** 2753 spike
versare 2754 to spill	**far girare** 2755 to spin	**gli spinaci** 2756 spinach	**la spina dorsale** 2757 spine
la spirale 2758 spiral	**la guglia** del campanile 2759 spire	**Sputare** non è da persona educata. 2760 to spit	**schizzare**, **sguazzare** 2761 to splash

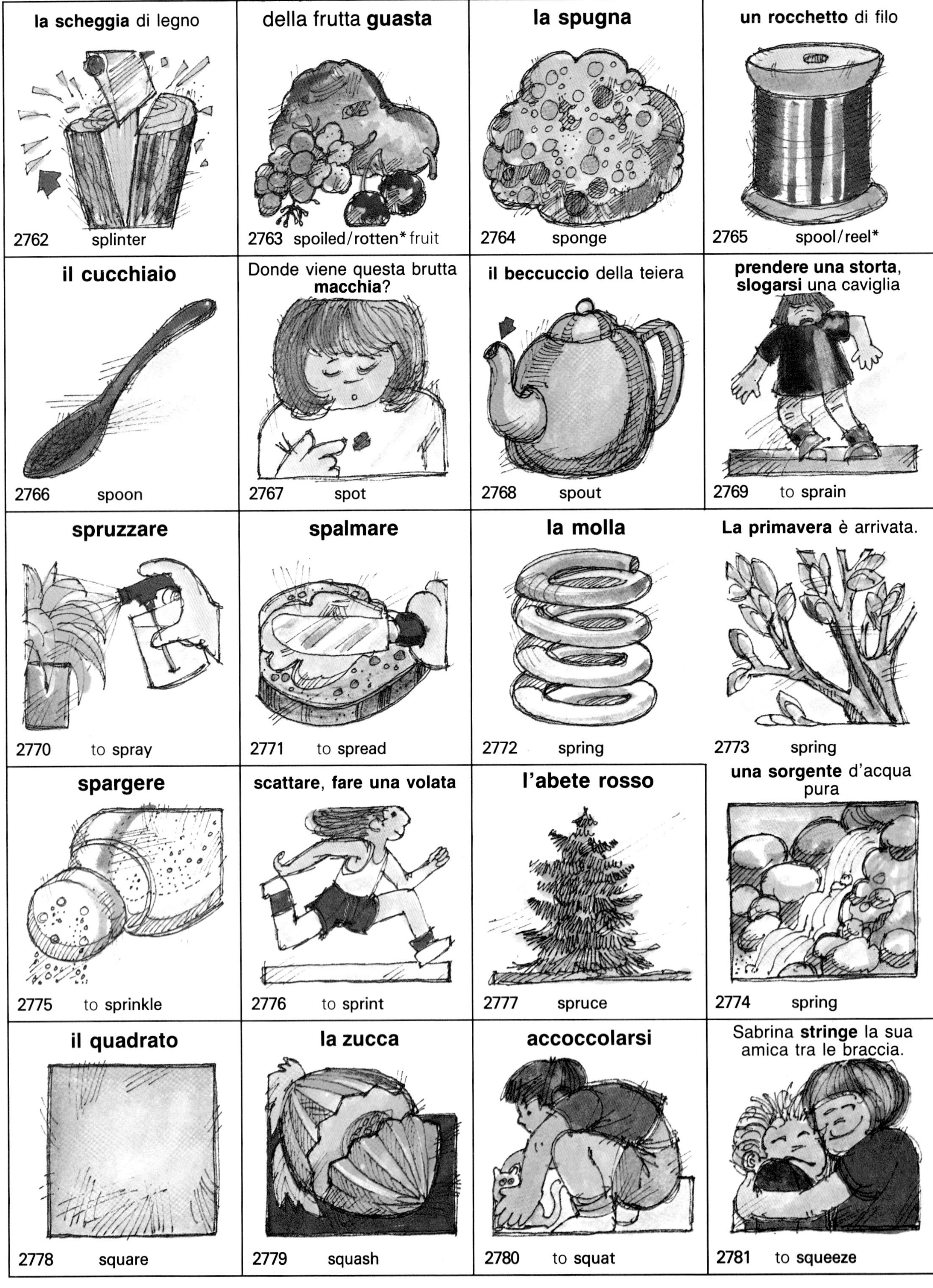
la scheggia di legno
2762 splinter
della frutta guasta
2763 spoiled/rotten* fruit
la spugna
2764 sponge
un rocchetto di filo
2765 spool/reel*
il cucchiaio
2766 spoon
Donde viene questa brutta macchia?
2767 spot
il beccuccio della teiera
2768 spout
prendere una storta, slogarsi una caviglia
2769 to sprain
spruzzare
2770 to spray
spalmare
2771 to spread
la molla
2772 spring
La primavera è arrivata.
2773 spring
spargere
2775 to sprinkle
scattare, fare una volata
2776 to sprint
l'abete rosso
2777 spruce
una sorgente d'acqua pura
2774 spring
il quadrato
2778 square
la zucca
2779 squash
accoccolarsi
2780 to squat
Sabrina stringe la sua amica tra le braccia.
2781 to squeeze

il calamaro

2782 squid

lo scoiattolo

2783 squirrel

sprizzare

2784 to squirt

la stalla per i cavalli

2785 stable

il palcoscenico del teatro

2786 stage

la macchia, **la chiazza**

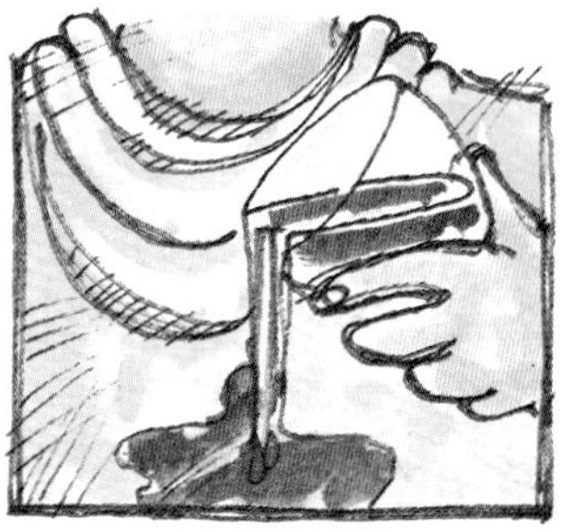

2787 stain

Dove porta questa **scala**?

2788 staircase

un paletto di legno

2789 wooden stake

stantio

A Sabrina non piace il pane **stantio**; lo preferisce fresco.

Sabrina does not like stale bread; she prefers it fresh.

2790 stale bread

un gambo di sedano

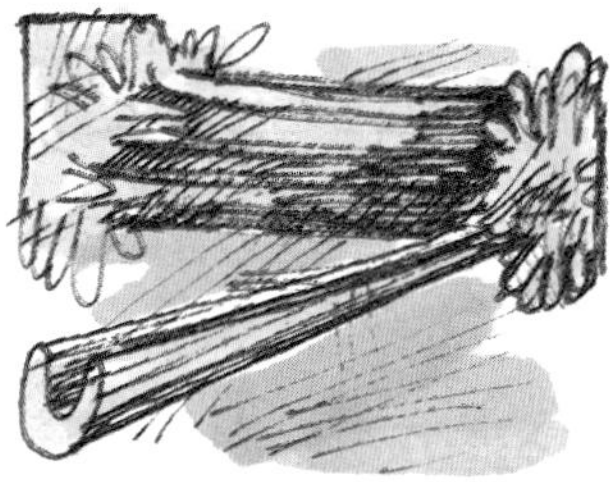

2791 celery stalk

Lo stallone è un cavallo maschio.

2792 stallion

il francobollo

2793 stamp

essere in piedi

2794 to stand

la stella

2795 star

Sabrina **guarda fisso** davanti a sè.

2796 to stare

lo storno

2797 starling

avviare il motore dell'auto

2798 to start a car

morire di fame, **avere una fame da lupo**

Quando Sabrina arriva da scuola, grida sempre: "**Muoio di fame**!"
Ha una fame da lupo, ma non **muore** veramente **di fame**.

When Sabrina comes home from school, she always shouts: "I am starving."
She is very hungry but she will not really starve.

2799 to starve

una stazione di servizio, **un distributore** di benzina

2800 gas/petrol* station

una stazione ferroviara

2801 train/railway* station

la statua
2802 statue
Midoro! Sta lì fermo!
2803 Stay there!
la bistecca
2804 steak
rubare
2805 to steal
il vapore
2806 steam
I coltelli sono fatti d'acciaio.
2807 Kinves are made of steel.
ripido
2808 steep
il manzo
2809 steer/bullock*
lo stelo della rosa
2811 stem
il gradino
2812 step
E' entrata in una pozzanghera.
2813 to step in
sterzare
2810 to steer
Papà ha preparato lo stufato.
2815 stew
il rametto
2816 stick
uscire per un minuto
2814 to step out
Armando ha le mani appiccicose.
2817 sticky
rigido, duro
Lo zio Giovanni ha una gamba rigida.
Questo spazzolino da denti è troppo duro.
Uncle Giovanni has a stiff leg.
This toothbrush is too stiff.
2818 stiff
Un'ape l'ha punta.
2819 to sting
la puntura dell'ape
2820 sting
puzzare
2821 to stink

Mescolare prima di bere.
2822 to stir
le calze
2823 stockings
caricare una caldaia
2824 to stoke
lo stomaco
2825 stomach
Tirare sassi è pericoloso.
2826 stone
lo sgabello
2827 stool
Si china per raccogliere la palla.
2828 to stoop/bend down*
lo stop, il segnale di stop
2829 stop
il negozio
CRAWZI
2832 store/shop*
la cicogna
2833 stork
il temporale, un uragano
2834 storm
Riesce a fermare il treno.
2830 He stops the train.
Zia Anna legge una storia.
2835 story
la cucina elettrica
2836 stove/cooker*
diritto
2837 straight
L'aereo ha fatto uno scalo.
2831 to stop over
colare, filtrare
2838 to strain
sforzare, affaticare
2839 to strain
un animaletto strano
2840 strange
Lo scimmione lo vuole strangolare.
2841 to strangle

la bretella
2842 strap
Ti piace sorbire la bibita con la cannuccia?
2843 straw
la fragola
2844 strawberry
il corso d'acqua, il ruscello
2845 stream
la bandierina
2846 streamer/pennant*
La strada è deserta.
2847 street
il lampione
2848 street light/lamp*
estendere
2849 to stretch
la barella
2850 stretcher
lo sciopero
Gli operai sono in sciopero. Fanno sciopero per ottenere più denaro.
The workers are on strike. They strike for more money.
2851 strike
Non bisogna picchiare la gente.
2852 to strike
Lo spago è avvolto sul rocchetto.
2853 string
un asciugamano a strisce
2854 stripe
E' molto forte.
2855 strong
lo scolaro
2856 student
Pino studia assiduamente.
2857 to study
un animale imbottito
2858 a stuffed animal
il ceppo di un albero
2859 stump
Il sottomarino naviga sott'acqua.
2860 submarine
sottrarre
5-2=3
2861 to subtract

succhiare

2862 to suck

improvvisamente, ad un tratto

Albina andò via **improvvisamente**.
Tutto **ad un tratto** cominciò a piovere.

Albina left suddenly.
Suddenly, it began to rain.

2863 suddenly

Non mangiare troppo **zucchero**.

2864 sugar

Luigi porta **un abito completo**.

2865 suit

la valigia

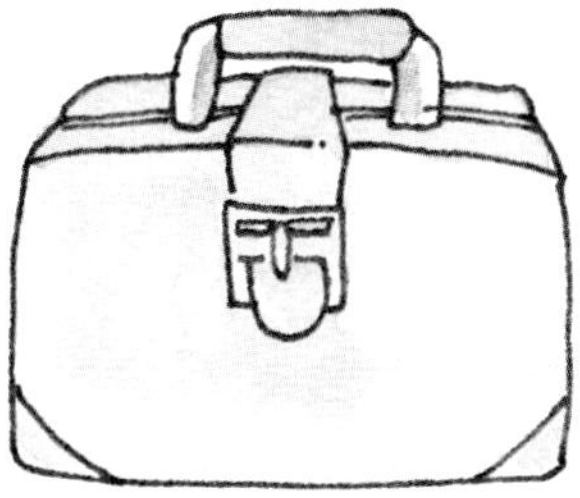

2866 suitcase

la scorsa **estate** al mare

2867 summer

il sole

2868 sun

domenica

La domenica è il settimo giorno della settimana.
Ogni **domenica** la mamma fa un dolce.

Sunday is the seventh day of the week.
Every Sunday, Mother bakes a cake.

2869 Sunday

La meridiana segna le ore.

2870 sundial

Il girasole guarda sempre il sole.

2871 sunflower

il levar del sole

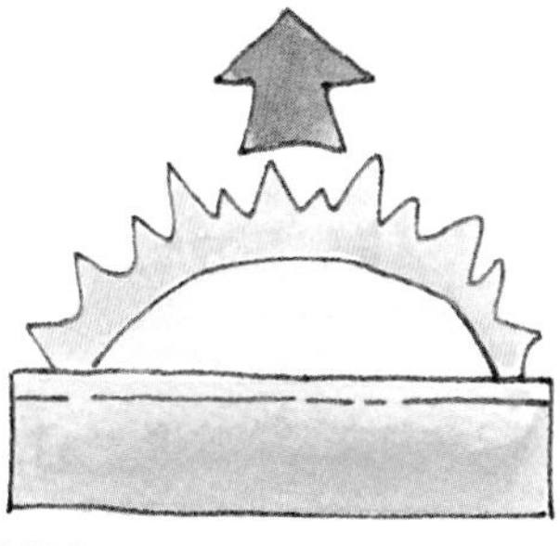

2872 sunrise

il tramonto del sole

2873 sunset

La signora Ida fa la spesa al **supermercato**.

2874 supermarket

la cena

2875 supper/dinner*

sicuro, certo

Questo è un modo **sicuro** per vincere.
Sono **certo** che domani farà bello.

That is a sure way to win.
I am sure it will be nice tomorrow.

2876 sure

la superficie

2877 surface

il chirurgo

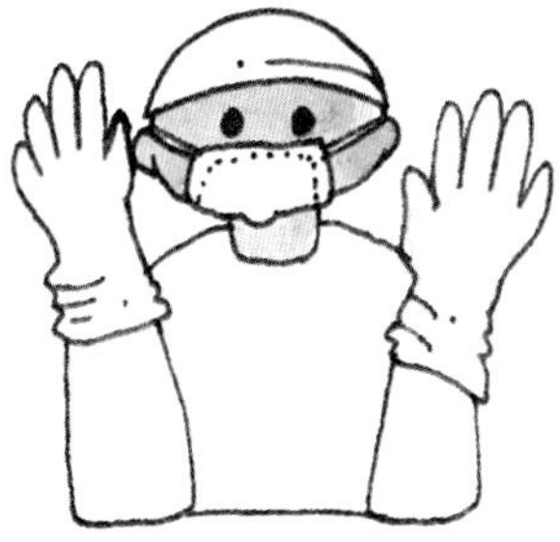

2878 surgeon

il cognome

Il mio nome è Sabrina; **il** mio **cognome** è Borello.

My first name is Sabrina; my surname is Borello.

2879 surname

una festa **a sorpresa**, **inattesa**

2880 surprise party

Non sparate! **Mi arrendo**!

2881 to surrender

circondare, **attorniare**
2882 to surround
Le bretelle servono a tenere su i pantaloni.
2883 suspenders/braces*
inghiottire, **ingoiare**
2884 to swallow
Il cigno è maestoso.
2885 swan
scambiare
2886 to swap
uno sciame di api
2887 swarm
sudare a profusione
2888 to sweat
il maglione
2889 sweater/sweatshirt*
scopare
2890 to sweep
dolce
2891 sweet
Per fortuna l'auto **ha deviato**.
2892 to swerve
Lucia **nuota** molto bene.
2893 to swim
l'altalena
2894 swing
dondolare
2895 to swing
un interruttore
2896 switch
accendere, **spegnere**
Accendi la luce, per favore.
E' meglio **spegnere** il televisore.
Switch on the light, please.
It is best to switch off the television.
2897 to switch
piombare sulla preda
2898 to swoop
la spada
2899 sword
il sicomoro
2900 sycamore
Lo sciroppo d'acero si mette sulle cialde calde.
2901 syrup

la tavola, il tavolo

2902 table

la tovaglia

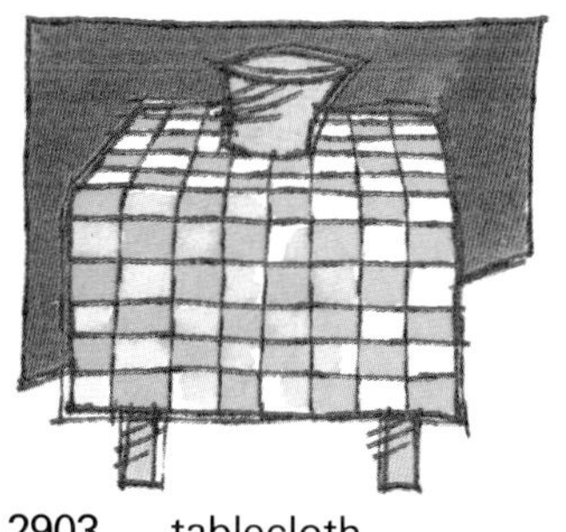

2903 tablecloth

la compressa, la pillola

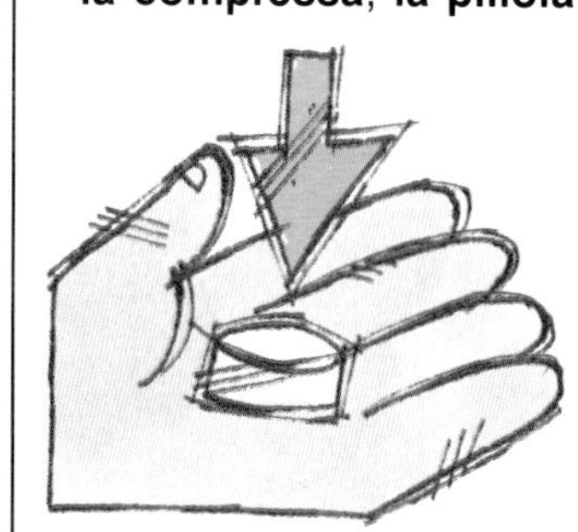

2904 tablet

la bulletta

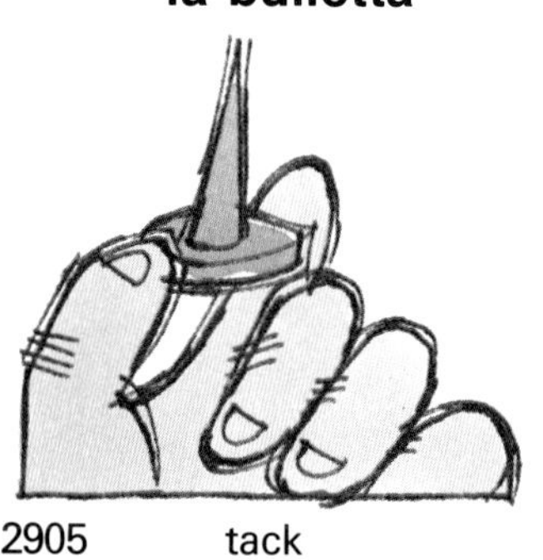

2905 tack

affrontare, contrastare

Sabrina deve **affrontare** la questione al più presto.
Aldo **contrastò** Giuseppe durante la partita di football.

Sabrina must tackle that problem as soon as possible.
Aldo tackled Giuseppe during the football game.

2906 to tackle

Il girino diventerà una rana.

2907 tadpole

la coda

2908 tail

prendere

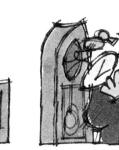

2910 to take

smontare

2911 to take apart

estrarre

2912 to take away

riportare, portare indietro

2913 to take back

togliere, togliersi

2914 to take off

decollare

2915 to take off

portare fuori

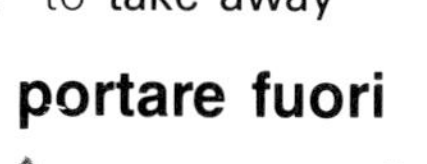

2916 to take out

Lucilla **ritira** il pollo arrosto per la famiglia.

2917 take-out/take-away*

Il sarto confeziona vestiti.

2909 tailor

la favola, la storia

2918 tale

il talento

Sabrina ha un grande **talento** per la danza.
La danza classica richiede sia **il talento** che l'esercizio continuo.

Sabrina has a great talent for dancing.
Dance requires both talent and hard work.

2919 talent

parlare

2920 to talk

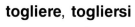

alto di statura
2921 tall

il tamburello
2922 tambourine

I leoni da circo sono **addomesticati**.
2923 tame

Erica ha **una** bella **abbronzatura**.
2924 tan

il mandarino
2925 tangerine

Il filo si è **ingarbugliato**.
2926 tangled

la cisterna, **il serbatoio**
2927 tank

la petroliera, la nave cisterna
2928 tanker

Il rubinetto non chiude bene.
2929 tap

il nastro adesivo
2930 tape

fissare col nastro adesivo
2931 to tape

il registratore, il magnetofono
2932 tape recorder

il catrame
2933 tar

Ha colpito **il bersaglio** in pieno.
2934 target

il targone
2935 tarragon

la pasta
2936 tart

Il suo **incarico** è di scopare il pavimento.
2937 task

Assaggia e dimmi se ti piace.
2938 to taste

gustoso, **saporito**

E' stata una cena veramente **gustosa**.
Questa salsa è molto **saporita**.

That was a tasty meal.
This sauce is really tasty.

2939 tasty

il tassì
2940 taxi

una tazza di **tè**
2941 a cup of tea
La signorina Perfetti **insegna** l'aritmetica.
2942 to teach
E' la nostra **insegnante**.
2943 teacher
una squadra affiatata
2944 team
la teiera
2945 teapot
la lacrima
2946 tear
stracciare
2947 to tear
Non bisogna **strappare via** le pagine dai quaderni.
2948 to tear out
il telegramma
2949 telegram
il telefono
2950 telephone
telefonare
2951 to telephone
Il telescopio è puntato verso il cielo.
2952 telescope
Il televisore è anche chiamato "la TV".
2953 television
dire
2954 to tell
temperamento
Nicola ha un pessimo **temperamento**.
Non riesce a controllare il suo **temperamento**.
Nicola has a bad temper.
He cannot control his temper.
2955 temper
Il termometro segna **la temperatura**.
2956 temperature
dieci mele
2957 ten apples
una racchetta e una palla da **tennis**
2958 tennis racquet and ball
una scarpa **da tennis**
2959 tennis shoe
Sabrina ha dormito sotto **la tenda**.
2960 tent

La decima lumaca è verde.
2961 tenth
il terminal del calcolatore elettronico
2962 terminal
provare la temperatura dell'acqua
2963 to test the water
Lei lo ringrazia di tutto cuore.
2964 to thank
sgelare, fondere
2965 to thaw
il teatro
2966 theater/theatre*
La palla è là.
2967 there
Il termometro è graduato.
2968 thermometer
Quest'albero ha un tronco molto grosso.
2969 thick
Ladro oggi . . . . . . galeotto domani!
2970 thief
la coscia
2971 thigh
il ditale per cucire
2972 thimble
Questo è sottile.
2973 thin
la cosa
Una persona non è una cosa.
Sabrina dice molte cose divertenti.
A person is not a thing.
Sabrina says many funny things.
2974 thing
pensare
2975 to think
la terza lumaca
2976 third
assetato
2977 thirsty
Sta attenta! Il cardo punge.
2978 thistle
Anche la spina punge.
2979 thorn
il filo
2980 thread

Sei capace di **infilare** il filo nell'ago?
2981 to thread

tre mele
2982 three

la soglia della porta
2983 threshold

la gola
2984 throat

il trono della regina
2985 throne

lanciare, **gettare**
2986 to throw

Vomita perché soffre il mal di mare.
2987 to throw up/be sick*

il pollice
2988 thumb

un tuono assordante
2989 thunder

il temporale
2990 thunderstorm

giovedì

Giovedì è il quarto giorno della settimana.
Sabrina prende lezioni di nuoto al **giovedì**.

Thursday is the fourth day of the week.
Sabrina has a swimming class on Thursdays.
2991 Thursday

Il timo insaporisce l'arrosto.
2992 thyme

il biglietto della ferrovia
2993 ticket

fare il solletico, **solleticare**
2994 to tickle

ordinato, **pulito**
2995 tidy

Mi annodo **la cravatta** da solo.
2996 tie

La tigre va a caccia.
2998 tiger

stringere la cintura
2999 to tighten

le piastrelle, **le mattonelle**
3000 tiles

legare, **annodare**
2997 to tie

La barca **si inclina** pericolosamente.
3001 to tilt
Che **ora** è?
3002 What **time** is it?
minuscola
3003 tiny
La barca **si è rovesciata**.
3004 to tip
camminare in punta di piedi
3006 tiptoe
un vecchio pneumatico
3007 tire/tyre*
stanco, affaticato
3008 tired
dare la mancia
3005 to tip
Il rospo vive nello stagno.
3009 toad
il pane tostato, il crostino
3010 toast
il tostapane
3011 toaster
oggi
La scuola comincia **oggi**.
Oggi Sabrina si alza presto a preparare la colazione.
School starts today.
Today, Sabrina gets up early to prepare breakfast.
3012 today
le dita dei piedi
3013 toes
Siamo seduti **insieme**.
3014 We are sitting **together**.
il gabinetto
3015 toilet
il pomodoro
3016 tomato
la tomba
3017 tomb
domani
Oggi verrà seguito da **domani**.
Domani Sabrina andrà a vedere i dinosauri al museo.
Today is followed by tomorrow.
Tomorrow Sabrina is going to see dinosaurs at the museum.
3018 tomorrow
le pinze, le molle
3019 tongs
Non mostrare **la lingua**!
3020 tongue

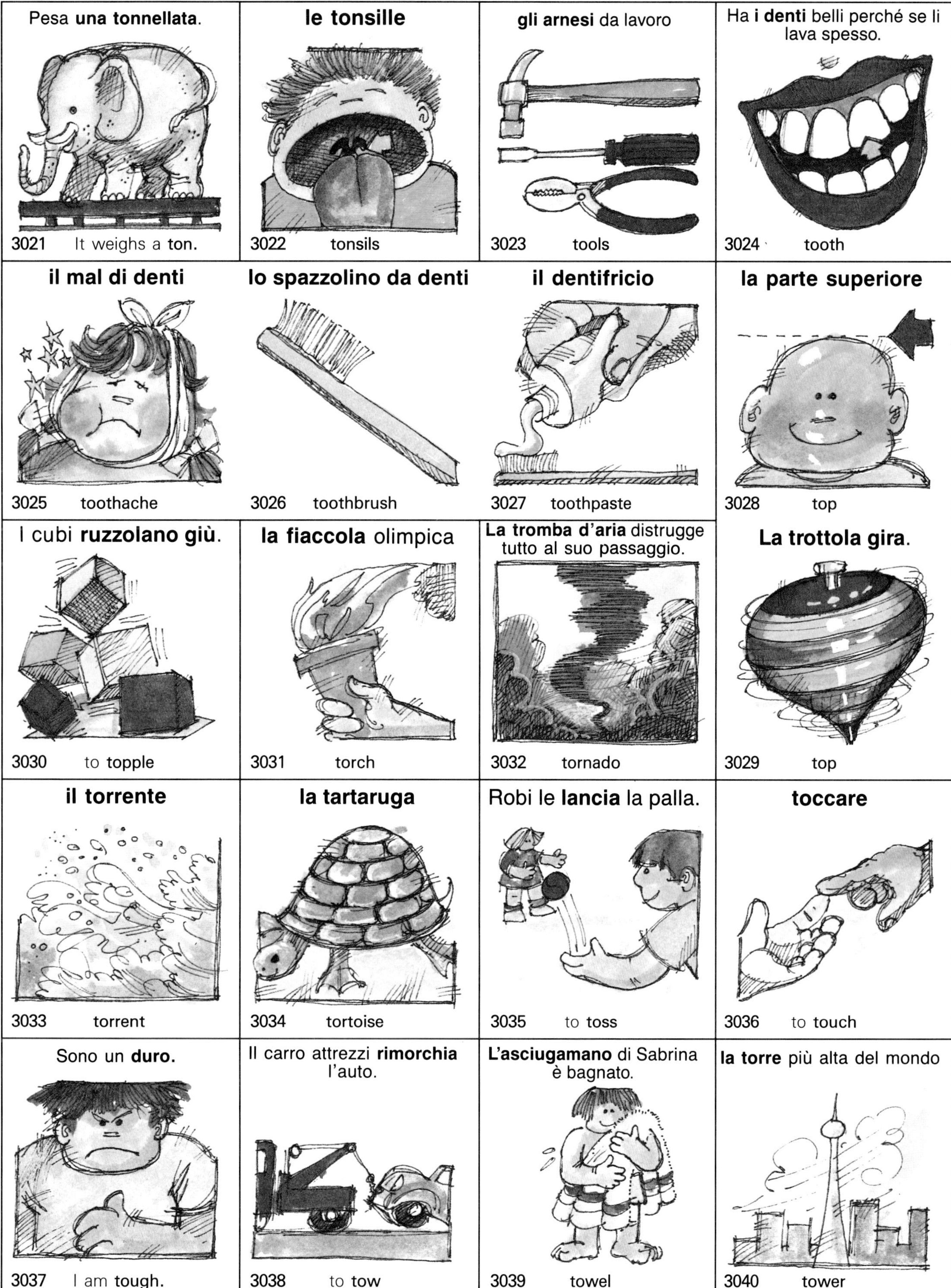
Pesa **una tonnellata**.
3021 It weighs a **ton**.
le tonsille
3022 tonsils
gli arnesi da lavoro
3023 tools
Ha **i denti** belli perché se li lava spesso.
3024 tooth
il mal di denti
3025 toothache
lo spazzolino da denti
3026 toothbrush
il dentifricio
3027 toothpaste
la parte superiore
3028 top
I cubi **ruzzolano giù**.
3030 to topple
la fiaccola olimpica
3031 torch
La tromba d'aria distrugge tutto al suo passaggio.
3032 tornado
La trottola gira.
3029 top
il torrente
3033 torrent
la tartaruga
3034 tortoise
Robi le **lancia** la palla.
3035 to toss
toccare
3036 to touch
Sono un **duro.**
3037 I am **tough.**
Il carro attrezzi **rimorchia** l'auto.
3038 to tow
L'asciugamano di Sabrina è bagnato.
3039 towel
la torre più alta del mondo
3040 tower

La casa di Sabrina è nei pressi di questa città.
3041 town
Raccogli i tuoi giocattoli, per favore!
3042 toys
tracciare
3043 to trace
Il treno corre sui binari.
3044 track
il trattore
3045 tractor
scambiare, commerciare
3046 to trade
Il traffico è intenso.
3047 traffic
il semaforo
3048 traffic light
Segue una buona pista.
3049 trail
Che cosa trasporta questo rimorchio?
3050 trailer
il treno
3051 train
Addestra il cane.
3052 to train
il vagabondo
R
3053 tramp
Non calpestate i fiori!
3054 to trample
il trampolino
3055 trampoline
La mamma di Marisa non è trasparente.
3056 transparent
trasportare
3057 to transport
l'autocarro
3058 transporter/lorry*
la trappola
3059 trap
il trapezio
3060 trapeze

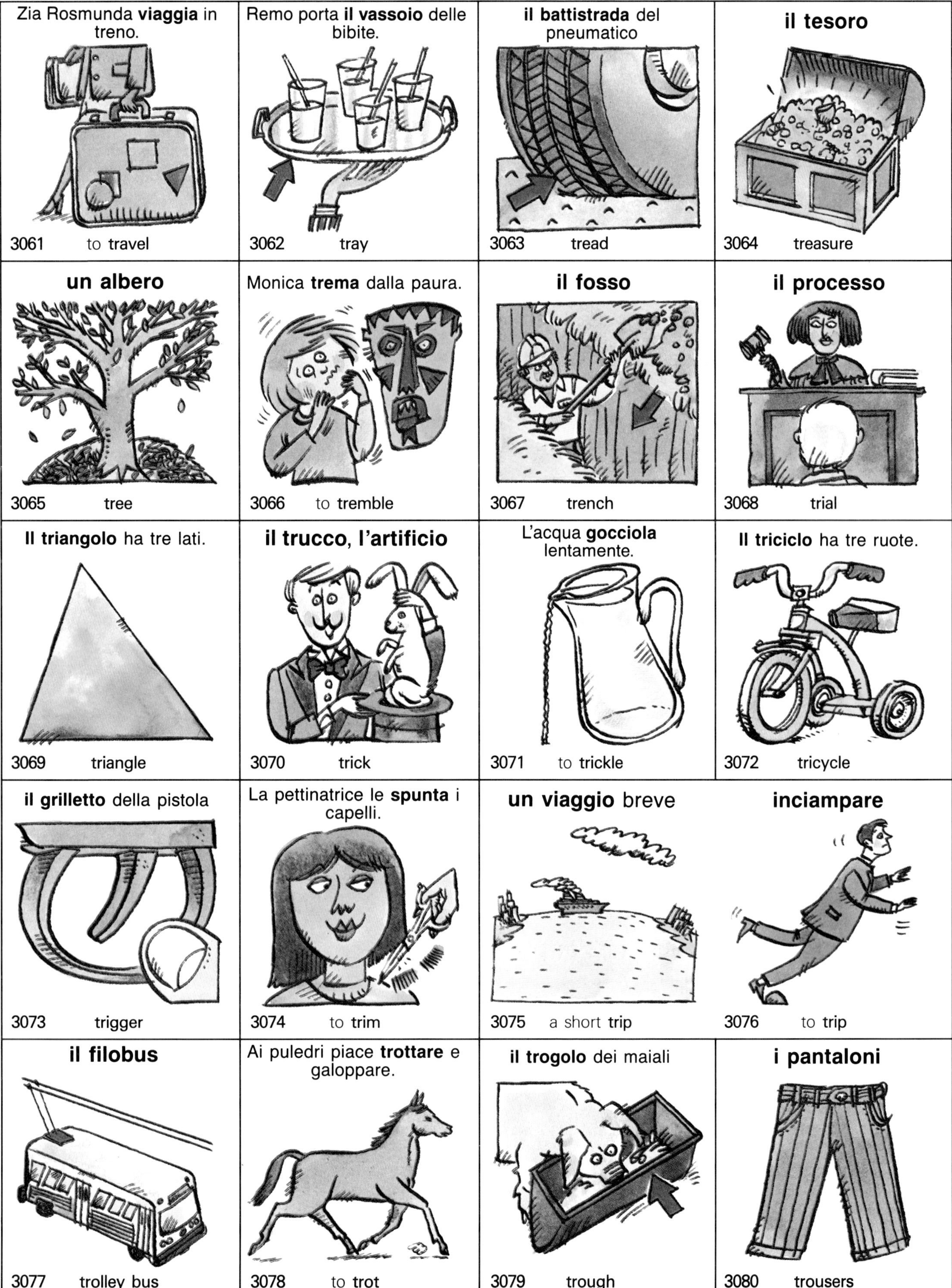
Zia Rosmunda **viaggia** in treno.
3061 to travel
Remo porta **il vassoio** delle bibite.
3062 tray
il battistrada del pneumatico
3063 tread
il tesoro
3064 treasure
un albero
3065 tree
Monica **trema** dalla paura.
3066 to tremble
il fosso
3067 trench
il processo
3068 trial
Il triangolo ha tre lati.
3069 triangle
il trucco, l'artificio
3070 trick
L'acqua **gocciola** lentamente.
3071 to trickle
Il triciclo ha tre ruote.
3072 tricycle
il grilletto della pistola
3073 trigger
La pettinatrice le **spunta** i capelli.
3074 to trim
un viaggio breve
3075 a short trip
inciampare
3076 to trip
il filobus
3077 trolley bus
Ai puledri piace **trottare** e galoppare.
3078 to trot
il trogolo dei maiali
3079 trough
i pantaloni
3080 trousers

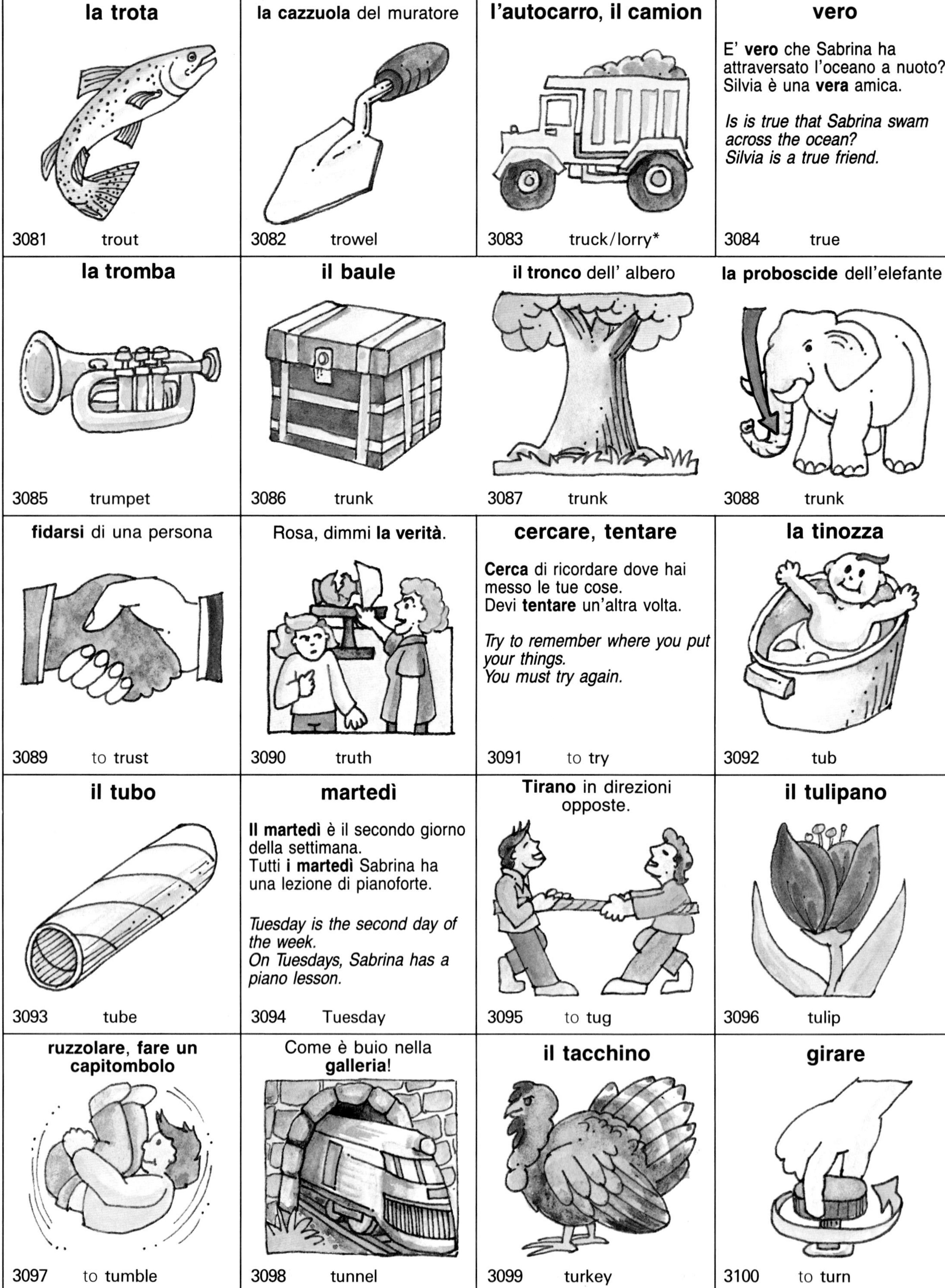

la trota
3081 trout

la cazzuola del muratore
3082 trowel

l'autocarro, il camion
3083 truck/lorry*

vero
E' **vero** che Sabrina ha attraversato l'oceano a nuoto?
Silvia è una **vera** amica.
Is is true that Sabrina swam across the ocean?
Silvia is a true friend.
3084 true

la tromba
3085 trumpet

il baule
3086 trunk

il tronco dell' albero
3087 trunk

la proboscide dell'elefante
3088 trunk

fidarsi di una persona
3089 to trust

Rosa, dimmi **la verità**.
3090 truth

cercare, tentare
Cerca di ricordare dove hai messo le tue cose.
Devi **tentare** un'altra volta.
Try to remember where you put your things.
You must try again.
3091 to try

la tinozza
3092 tub

il tubo
3093 tube

martedì
Il martedì è il secondo giorno della settimana.
Tutti **i martedì** Sabrina ha una lezione di pianoforte.
Tuesday is the second day of the week.
On Tuesdays, Sabrina has a piano lesson.
3094 Tuesday

Tirano in direzioni opposte.
3095 to tug

il tulipano
3096 tulip

ruzzolare, **fare un capitombolo**
3097 to tumble

Come è buio nella **galleria**!
3098 tunnel

il tacchino
3099 turkey

girare
3100 to turn

spegnere la luce
3101 to turn off
accendere la luce
3102 to turn on
diventare, **riuscire**
Carletto **è diventato** un vero discolo.
Tutto **è riuscito** bene.
Carletto turned out a real brat.
Things turned out well.
3103 to turn out
Silvia **gira** la bistecca.
3104 to turn over
la rapa
3105 turnip
il giradischi
3106 turntable
turchese
3107 turquoise
Sulla **torretta** sventola la bandiera rossa.
3108 turret
la tartaruga
3109 turtle
Le zanne dell'elefante sono d'avorio.
3110 tusk
le pinzette
3111 tweezers
due volte, **il doppio**
Sabrina è andata **due volte** allo zoo.
Carla ha **il doppio** dei libri di Sabrina.
Sabrina has been to the zoo twice.
Carla has twice as many books as Sabrina.
3112 twice
il rametto
3113 twig
I gemelli sono identici.
3114 twins
Le stelle **scintillano**.
3115 Stars twinkle.
far girare, **mulinare**
3116 to twirl
torcere
3117 to twist
due
1
2
3118 two
scrivere a macchina, **dattilografare**
3119 to type
la macchina da scrivere
3120 typewriter

E' brutta, ma è molto gentile.

3121 ugly

l'ombrello

3122 umbrella

lo zio

Mio **zio** è il fratello di mia madre.
L'altro mio **zio** è fratello di mio padre.

My uncle is my mother's brother.
My other uncle is my father's brother.

3123 uncle

sotto

Sabrina si è nascosta **sotto** le coperte.
I bambini **sotto** i 5 anni non possono andarvi.

Sabrina is hiding under the covers.
Children under 5 cannot go.

3124 under

comprendere

3125 to understand

la biancheria intima

3126 underwear

svestirsi

3127 to undress

infelice, scontenta

3128 unhappy

L'unicorno esiste solo nelle favole.

3129 unicorn

Zio Riccardo porta **l'uniforme**.

3130 uniform

un'università

3131 university

Che cosa **sta scaricando** l'autocarro?

3132 to unload

aprire con la chiave

3133 to unlock

aprire un pacco, scartocciare

3134 to unwrap

in piedi

3135 upright

capovolto, sottosopra

3136 upside-down

Mamma **usa** il pepe in cucina.

3137 to use

Ha **esaurito** il pepe.

3138 to use up

Questo temperino è molto **utile**.

3139 useful

Viva **le vacanze**!

3140 vacation/holiday*

il vapore

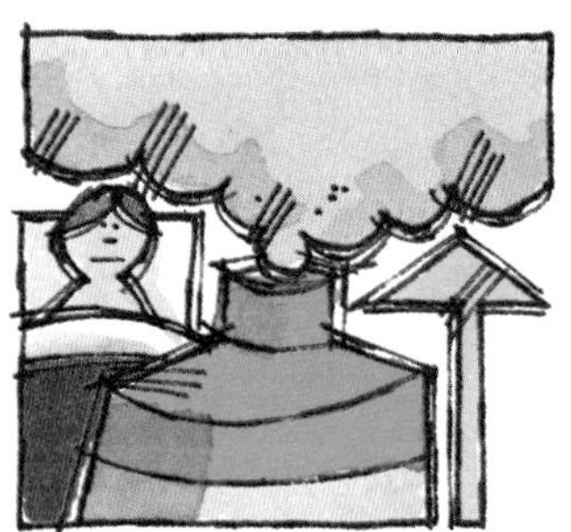

3141 vapor/vapour*

Vernicia il legno per proteggerlo.

3142 to varnish

Sabrina ha regalato **un vaso** alla mamma.

3143 vase

una bistecca di **vitello**

3144 veal

la verdura

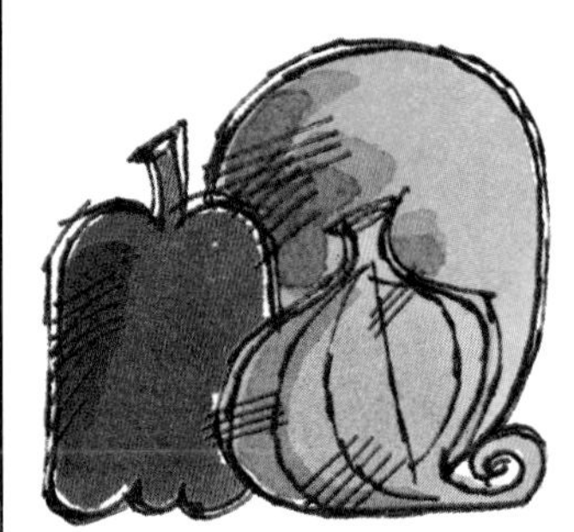

3145 vegetable

il veicolo

3146 vehicle

la veletta, **il velo**

3147 veil

la vena

3148 vein

il veleno

Certi serpenti producono del **veleno**.
Anche alcuni insetti hanno **il veleno**.

Some snakes produce venom.
Some insects also have venom.

3149 venom

Una linea **verticale** va diritta dall'alto in basso.

3150 vertical

molto, **proprio**

Sabrina pensa che suo fratello sia **molto** furbo.
Te l'ha fatta **proprio** sotto gli occhi.

Sabrina thinks her little brother is very clever.
He did it under your very eyes.

3151 very

il panciotto

3152 vest/waistcoat*

Il veterinario cura gli animali.

3153 veterinarian/veterinary surgeon*

la vittima del delitto

3154 victim

il video registratore

3155 video recorder

Non bisogna giocare con **il nastro della videocassetta**.

3156 video tape

il panorama, **la veduta**

Che bel **panorama**, dalla cima della montagna!
Ciascuno di noi ha **le** proprie **vedute**.

What a wonderful view from the top of the mountain!
We each have our own point of view.

3157 view

il villaggio, **il paese**

3158 village

il furfante, **il mascalzone** 3159 villain	**La vite** produce i grappoli d'uva. 3160 vine	A Sabrina piace mettere **l'aceto** sulle patatine. 3161 vinegar	Alla nonna piace il profumo delle **violette**. 3162 violet
il violino 3163 violin	Per entrare in certi paesi occorre **un visto**. 3164 visa	**visibile** Ci sono molte nuvole questa sera e le stelle sono appena **visibili**. Un uomo invisibile non è **visibile** per nulla. *There are many clouds tonight and the stars are barely visible.* *An invisible man cannot be seen.* 3165 visible	Lorenzo **visita** sua zia, che è ammalata. 3166 to visit
la visiera 3167 visor	**il vocabolario** Sabrina ha **un** buon **vocabolario**; conosce molte parole. Questo dizionario vi aiuterà ad aumentare **il** vostro **vocabolario**. *Sabrina has a good vocabulary; she knows many words.* *This dictionary will help increase your vocabulary.* 3168 vocabulary	**la voce** 3169 voice	**Il vulcano** è in eruzione. 3170 volcano
la pallovolo 3171 volleyball	**La volontaria** aiuta la signora Bea. 3172 volunteer	**vomitare** 3173 to vomit	**votare** 3174 to vote
un elettore 3175 voter	**la vocale** A,E,I,O,U sono **le vocali** dell'alfabeto italiano. *A, E, I, O, U are the vowels of the Italian alphabet.* 3176 vowel	**la traversata** 3177 voyage	**un avvoltoio** 3178 vulture

guadare
3179 to wade
la cialda
3180 waffle
Il cavallo tira **il carro**.
3181 wagon/cart*
gemere, **lamentarsi**
3182 to wail
Debora ha **la vita** sottile.
3183 waist
Carmela **aspetta** l'autobus.
3184 to wait
La mamma **sveglia** Golia.
3185 to wake
Cammina a grandi passi.
3186 to walk
il muro
3187 wall
il portafogli
5
5
3188 wallet
la noce
3189 walnut
il tricheco
3190 walrus
la bacchetta magica
3191 wand
vagare
3192 to wander
volere
Papà **vuole** che Sabrina lo aiuti a lavare i piatti.
Ella lo **vorrebbe** aiutare, ma non c'è acqua.
Dad wants Sabrina to help him wash the dishes.
She wants to help him but there is no water.
3193 to want
Sabrina odia **la guerra**.
3194 war
il corredo
3195 wardrobe
il magazzino
3196 warehouse
un maglione bello **caldo**
3197 warm

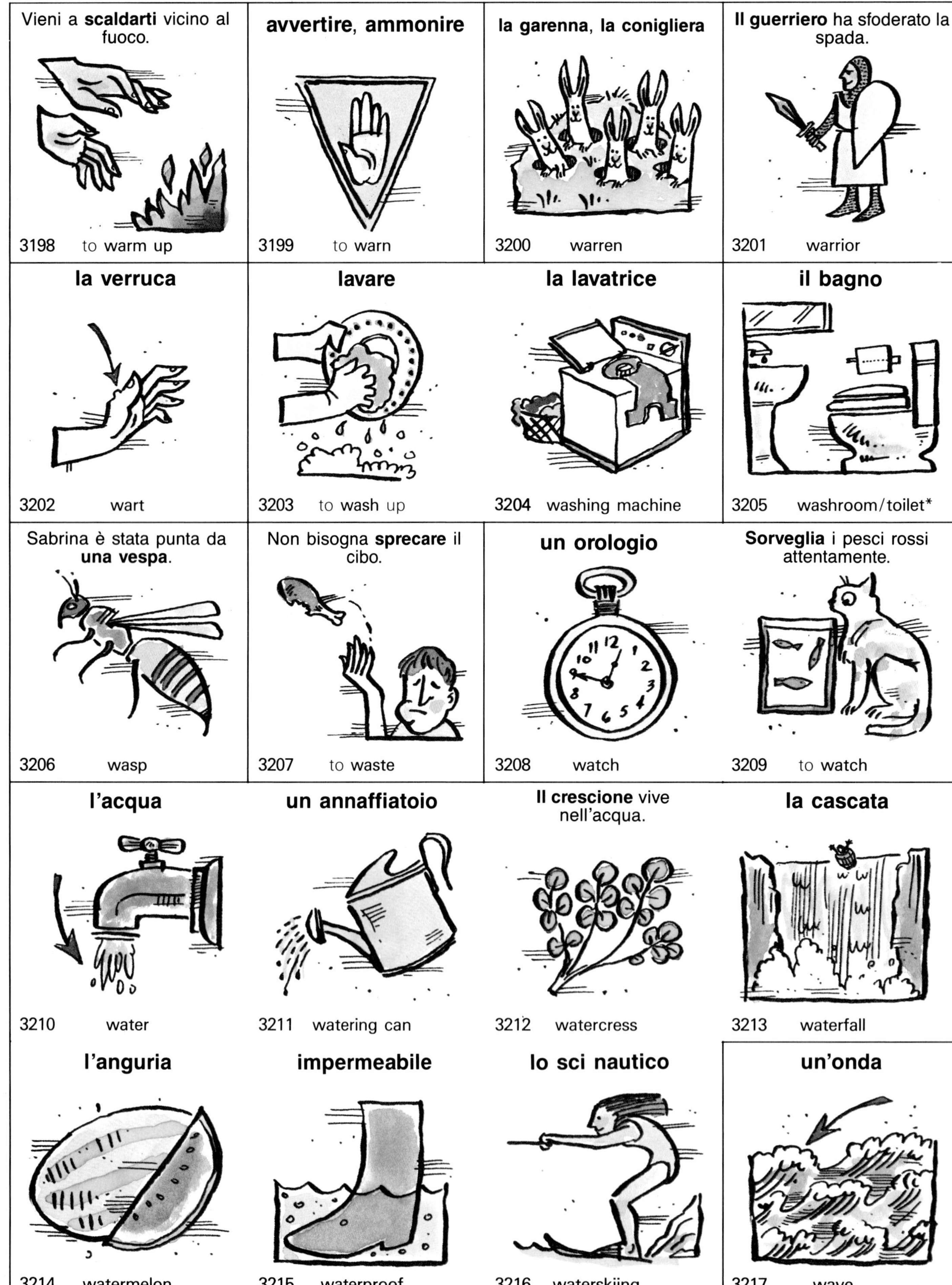
Vieni a **scaldarti** vicino al fuoco.
3198 to warm up
avvertire, ammonire
3199 to warn
la garenna, la conigliera
3200 warren
Il guerriero ha sfoderato la spada.
3201 warrior
la verruca
3202 wart
lavare
3203 to wash up
la lavatrice
3204 washing machine
il bagno
3205 washroom/toilet*
Sabrina è stata punta da **una vespa**.
3206 wasp
Non bisogna **sprecare** il cibo.
3207 to waste
un orologio
3208 watch
Sorveglia i pesci rossi attentamente.
3209 to watch
l'acqua
3210 water
un annaffiatoio
3211 watering can
Il crescione vive nell'acqua.
3212 watercress
la cascata
3213 waterfall
l'anguria
3214 watermelon
impermeabile
3215 waterproof
lo sci nautico
3216 waterskiing
un'onda
3217 wave

Katia fa **un cenno** con la mano a Luigi.
3218 to wave

Ha i capelli **ondulati**.
3219 wavy

La cera della candela cola.
3220 wax

Uno è **debole**, l'altro è forte.
3221 weak

un'arma pericolosa
3222 weapon

Indossa un cappotto pesante.
3223 to wear

la donnola
3224 weasel

Che **tempo** fa?
3225 weather

intrecciare
3226 to weave

un piede palmato
3227 web foot

lo sposalizio, le nozze
3228 wedding

il cuneo, lo spicchio
3229 wedge

mercoledì

Mercoledì è il terzo giorno della settimana.
Al mercoledì Sabrina porta fuori i rifiuti.

Wednesday is the third day of the week.
On Wednesdays, Sabrina takes out the garbage.

3230 Wednesday

Il giardino è stato invaso dalle **erbacce**.
3231 weed

la settimana
3232 week

il fine settimana, il weekend

Il fine settimana comprende il sabato e la domenica.
Zia Lucia ci farà visita questo **weekend**.

Saturday and Sunday make a weekend.
Aunt Lucie will visit us this weekend.

3233 weekend

Piange perché è triste.
3234 to weep

pesare
3235 to weigh

Questa figura è **bizzarra**.
3236 weird

dare il benvenuto
3237 to welcome

Non cadere nel **pozzo**!
3238 well
Mi sento **bene**.
3239 I feel well.
L'ovest è opposto all'est.
N
W
E
S
3240 west
bagnato, fradicio
3241 wet
la balena
3243 whale
il molo
3244 wharf
cosa, che cosa
Cosa è successo al pelo di Tigre?
Sabrina, **che cosa** hai fatto al gatto?
What has happened to the Tiger's fur?
Sabrina, what did you do to your cat?
3245 what
inzuppare
3242 to wet
Il grano serve a fare il pane.
3246 wheat
la ruota
3247 wheel
la carriola
3248 wheelbarrow
la sedia a rotelle
3249 wheelchair
quando
Quando verrà zia Emilia a trovarci, papà?
Quando verrà in vacanza.
When is Aunt Emilia coming to see us?
When she takes her holidays.
3250 when
dove
Ci siamo persi e la mamma non sa **dove** siamo.
So **dove** è, ma non riesco a trovarlo.
We are lost and Mom has no idea where we are.
I know where it is but I cannot find it.
3251 where
Non sa **quale** scegliere.
3252 which one
frignare, piagnucolare
3253 to whine
la frusta
3254 whip
il caprimulgo
3255 whippoorwill
Il frullino serve a montare la panna.
3256 whisk
i baffi del gatto
3257 whisker

Che cosa le **sussurra** all'orecchio? 3258 to whisper	**il fischietto** 3259 whistle	**fischiare** 3260 to whistle	**bianco** 3261 white
Chi ci va? 3262 Who is going?	**perché** Voglio sapere **perché** Sabrina ha preso la mia cravatta. **Perché** non riesce a ricordarsene? *I want to know why Sabrina took my tie. Why can she not remember?* 3263 why	**Lo stoppino** brucia lentamente. 3264 wick	**malvagio, perfido** 3265 wicked
più **larga** che lunga 3266 wide	**la moglie** del signor Paolo 3267 wife	Il leone è un animale **selvaggio**. 3268 The lion is a **wild** animal.	**Il salice** ha lunghi rami. 3269 willow
I fiori **appassiscono** quando non sono innaffiati. 3270 to wilt	**astuto, scaltro** 3271 wily	**vincere** 3272 to win	Luigi **trasalì** per il dolore. 3273 to wince
Il vento soffia furiosamente. 3274 wind	**caricare** un orologio 3275 to wind	**giacca a vento** 3276 windbreaker	**Il mulino a vento** ha lunghe pale. 3277 windmill

la finestra
3278 window

il parabrezza
3279 windshield/windscreen*

Il vino è una bevanda per adulti.
3280 wine

un'ala
3281 wing

ammiccare, strizzare l'occhio
3282 to wink

Ti piace **l'inverno**?
3283 winter

Strofinalo bene, per favore.
3284 to wipe

Gli uccelli sono appollaiati sui **fili**.
3285 wire

saggio, **prudente**

Il nonno è un vecchio **saggio**. Sabrina, pensi che sia **prudente** camminare nel bosco da sola?

Grandfather is a wise old man. Sabrina, do you think it is wise to walk in the forest alone?

3286 wise

formulare **un desiderio**
3287 to make a wish

la strega
3288 witch

il mago
3289 wizard

il lupo
3290 wolf

la donna
3291 woman

chiedersi, **meravigliarsi**
3292 to wonder

meraviglioso
3293 wonderful

la legna da ardere
3294 wood

Il picchio scava i tronchi degli alberi.
3295 woodpecker

Passeggiano nei **boschi**.
3296 woods

la falegnameria
3297 woodwork

Lavora a maglia con la lana.
3298 wool
Che parola strana!
GLÜRP
3299 word
Un tipo di lavoro.
3300 work
Lavora in giardino.
3301 to work
l'officina
3303 workshop
il mondo
3304 world
Il verme striscia.
3305 worm
fare ginnastica
3302 to work out
La mamma si preoccupa per Sabrina.
3306 to worry
la ferita
3307 wound
avviluppare, incartare
3308 to wrap
la ghirlanda, la corona di fiori
3309 wreath
il relitto
3310 wreck
lo scricciolo
3311 wren
Lottano strenuamente.
3312 to wrestle
torcere, strizzare
3313 to wring
il polso
3314 wrist
un orologio da polso
3315 wristwatch
scrivere
3316 to write
male, sbagliato
E' male copiare e mentire.
Penso che il nostro autobus stia andando nella direzione sbagliata.
It is wrong to cheat and to lie.
I think our bus is going the wrong way.
3317 wrong

i raggi x, la radiografia

3318 X-ray

lo xilofono

3319 xylophone

un piccolo **panfilo**

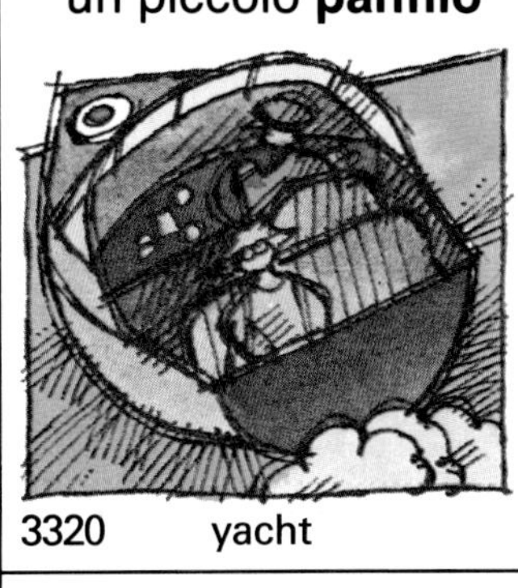

3320 yacht

il giardino, la corte

3321 yard/garden*

Sbadiglia dalla noia o dal sonno?

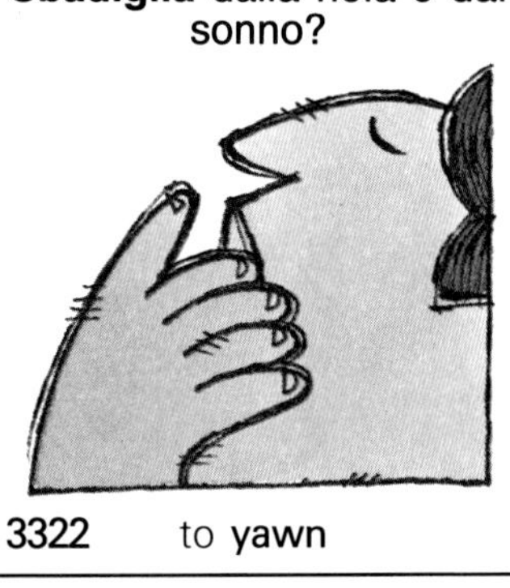

3322 to yawn

un altro anno

3323 year

gridare, urlare

3324 to yell

giallo

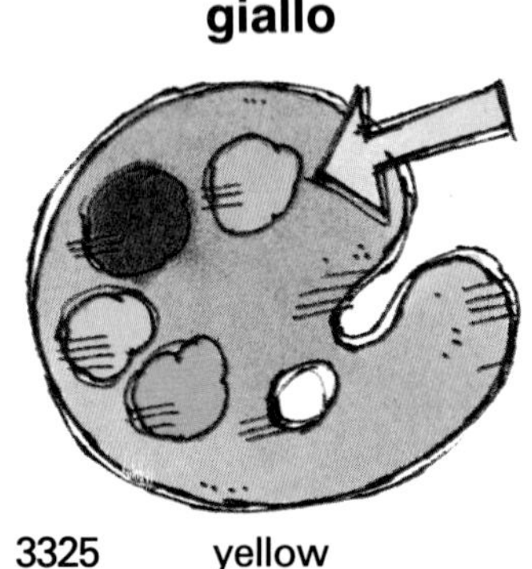

3325 yellow

sì

E' **sì**, è no, oppure è forse?
Se dici di **sì**, devi essere ben sicuro.

Is it yes, is it no, or is it maybe?
If you say yes, you had better be sure.

3326 yes

ieri

Ieri Sabrina non stava bene, perché aveva mangiato troppo gelato.
Che cosa hai fatto **ieri**?

Yesterday Sabrina was sick from eating too much ice cream.
What did you do yesterday?

3327 yesterday

Deve **cedere** il passo.

3328 to yield/give way*

il tuorlo dell'uovo

3329 yolk

giovane e vecchio

3330 young

la zebra disegnata da Sabrina

3331 zebra

lo zero

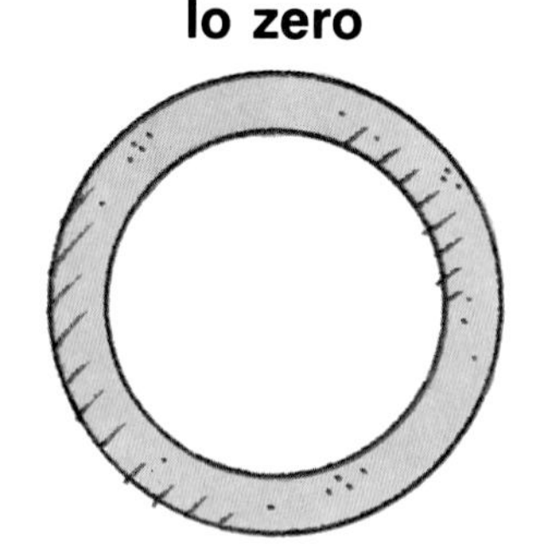

3332 zero

la chiusura lampo

3333 zipper/zip*

lo zoo

3334 zoo

sfrecciare

3335 to zoom

Gli zucchini sono l'ultima parola di Sabrina.

3336 zucchini/courgette*

a

a 117
a buon mercato 497
a casa 1355
a pagamento 2054
a reazione 1485, 1486
a sorpresa 2880
abbaco (il) 1
abbaiare 174
abbandonare 839
abbassare 1699
abbastanza 900
abbozzare 2660
abbracciare 890
abbronzatura (la) 2924
abete (il) 996
abete rosso (il) 2777
abitare 1439, 1667
abito completo (il) 2865
abitudine (la) 1234
accalcarsi 1395
accanto 238
accaparrare 1341
accarezzare 2093
accelerare 2747
acceleratore (il) 5, 1111
accendere 1638, 2897, 3102
accento (il) 6
accetta (la) 1278
acchiappare 1127
acciaio (il) 2807
accidentato 2470
accigliarsi 1079
accoccolarsi 2780
accorciarsi 2629
accurato 1882
accusare 9, 492
aceto (il) 3161
acetosella (la) 2730
acido (il) 12
acqua (la) 3210
acquario (il) 90
acrobata (il) 14
aculeo (il) 2238, 2318, 2753
ad alta voce 53
ad un tratto 2863
addentare 256
addestrare 3052
addio 956
additare 2177
addizionare 16
addomesticato 2923
addormentato 111
adirato 65
adorare 19
adulto (il) 20, 1221
aeroplano (il) 39
aeroporto (il) 40
affaticare 2839
affaticato 3008
afferrare 459, 559, 1175, 2550
affettare (709)
affilato 2584
affilatoio (il) 2585
affilatrice (la) 2586
affittare 2398
affondare 2649
affrettarsi 1405
affrontare 2906
Africa (la) 25
agente di polizia (il) 2185
agile 31
agitare 2579
aglefino (il) 1235
aglio (il) 1107
agnello (il) 1561
ago (il) 1890
agosto (il) 126
agricoltore (il) 958
agrifoglio (il) 1353
agro 2734
aiutare 1308
ala (la) 3281
albergo (il) 1386
albero (il) 1745, 3065
albicocca (la) 87
albo (il) 43
alce (il) 887
alce americano (il) 1833
alfabeto (il) 54
alga marina (la) 2553
aliante (il) 1154
alito (il) 341
all'aria aperta 1971
allacciare 960, 1553
alleggerire 1640
allegro 1775
allenare 562
allenatore (il) 560
allentato 1689
alligatore (il) 48
allodola (la) 1577, 2670
alluminio (il) 58
altalena (la) 2557, 2894
altercare 2308
altipiano (il) 2152
alto 1328, 2921
altro 69
alveare (il) 80, 218, 1340
alzare 2340
alzarsi 1133
amaca (la) 1248
amaro 258
amarsi 1696
ambedue 315
ambulanza (la) 60
amico (il) 1073
ammaccare 747
ammalato 2634
ammiccare 3282
ammiraglio (il) 18
ammonire 3199
amo (il) 1007, 1366
amore (il) 1695
ananas (il) 2126
anca (la) 1336
anche 57
ancora (la) 62
andare 1157
andare a cavallo 2419
andare alla deriva 825
andare in letargo 1323
anello (il) 2425
angelo di mare (il) 1826
angolo (il) 64, 630
anguilla (la) 875
anguria (la) 3214
animale (il) 66
animale favorito (il) 2092
anitra (la) 847
annaffiatoio (il) 3211
anno (il) 3323
annodare 2997
annoiare 311
annunciare 68
ansimare 2013
Antartico (il) 72
anticipo (in) 33
antico 63
antilope (la) 73
ape (la) 216
aperto 1952
apparire 82
appartenere 231
appassire 3270
appena 1510, 2370
appendere 1259, 1261
appiccicoso 2817
applaudire 83, 537
appollaiarsi 2453
appuntito 2178
apribottiglie (il) 317
aprile (il) 88
aprire 1953, 3133
aprire un pacco 3134
apriscatole (il) 418
aquila (la) 858
aquilone (il) 1537
arachide (la) 2060
aragosta (la) 1675
arancia (la) 1958
arancione 1959
aratro (il) 2162
arbitro (il) 2382
arbusto (il) 2630
architetto (il) 92
arco (il) 91, 322
arcobaleno (il) 2338
ardere 386
arenarsi 32
argento (il) 2644
argilla (la) 540
argomentare 2365
aria (la) 36
aringa (la) 1320, 1533
arma (la) 3222
armadietto (il) 401
armatura (la) 97
armonica (la) 1271
arnese (il) 3023
arpa (la) 1273
arrampicarsi 544
arrendersi 1147, 2881
arrestare 101
arricciare 700

b

C

d

festeggiare 468
fiaccola (la) 3031
fiamma (la) 1013
fiammifero (il) 1748
fianco (il) 2635
fibbia (la) 369
fidarsi 3089
fiducia (la) 943
fienile (il) 177
fieno (il) 1283
fiera (la) 941
fiero 2266
figlia (la) 734
figlio (il) 2725
figura (la) 1056
fila (la) 2562
filo (il) 2980, 3285
filo per stendere (il) 552
filo spinato (il) 169
filobus (il) 3077
filtrare 2838
fine (la) 894
fine settimana (il) 3233
finestra (la) 3278
finimento (il) 1272
fiocco (il) 1012
fiocco d'avena (il) 477
fiocco di neve (il) 2713
fioco 768
fionda (la) 2687
fiore (il) 1032
fiorire 286
fioritura (la) 285
firma (la) 2640
fisarmonica (la) 8
fischiare 3260
fischietto (il) 3259
fissare col nastro adesivo 2931
fiume (il) 2436
foca (la) 2546
fodera (la) 1655
fodero (il) 2591
foglia (la) 1599
foglia d'alloro (la) 197
folla (la) 682
fondamento (il) 1061
fondere 1770, 2965
fondo (il) 318
fontana (la) 1062
football (il) 1045
forare 826, 2286
forbici (le) 2528
forbicine per le unghie (le) 1870
forchetta (la) 1045
forcina (la) 299
forcone (il) 2134
foresta (la) 1051
formaggio (il) 501
formica (la) 71
fornaio (il) 150
forno (il) 1524, 1974
forno a microonde (il) 1787
forse 1753
forte (il) 1057
forte 53, 1692, 2855
fortunato 1700
foruncolo (il) 2122
forzare 1049
foschia (la) 1284, 1809
fossato (il) 792, 1814
fossetta (la) 769
fossile (il) 1059
fosso (il) 3067
foto (la) 2100
fotografia (la) 2100
fracassare 2699
fracasso (il) 2328
fradicio 3241
fragile 353, 1065
fragola (la) 2844
francobollo (il) 2793
frantumare 2588
frase (la) 2566
frastagliato 1475
frastuono (il) 2328
fratello (il) 358
frazione (la) 1064
freccia (la) 103
freddo (il) 575
fregare 2541
frenare 333
freno (il) 332
freno a mano (il) 1252
fresco 522, 1070
friggere 1081
frignare 3253
frigo (il) 1072
frigorifero (il) 1072, 2384
frittata (la) 1946
frittella (la) 2008
frizione (la) 558
fronte (la) 1050
frontiera (la) 309
frullatore (il) 1813
frullino (il) 3256
frusta (la) 3254
frutta (la) 1080
frutteto (il) 1960
fuggire 1023
fumare 2703
funerale (il) 1087
fungo (il) 1861
fuoco (il) 997
fuoco di Sant'Antonio (il) 2602
fuori 1971
furfante (il) 3159
fusibile (il) 1094

g

gabbia (la) 404, 660
gabbiano (il) 1230, 2545
gabinetto (il) 3015
galleggiare 1026
galleria (la) 1096, 3098
gallina (la) 1312
galoppare 1097
gamba (la) 1611
gamberetto (il) 2628
gambero (il) 662
gambo (il) 2791
gara (la) 1747
garenna (la) 3200
gargarismo (il) 1106
garofano (il) 443
gas (il) 1109
gatto (il) 457
gazza (la) 1716
gelare 1069
gelatina (la) 1484
gelato (il) 1414
gelo (il) 1078
gemello (il) 3114
gemere 1208, 3182
generale (il) 1118
generoso 1119
gengiva (la) 1231
genitore (il) 2023
gennaio (il) 1479
gente (la) 2080
gentile 1120, 1529
gentiluomo (il) 1121
geranio (il) 1124
gerbillo (il) 1125
germe (il) 1126
gesso (il) 483
gettare 2986
gettare i rifiuti per terra 1665
getto (il) 1487
ghiacciaio (il) 1148
ghiaccio (il) 1413
ghiacciolo (il) 1416
ghiaia (la) 1192
ghianda (la) 13
ghirlanda (la) 3309
già 55
giacca (la) 1473
giacca a vento (la) 2026, 3276
giacca sportiva (la) 272
giacinto (il) 1410
giaggiolo (il) 1463
giallo 3325
giardino (il) 3321
giarrettiera (la) 1108
gigante (il) 1135
gigantesco 1137
giglio (il) 1647
ginocchio (il) 1540
giocare 2154
giocattolo (il) 3042
gioco (il) 1098
gioco della settimana (il) 1371
gioco delle composizioni (il) 1489
giocoliere (il) 1497
giocondo 1775
gioiello (il) 1488
giornale (il) 1904
giornata (la) 735
giovane 3330
giovedì (il) 2991

giradischi (il) 2374, 3106
giraffa (la) 1143
girare 3100, 3104
girasole (il) 2871
girino (il) 2907
gitano (il) 1142
giudice (il) 1496
giugno (il) 1506
giumenta (la) 1735
giunca (la) 1508
giunchiglia (la) 718
giungla (la) 1507
giusto 1510. 2422
gobba (la) 1399
goccia (la) 835
gocciolare 830, 3071
godere 898
godersi 898
gola (la) 2984
goletta (la) 2527
golf (il) 1166
golfo (il) 1229
gomito (il) 881
gomma (la) 1232, 2465
gonfiare 2282
gonfiore (il) 1705
gonna (la) 2667
gonnellino scozzese (il) 1527
gorilla (il) 1172
governare 1173
governo (il) 1174
gradino (il) 2812
graffiatura (la) 2537
graffio (il) 2537
grafico (il) 494, 1187, 2537
grammo (il) 1179
granchio (il) 653
grande 245, 1576
grande magazzino (il) 749
grandine (la) 1236
granello (il) 2031
granito (il) 1183
grano (il) 1178, 3246
granoturco (il) 629
grasso (il) 1195
grasso 961
grassoccio 2168
grattacielo (il) 2671
grattugia (la) 1190
gravità (la) 1193
grazioso 1697
grembiule (il) 89
grembo (il) 1573
gridare 2627, 3324
grigio 1202
grilletto (il) 3073
grillo (il) 670
grosso 1576, 2969
grossolano 564
gru (la) 657, 658
gruccia (la) 688
gruppo (il) 1218
guadagnare 861
guadare 3179
guaina (la) 2591
guancia (la) 500
guanto (il) 1155, 1811
guardare 1686
guardare fisso 2796
guardaroba (il) 549
guarire 1290, 2375
guarito 699
guasto 2763
guerra (la) 3194
guerriero (il) 3201
gufo (il) 1981
guglia (la) 2759
guidare 831
guidatore (il) 832
guinzaglio (il) 1603
gusto (il) 1021
gustoso 2939

h

Halloween 1243
handicap (il) 1254
hockey (il) 1344
hovercraft (il) 1390

i

iceberg (il) 1415
idea (la) 1418
identico 1419, 2497
idiota (il) 1420
idraulico (il) 2167
ieri 3327
iglù (il) 1423
illuminare 1426
illustrazione (la) 1427
imbarazzare 889
imbianchino (il) 2000
imbottito 2858
imbrattare 2700
imbrogliare 498
imbroglione (il) 674
imbucare 1717, 2208
imbuto (il) 1088
immagine riflessa (la) 2383
immondizia (la) 775, 2466
impalcatura (la) 2513
imparare 1602
impaurito 24
impennarsi 2225
impermeabile (il) 2339, 3215
importante 1428
importunare 2091
imposta (la) 2632
impronta (la) 1046, 1047
impronta digitale (la) 994
improvvisamente 2863
in 1429
in fiamme 44
in mare 1975
in nessun posto 77
in piedi 3135
in ritardo 1582
in voga 2199
inatteso 2880
incarico (il) 2937
incartare 3308
incendio (il) 271
incenso (il) 1430
inchiodare 1871
inchiostro (il) 1443
inciampare 3076
incidente (il) 7
incinta 2228
inclinarsi 3001
inclinato 676, 2673
incollare 2041
incolpare 266
incontrare 1767
incontro (il) 1747
incoronare 684
increspatura (la) 2432
incrinatura (la) 654
incrocio (il) 1453
incrollabile 1003
incubo (il) 1913
incursione (la) 2334
indaco 1433
indicare 2176
indice (il) 1432
indietreggiare 143
indirizzo (il) 17
indizio (il) 557
indossare 3223
indovinare 1223
inerme 1309
infelice 3128
inferno (il) 1304
infestato dagli spettri 1280
infettivo 1437
infezione (la) 1436
infilare 2981
influenza (la) 1033
informare 1438
ingarbugliato 2926
inghiottire 2884
inginocchiarsi 1541
ingoiare 2884
ingranaggio (il) 1116
iniezione (la) 1441
iniziali (le) 1440
inno (il) 1411
inoltre 239
inondazione (la) 1028
insalata (la) 2492
insegnante (la) 2943
insegnare 2942
inseguire 2295
insetto (il) 372, 1444
insetto nocivo (il) 2090
insieme 3014
insistere 1446
insurrezione (la) 2429
intelligente 2698
intelligenza (la) 1795

interno (il) 1434
interruttore (il) 2896
intervista (la) 1454
intonacare 2148
intonaco (il) 2147
intrecciare 3226
invadere 1457
invalido 1458
invece di 1449
inventare 1459
inverno (il) 3283
investigatore (il) 755
investire 2477
invisibile 1460
invitare 1462
invito (il) 1461
inzuppare 3242
ippopotamo (il) 1337
iris (il) 1463
iscriversi 2387
isola (la) 1467
isolamento (il) 1452
isolato (il) 281
ispettore (il) 1448
ispezionare 1447
istrice (il) 1301
istruttore (il) 1451
istruzione (la) 1450

j

jeans (i) 1482
jeep (la) 1483

k

kilt (il) 1527
kiwi (il) 1539
koala (il) 1549

l

là 2967
labbro (il) 1659
labirinto (il) 1755
laboratorio (il) 1551
lacerare 2430
lacerazione (la) 2535
lacrima (la) 2946
ladro (il) 2440, 2970
lago (il) 1560
lama (la) 265
lamentarsi 1208, 3182
lampada (la) 214, 1563
lampada elettrica (la) 1017
lampadina (la) 1639
lampione (il) 1564, 2848
lampo (il) 1016, 1642
lampone (il) 2347
lana (la) 3298
lancia (la) 1565, 2746
lanciare 1403, 1586, 2986, 3035
lanciare la palla 2132
lancio (il) 2133
lanterna (la) 1572
lanuggine (la) 1657
lanugine (la) 1034
lardo (il) 1575
largo 3266
larice (il) 1574
larva (la) 1710
lasciar cadere 836
lasciare 838, 1605, 1621
latte (il) 1793
lattina (la) 417
lattuga (la) 1624
lavagna (la) 262
lavagnetta (la) 2676
lavanda (la) 1590
lavanderia a secco (la) 844
lavandino (il) 2648
lavare 2541, 3203
lavatrice (la) 3204
lavorare 3301
lavorare a maglia 1543
lavorato 2139
lavoro (il) 1490, 3300
lecca-lecca (il) 1683
leccare 1630
legaccio (il) 2610
legare 250, 2997
legge (la) 1591
leggenda (la) 1612
leggere 2358
legna (la) 3294
legname da costruzione (il) 1704
legno compensato (il) 2171
lente (la) 1616, 1715
lentiggine (la) 1067
lenzuolo (il) 2593
leone (il) 1658
leopardo (il) 1617
lepre (la) 1269
lettera (la) 1622, 1623
lettino per bimbi (il) 669
letto (il) 213
leva (la) 1626
levar del sole (il) 2872
levigare 2187
lezione (la) 1620
libbra (la) 2217
libellula (la) 814
liberare 2394
liberarsi 1132
libero 1068
libro (il) 305
lillà (il) 1646
limare 985
limite (il) 1650
limonata (la) 1614
limone (il) 1613
lindo 1882
linea (la) 1652
linfa (la) 2501
lingua (la) 1571, 3020
lingua di gatto (la) 1558
liquido (il) 1035, 1661
liscio 1019, 2704
lista (la) 1662
litro (il) 1664
livido (il) 361
locomotiva (la) 1678
lontano 955
lontra (la) 1969
lottare 3312
lozione (la) 1691
lucchetto (il) 1992
luce (la) 1637
lucertola (la) 1670
lucidare 2187
luglio (il) 1499
lumaca (la) 2706
luna (la) 1832
lunedì (il) 1823
lungo 52, 1685
lupo (il) 3290

m

ma 393
macchiare 2700
macchia (la) 287, 2767, 2787
macchina (la) 436
macchina da cucire (la) 2574
macchina da scrivere (la) 3120
macchina dei pompieri (la) 998
macchina fotografica (la) 414
macchinista (il) 897
macellaio (il) 394
macinare 1206
madre (la) 1839
magazzino (il) 3196
maggio (il) 1752
magia (la) 1711
maglio (il) 1722
maglione (il) 2279, 2889
magnetofono (il) 2932
magnifico 1196, 1714
mago (il) 1712, 2728, 3289
mai 1901
maiale (il) 2113
maiuscolo 433
mal di denti (il) 3025
mal di testa (il) 1288
malato 1425
malattia (la) 782
male 3317
maleducato 2469
malvagio 3265
mamma (la) 1839

mancino 1610
mandare 2564
mandarino (il) 1724, 2925
mandolino (il) 1725
mandorla (la) 49
mandria (la) 1315
manetta (la) 1253
mangiare 868
mango (il) 1727
manica (la) 2682
maniera (la) 1728
manifesto (il) 2211
maniglia (la) 805, 1255, 1544
mano (la) 1250
manopola (la) 1811
manzo (il) 2809
mappa (la) 1730
marciapiede (il) 2636
marciare 1733
marcio 2459
mare (il) 2544
margherita (la) 722
marinaio (il) 2491
marionetta (la) 2289
marito (il) 1407
marmellata (la) 1477
marmo (il) 1731
marmotta americana (la) 1217
marrone 360
martedì (il) 3094
martellare 1247
martello (il) 1246
martin pescatore (il) 1531
marzo (il) 1734
mascalzone (il) 3159
maschera (la) 1743
maschio (il) 1721
massa (la) 1744
masso (il) 319, 2442
masticare 506
mastice (il) 2300
matematica (la) 1749
materassino pneumatico (il) 37
materasso (il) 1751
materiale isolante (il) 1452
matita (la) 2075
matraccio (il) 1018
mattarello (il) 2450
mattino (il) 1834
mattone (il) 343
mattonella (la) 3000
maturo 2431
mazza (la) 190
mazzo (il) 321, 382
mazzuolo (il) 1722
meccanico (il) 1763
medaglia (la) 1764
medicina (la) 1765
medio 1766
megafono (il) 378, 1693
meglio 241
mela (la) 84
mela cotogna (la) 2320
melagrana (la) 2190
melanzana (la) 877
melone (il) 428, 1769
melone verde (il) 1360
membro (il) 1771
mendicare 223
meno 1801
mensola (la) 2594
menta (la) 1800
menta peperita (la) 2082
mente (la) 1795
mento (il) 515
menu (il) 1772
meraviglioso 3293
mercato (il) 1739
mercè (la) 1773
mercoledì (il) 3230
merenda all'aperto (la) 2107
meridiana (la) 2870
meritare 861
merlo (il) 261
merluzzo (il) 570
mescolare 586, 1812, 2631, 2822
mese (il) 1828
messaggero (il) 1778
messaggio (il) 1777
mestolo (il) 1555
metà (la) 1241
metallo (il) 1779
meteorite (la) 1780
metodo (il) 1783
metro (il) 1782
metronomo (il) 1784
mettere 2297
mettere il chiavistello 1581
mettere in comune 2194
mettere in pratica 2222
mettere insieme 2111
mettere la sicura 1676
mettere sotto aceto 2106
mettere via 2298
mettersi in mostra 2624
mezzanotte 1791
mezzo (il) 1789
mezzogiorno 1788, 1921
micino (il) 1538
microfono (il) 1785
microscopio (il) 1786
miele (il) 1358
mietere 1275
miglio (il) 1792
migliore 240, 241
millepiedi (il) 475
minatore (il) 1797
minerale (il) 1798
minestra (la) 2733
miniera (la) 1796
minuscolo 3003
minuto (il) 1802
miracolo (il) 1803
miraggio (il) 1804
mirare 35
mirtillo (il) 292, 1394
missile (il) 1808
misurare 1761
mobile (il) 1093
modello (il) 1817, 2049
moderno 1818
moglie (la) 3267
molla (la) 2772
molle (le) 3019
molletta (la) 181
mollusco (il) 535
molo (il) 2112, 3244
moltiplicare 1856
molto 1729, 3151
momento (il) 1822
mondo (il) 3304
moneta (la) 574
mongolfiera (la) 159
montagna (la) 1845
montare 1131, 1844
monticello (il) 1843
monumento (il) 1829
mora (la) 260
morbillo (il) 1760
morire 763
morire di fame 2799
morsa (la) 536
mortaio (il) 1835
mortale 962
morto 736
mosaico (il) 1836
mosca (la) 1036
mostarda (la) 1866
mostrare 2623
mostro (il) 1827
motocicletta (la) 1841
motore (il) 896, 1840
motoretta (la) 2530
movimento (il) 1850
mucca (la) 650
mucchio (il) 1292, 2116
mulinare 3116
mulinello (il) 2381
mulino (il) 1794
mulino a vento (il) 3277
mulo (il) 1855
multa (la) 991
muoversi 1849
muratore (il) 344
muro (il) 3187
muschio (il) 1838
muscolo (il) 1859
museo (il) 1860
museruola (la) 1867
musica (la) 1862
musicista (la) 1863
muso (il) 1867

nailon (il) 1926
nano (il) 856, 1790
nascita (la) 253
nascondersi 1326
nascondiglio (il) 1327

p

q

r

raschietto (il) 2536
raso (il) 2504
rasoio (il) 2356
rastrello (il) 2342
ratto (il) 2348
ravanello (il) 2331
razzo (il) 1015, 2444
re (il) 1530
recitare 2372
recuperare 2375
redini (le) 2391
regale 2464
regalo (il) 1136, 2230
reggipetto (il) 328
regina (la) 2312
regione (la) 2386
registratore (il) 2932
regola (la) 2472
relitto (il) 3310
remare 1991, 2463
remo (il) 1928
remoto 2396
rendere 2562
rendersi conto 2361
rene (il) 1522
renna (la) 2390
respirare 342
responsabile 2406
restituire 1146, 2409
rettangolo (il) 2376
rettile (il) 2403
ribellarsi 2367
ribes (il) 263, 703
ricamo (il) 891
ricaricare 492
riccio 701
ricco 2417
ricetta (la) 2371
ricevere 2369
ricordarsi 2368, 2395
ridacchiare 1138
ridere 1584
riempire 986
rifiutare 2385
rifiuto (il) 1103, 1509, 2466
riflesso (il) 2383
riflettore (il) 2549
rifugio (il) 2596
rigido 512, 1274, 2818
rigogolo (il) 1966
rilasciare 2394
rilassarsi 2393
rima (la) 2413
rimbalzare 320
rimorchiare 3038
rimorchio (il) 3050
rimpiangere 2388
rincorrere 495
ringhiare 1220
ringraziare 2964
rinoceronte (il) 2411
rinviare 2299
riparare 1010, 2399
ripetere 2400
ripido 2808
riportare 352, 2913
riposare 2393, 2407
riprendersi 589
riscaldare 1295
rischio (il) 2434
risciacquatura (la) 786
riso (il) 2416
risolvere 2723
risparmiare 2508
risplendere 2600
rispondere 2402
risposta (la) 70
ristorante (il) 2408
ritagliare 711
ritirare 2917
ritornare 2409
ritratto (il) 2206
riunione (la) 1768
riuscire 426, 3103
rivale (il) 2435
rivista (la) 1709
rivoltarsi 2367
rocchetto (il) 2765
roccia (la) 2442
roco 1342
rompere 337, 2588
rompersi 338, 940
rompicapo (il) 2301
rosa (la) 2456
rosa 2127
roseo 2458
rosicchiare 1906
rosmarino (il) 2457
rospo (il) 3009
rossetto (il) 1660
rosso 2377
rotolare 2448
rotolo (il) 2447
rotondo 2461
rottame (il) 1509
rovesciarsi 1979, 3004
rovina (la) 2471
rubare 2805
rubinetto (il) 964, 2929
rubino (il) 2467
ruggine (la) 2480
ruggire 2438
rugiada (la) 756
rumore (il) 1920
ruota (la) 3247
ruota del timone (la) 1306
ruota di scorta (la) 2741
rupe (la) 543
ruscello (il) 356, 2845
ruvido 564, 2460
ruzzolare 3030, 3097

S

sabato (il) 2505
sabbia (la) 2498
sabbia mobile (la) 2315
sacchetto (il) 2215
sacco (il) 2483
sacco a pelo (il) 2679
sacro 1354, 2484
saggio 3286
sailboard (il) 2489
sala cinematografica (la) 1851
sala da pranzo (la) 771
saldo (il) 172
sale (il) 2495
salice (il) 3269
salire 1160
salmone (il) 2494
salotto (il) 1669
salsa (la) 2506
salsa di senape (la) 1866
salsiccia (la) 2507
saltare 1500, 2665
saltare dentro 1501
saltare sopra 1502
saltatore (il) 1503
saltellare 1368
salutare 1201, 2496
salvare 2404
salve 1305
salvietta (la) 1874
sandalo (il) 2499
sangue (il) 284
sanguinare 274
sano 1291
sapere 1547
saponata (la) 1583
sapone (il) 2715
saporito 2939
sardina (la) 2502
sarto (il) 2909
sasso (il) 2826
sassolino (il) 2065
satellite (il) 2503
sbadigliare 3322
sbagliato 3317
sbarra (la) 167, 182
sbattere 2672
sbattere le palpebre 277
sbavare 824, 834
sbucciare 2072
sbuffare 2275
scadente 2195
scaffale (lo) 306
scafo (lo) 1397
scagliare 1403
scala (la) 1554, 2788
scala mobile (la) 907
scalare 544
scaldare 1295
scaldarsi 3198
scalo (lo) 2831
scalpello (lo) 518
scaltro 3271
scambiare 2886, 3046
scamiciato (lo) 1504
scampagnata (la) 2107
scampanio (lo) 2059
scampare 2476
scanalatura 1214
scappare 908, 2476
scarafaggio (lo) 221

scaricare 851, 3132
scarico (lo) 815
scarlatto 2522
scarpa (la) 2609
scarpa da tennis (la) 2709
scartocciare 3134
scassinare 339
scassinatore (lo) 385
scatola (la) 325, 451
scattare 2776
scegliere 524, 2102
scena (la) 2523
scendere 1130, 1158
scheggia (la) 517, 2762
scheletro (lo) 2659
scherzo (lo) 1495
schiaccianoci (lo) 1925
schiacciare le patate 1742
schiaffeggiare 2674
schiantarsi 659
schiena (la) 142
schiudere 1277
schiuma (la) 1039
schiuma di sapone (la) 1583
schizzare 2761
sci (gli) 2661
sci nautico (lo) 3216
sciacquare 2428
scialuppa (la) 1585
scialuppa di salvataggio (la) 1635
sciame (lo) 2887
sciare 2662
sciarpa (la) 2521
scimmia (la) 79, 1825
scimpanzè (lo) 514
scintilla (la) 2742
scintillare 2743, 3115
sciocco 2643
sciogliersi 788, 1770
sciopero (lo) 2851
sciroppo (lo) 2901
sciupato 2575
scivolare 1153, 2688
scivolo (lo) 2683
scodella (la) 324
scogliera (la) 2379
scoiattolo (lo) 2783
scolaro (lo) 2856
sconsiderato 441
scontento 3128
scontrarsi 579, 659
scontro (lo) 580
scopa (la) 357
scopare 2890
scoppiare 387
scoppio (lo) 269
scoprire 780
scordarsi 1052
scorrere 1031
scorticatura (la) 2535
scorza (la) 2424
scossa (la) 2608
scottare 2514
scricciolo (lo) 3311
scrivania (la) 751
scrivere 3316
scrivere a macchina 3119
scrivere lettera per lettera 2748
scrofa (la) 2736
scudo (lo) 2598
sculacciare 2740
scultore (lo) 2542
scuola (la) 2526
scuola secondaria (la) 1330
scuotere 2579
scusare 919
scusarsi 81
se 1422
secchio (il) 368, 1994
secolo (il) 476
seconda colazione (la) 1706
secondo (il) 2554
sedano (il) 469
sedere 2653
sedia (la) 482
sedia a dondolo (la) 2445
sedia a rotelle (la) 3249
sedile (il) 2551
sega (la) 2509
sega a motore (la) 481
segale (la) 2482
segare 2510
segatura (la) 2511
segnalare 2639
segnale di stop (il) 2829
segnare 1737, 2532
segreto (il) 2555
seguire 1042
sei 2654
selciato (il) 2051
sella (la) 2486
selvaggio 3268
semaforo (il) 3048
sembrare 2559
seme (il) 2558
semicerchio (il) 2563
seminare 2737
seminterrato (il) 186, 471
semplice 2645
sempre 59
sempreverde 913
sentenza (la) 2566
sentiero (il) 2046
sentinella (la) 2567
sentire 1293
sentire la mancanza 1807
sentirsi bene 973
sentirsi soffocare 523
senza scosse 2704
separare 2732
separato 78
sequestrare 1332, 1521
serbatoio (il) 2405, 2927
serpente (il) 2707
serpente a sonagli (il) 2350
serpentina (la) 573
serra (la) 1200
serratura (la) 1677
servire 2569
sesto 2655
sette 2570
settembre (il) 2568
settimana (la) 3232
settimo 2571
sfera (la) 2750
sforzare 2839
sfrecciare 3335
sfregiare 2675
sgabello (lo) 2827
sgelare 2965
sgraziato 137
sguazzare 2761
shampoo (lo) 2581
sì 3326
sia...che 315
sicomoro (il) 2900
sicuro 2876
sicuro di sè 610
siepe (la) 1300
sigaretta (la) 531
sigaro (il) 530
signora (la) 1556
silenzioso 2641
sindaco (il) 1754
singolare 2647
sinistra (la) 1609
sirena (la) 1774, 2651
siringa (la) 2011
skateboard (lo) 2658
slitta (la) 2677
slittare 2663
slogarsi 2769
smontare 2911
smussato 293
snello 2684
soccorrere 34, 2404
sofà (il) 2719
soffiare 290
soffice 2720
soffitta (la) 124
soffitto (il) 467
soglia (la) 2983
sogliola (la) 2722
sognare 820
sogno (il) 819
solaio (il) 1681
solco (il) 2481
soldato (il) 2721
sole (il) 2868
solitario 1684
solleticare 2994
sollevare 1297, 1636, 2103, 2340
solo 51, 1684
sonaglio (il) 2349
sonnecchiare 810
sopra 3
soprabito (il) 1976

sopracciglio (il) 359, 933
sopraccoperta (la) 1474
soprannome (il) 1909
soprascarpa (la) 1978
sordo 737
sorella (la) 2652
sorgente (la) 2774
sorgere 2433
sorridere 1205
sorseggiare 2650
sorvegliare 3209
sospirare 2637
sostenere 2261
sostituire 2401
sottaceti (i) 2105
sotterrare 388
sottile 2973
sotto 232, 3124
sottomarino (il) 2860
sottosopra 3136
sottrarre 2861
sovente 1941
sovrano (il) 2473
spada (la) 2899
spago (lo) 2853
spalla (la) 2619
spalmare 2771
sparare 2612
sparecchiare 542
spargere 2775
sparire 778
spartire 2582
spaventapasseri (lo) 2520
spaventare 1074, 2519
spazio (lo) 1101
spazzatura (la) 1103
spazzola (la) 363
spazzola per capelli (la) 1238
spazzolare 362
spazzolino (lo) 365
spazzolino da denti (lo) 3026
specchietto retrovisore (lo) 2364
specchio (lo) 1805
specie (la) 1528
spedire 2564
spedire per posta 1717
spegnere 2897, 3101
spendere 2749
spennare 2163
sperare 1369
spesso 1941
spezzarsi d'un colpo 2708
spiacente 2731
spiaggia (la) 200, 2616
spianare 1020
spicciolo (lo) 485
spiegare 928
spilla (la) 355
spina (la) 2164, 2979
spina dorsale (la) 2757
spinacio (lo) 2756
spingere 2296
spingere colla mano 2182
spirale (la) 2758
splendente 350, 2603
sporco 989, 1204
sposa (la) 345
sposalizio (lo) 3228
sposarsi 1740
sposo (lo) 346, 1211
sprecare 3207
sprizzare 2784
spruzzare 2770
spugna (la) 2764
spuntare 3074
sputare 2760
squadra (la) 2944
squalo (lo) 2583
staccarsi 588
staccionata (la) 975
stagione (la) 2550
stagno (lo) 2191
stalla (la) 177, 2785
stalliere (lo) 1212
stallone (lo) 2792
stampo (lo) 1842
stanco 3008
stantio 2790
stanza (la) 2452
stare bene 56, 992
stare fermo 2803
starnutire 2710
statua (la) 2802
stazione (la) 2801
stazione di servizio (la) 2800
stella (la) 2795
stella di Natale (la) 2179
stelo (lo) 2811
sterzare 2810
stesso 2497
stinco (lo) 2599
stirare 1464
stivale (lo) 308
stoffa (la) 550
stomaco (lo) 2825
stop (lo) 2829
stoppino (lo) 3264
storia (la) 1338, 2835, 2918
stormo (lo) 1027
stornello americano (lo) 1757
storno (lo) 2797
storto 675
stracciare 2947
strada (la) 2437, 2847
strada maestra (la) 1331
strangolare 522, 2841
strano 2840
strappare via 2948
strato (lo) 1595
strega (la) 3288
stretto 1875
strillare 2610, 2627
stringere 1207, 2781, 2999
stringersi insieme 1395
striscia (la) 2854
strisciare 661
strizzare 3313
strizzare l'occhio 3282
strofinaccio (lo) 550
strofinare 29, 3284
struzzo (lo) 1968
stucco (lo) 2147
studiare 1123, 2857
stufato (lo) 2815
stupendo 1171
stupido 2643
stupire 114
su 1947
succhiare 2862
succo (il) 1498
sud (il) 2735
sudare 2888
sudicio 1204
suggerimento (il) 557
suonare il campanello 2426
suonare il clacson 1361
suono delle campane (il) 2059
superficie (la) 2877
supermercato (il) 2874
supplicare 2157
susina (la) 2166
sussurrare 3258
svantaggio (lo) 1254
sveglia (la) 42
svegliarsi 3185
sveglio 134
svendita (la) 2493
svenire 2035
svestirsi 3127

t

tacchino (il) 3099
taglia (la) 2656
tagliare 546, 709
tagliare la strada 710
tagliente 2584
talento (il) 2919
talpa (la) 1820
tamburello (il) 2922
tamburo (il) 841
tana (la) 1559
tanto 106
tappeto (il) 446
tappo (il) 627, 2165
targa (la) 1629
targone (il) 2935
tartaruga (la) 3034, 3109
tasca (la) 2173
tassì (il) 2940
tavola (la) 296, 2144, 2902
tavolo (il) 2902
tavolozza (la) 2005
tazza (la) 696
tè (il) 2941

U

W

Z